T0301422

INTERNATIONAL POLICY RULES
AND INEQUALITY

INITIATIVE FOR POLICY DIALOGUE AT COLUMBIA:
CHALLENGES IN DEVELOPMENT AND GLOBALIZATION

INITIATIVE FOR POLICY
DIALOGUE AT COLUMBIA:
CHALLENGES IN DEVELOPMENT
AND GLOBALIZATION

JOSÉ ANTONIO OCAMPO AND JOSEPH E. STIGLITZ,
SERIES EDITORS

INTERNATIONAL POLICY RULES AND INEQUALITY

IMPLICATIONS FOR GLOBAL ECONOMIC GOVERNANCE

EDITED BY

José Antonio Ocampo

COLUMBIA UNIVERSITY PRESS

NEW YORK

Columbia University Press
Publishers Since 1893
New York   Chichester, West Sussex
cup.columbia.edu

Library of Congress Cataloging-in-Publication Data
Names: Ocampo, Jose Antonio, editor.
Title: International policy rules and inequality :
implications for global economic governance /
edited by Jose Antonio Ocampo.
Description: New York : Columbia University Press, [2018] |
Includes bibliographical references and index.
Identifiers: LCCN 2018040789 (print) |
LCCN 2018042142 (e-book) | ISBN 9780231549141 (e-book) |
ISBN 9780231190848 (hardback : alk. paper)
Subjects: LCSH: Equality. | Income distribution. | Economic policy—
International cooperation. | International economic relations. |
International law.
Classification: LCC HM821 (e-book) |
LCC HM821 .I68 2018 (print) |
DDC 305—dc23
LC record available at https://lccn.loc.gov/2018040789

Columbia University Press books are printed on permanent
and durable acid-free paper.

Printed in the United States of America

Cover image: *Broken Ways*, © Paulo Cesar Acosta Castaño
Cover design: Elliott S. Cairns

INITIATIVE FOR POLICY DIALOGUE AT COLUMBIA: CHALLENGES IN DEVELOPMENT AND GLOBALIZATION

JOSÉ ANTONIO OCAMPO AND JOSEPH E. STIGLITZ, SERIES EDITORS

The Initiative for Policy Dialogue (IPD) at Columbia University brings together academics, policy makers, and practitioners from developed and developing countries to address the most pressing issues in economic policy today. IPD is an important part of Columbia's broad program on development and globalization. The Initiative for Policy Dialogue at Columbia: Challenges in Development and Globalization presents the latest academic thinking on a wide range of development topics and lays out alternative policy options and trade-offs. Written in a language accessible to policy makers and students alike, this series is unique in that it both shapes the academic research agenda and furthers the economic policy debate, facilitating a more democratic discussion of development policies.

This book highlights trends in two research and policy issues that have been at the center of global debates in recent years. The first trend is the rising national income and wealth inequalities that have taken place in recent decades. The second is the large historical inequalities in living standards between developed and developing countries. The coincidence of these adverse distributive trends with the globalization process currently under way raises obvious questions about the extent to which the rules—or, equally important, the lack of them—that formally or informally govern the global economy are basic determinants of world inequality.

Chapter authors look at this interaction both from a general perspective and through a deep look at four types of rules: those related to foreign investment, cross-border financial flows, intellectual property rights, and lack of rules regarding taxation. The authors recommend improvements to global economic governance that would provide countries with the freedom to adopt national policies they deem necessary to avoid negative effects on domestic inequality and would strengthen the power of global institutions in their efforts to reduce the negative effects on both international and national inequalities.

CONTENTS

INTERNATIONAL POLICY RULES
AND INEQUALITY

CHAPTER 1

International Policy Rules and Inequality

IMPLICATIONS FOR GLOBAL ECONOMIC GOVERNANCE

José Antonio Ocampo

1. INTRODUCTION

Rising inequalities in national income and wealth are among the most adverse trends that the world has experienced over the past decades. This is mixed with large historical inequality in living standards between developed and developing countries, as well as rising inequalities in recent decades among emerging and developing countries—referred to in this chapter simply as "developing countries." These trends coincide with consolidation of what has come to be called the "second globalization" in the economic history literature. An obvious question to ask is: To what extent are the rules that govern the global economy—or the lack of them—basic determinants of these trends?

In this book we analyze this question from a general perspective as well as through a deep look at the rules related to foreign investment, cross-border financial flows, intellectual property rights, and taxation (in the latter case, the lack of rules). On the basis of this analysis, we make recommendations on how to improve global economic governance to give countries the freedom to adopt the national policies they deem necessary to avoid such negative effects on domestic inequality and to improve the global institutions and rules to avoid negative effects on both international and national inequalities. This chapter provides a framework for those that follow, analyzing cross-cutting issues and summarizing the major concerns raised by the other authors.

The book is the result of a joint project supported by Columbia University's Global Policy Initiative through the Initiative for Policy Dialogue (IPD). For this project, IPD partnered with the University of Waterloo, the South Centre, and the Global Economic Governance

Initiative (GEGI) at Boston University's Pardee School of Global Studies, as well as bringing in researchers from several other institutions.

2. RISING INEQUALITIES AND THEIR LINKS
WITH INTERNATIONAL POLICY RULES

As a growing literature has emphasized,[1] rising domestic income inequalities in a large number of countries is one of the most adverse global trends since the 1980s. Palma (2017) argues that this trend coincides with a broad range of inequality across countries (Gini coefficients in the 0.25–0.65 range), and particularly across middle-income countries. The main difference in inequality levels is the share of the top decile of the income distribution versus the bottom 40 percent and, in extremely unequal countries such as South Africa and several in Latin America), also against middle-income households. These dissimilarities reflect the nature of the social and political settlements, with long historical roots, among different countries. These are what Palma characterizes as the "distributional choice" of different societies.

The growing domestic inequalities that have characterized recent decades have been reflected in the rising share of the top decile of the income distribution, in most cases just the top 1 percent or even 0.1 percent. Although the deterioration of national income distributions has been a fairly generalized trend, some countries have avoided it. Some have even improved it, at least for particular periods, notably most Latin American countries in the early twenty-first century. In Palma's view, the ongoing second globalization has not mechanically led to the increase of inequality, but it has helped to create a set of *opportunities* for it—thus exacerbating the "distributional failures" in most countries. The financialization that has characterized the current globalization (massive growth in the stock of financial assets, increasing mobility of capital across borders, and the financial liberalization that has generated both of these phenomena) is, in his view, a major force behind rising inequality. Other forces include greater oligopolistic concentration, offshoring in search of lower wages, increasing rents from intellectual property rights, higher share of dividends in profits, and the short-termism of shareholders. Many of these processes reflect the reduction in the role of the state worldwide as a result of the market reforms undertaken since the 1980s.

As Ostry, Loungani, and Furceri argue in their contribution to this volume (chapter 3), the basic problem generated by these trends is that larger levels of inequality are bad not only for social and moral reasons but also from the point of view of growth and efficiency. Their statistical analysis illustrates a strong negative relation between the level of inequality and growth in income per capita, and that higher levels of inequality are associated with shorter periods of sustained growth.[2] They also show that fear of the adverse growth effects of redistributive policies is misplaced because the data do not support the supposedly adverse effects of redistribution on growth. To this they add that high levels of inequality may lead to latent social conflicts that may ultimately translate into political backlash against market-friendly policies. Even if market-friendly policies are considered desirable to ensure an increase in living standards, the distributional consequences of these policies should be recognized and addressed.

Growing domestic inequalities have been mixed with large inequalities in per capita income among countries, and particularly between developed and developing countries—in short, international inequalities. This is the result of the long-term historical divergence in development levels of the previous two centuries, particularly during the "first globalization" of the late nineteenth and early twentieth centuries. Average inequalities between developed and developing countries have been declining since the early twenty-first century (since the 1990s in the case of Asia), but inequalities among developing countries and regions have been increasing at the same time.[3]

These two trends have generated a very unequal world income distribution that worsened and then stabilized at very high levels during the ongoing second globalization. The sources of inequality also have been changing: international inequalities continue to dominate the world income distribution, but domestic inequalities have been playing a more significant role in recent decades.

The associated trends have received consideration in national and international policy circles. Concerns over international inequalities have been at the heart of international cooperation since the early post–World War II years, and were reflected in the sequence of United Nations' "Development Decades," beginning in the 1960s (United Nations 2017). The domestic distributive effects also appeared at the forefront of development debates in the 1970s, both in the "Redistribution with Growth" views expressed in the World Bank (Chenery et al. 1974) and in the "Basic Needs Approach" of the International Labor Organization (ILO 1976).

In the 1980s, both domestic and international inequalities were downplayed in international cooperation with the victory of the market reform agenda. Combating world poverty remained a global concern, nonetheless, and it was at the forefront of the Millennium Development Goals adopted by the United Nations in 2000. International and domestic distributive effects have come back with significant force in recent years, leading several multilateral institutions to place these issues at the center of their agendas. One of the World Bank's major objectives, adopted in 2013, is "promoting shared prosperity," which it defined as "fostering income growth of the bottom 40 percent of the population in every country." In turn, in 2015, the United Nations adopted Agenda 2030, which includes as its tenth Sustainable Development Goal the commitment to "reduce income inequality within and among countries." This goal includes not only the World Bank target of improving the living standards of the poorest 40 percent of the population, but also adopting policies to achieve greater equality, especially in the fiscal, wage, and social-protection areas. The International Monetary Fund (IMF) has also argued recently that inequality is a major cause of macroeconomic instability and slower economic growth.[4] This issue is high on the agenda of other major international institutions, including the specialized agencies of the United Nations (UN) system and the Organisation for Economic Co-operation and Development (OECD).

The coincidence of these adverse distributive trends with the globalization processes under way raises the obvious question: to what extent are the rules—or, equally important, the lack of them—that formally or informally govern the global economy basic determinants of world inequalities? To answer this question, we must put together two strains of ongoing research and debates—those that relate to global rules and those that relate to national and international inequalities—and analyze the interactions between the two to draw lessons on how international governance arrangements must be reformed to counteract these trends.

International policy rules encompass a broad set of norms included in global (World Trade Organization [WTO] and the IMF), regional (European Union [EU] and the North American Free Trade Agreement [NAFTA], among others), plurilateral (free trade agreements [FTAs] involving groups of countries), and bilateral (FTAs and investment protection) agreements. To these we should add the mega-regional trade agreements, notably the Trans-Pacific and Transatlantic Trade and Investment Partnerships, the first of which came into being without the participation of the United States. International policy rules also include a set of non-binding norms (for example, the standards and principles of the Extractive Industries Transparency Initiative) that operate as a sort of "soft law."

Existing norms are not necessarily consistent with one another. For example, the policy space given by the IMF Articles of Agreement to countries to regulate cross-border capital flows and the recent support by the IMF to countries to use them as "macroprudential" measures (IMF 2012) run in sharp contrast with the restrictions on doing so included in several investment-protection and free trade agreements, particularly those in which the United States is a partner. No less important are areas with international rules and others that have *no* rules (for example, international migration) or at best very limited rules (taxation), as well as areas with well-developed dispute-settlement mechanisms (trade and investment) and others that lack enforcement or even basic accountability mechanisms to guarantee the achievement of international commitments. This "variable geometry" of international norms also reflects, no doubt, the balance of power in the global economy.

Among international norms, trade rules have been the subject of most research, particularly in terms of their effects on labor markets and income distribution. For this reason, this topic was left out of this project, which focuses on four other families of rules that also have been at the center of global policy debates, including for their possible adverse distributive effects:

(i) Investment agreements, which can restrict the capacity of governments to introduce regulations that promote the public interest (for example, social and environmental regulations); these measures may trigger lawsuits by investors and result in rulings demanding that governments pay significant amounts of compensation to private investors.

(ii) Capacity of countries to manage international capital flows, particularly volatile financial flows, which are a major source of boom-bust cycles, particularly in developing countries but recently also in some developed ones (the European periphery).

(iii) Intense protection of intellectual property rights (IPRs), which has adverse effects on technology-importing countries and can increase the costs of life-saving medicines, agricultural technologies used by smallholders (for example. access to improved seeds), and managing environmental risks, among others.

(iv) Tax competition and, at best, highly insufficient tax cooperation, which may lead to both less progressive tax systems and reduced tax collection, affecting the capacity of countries to adopt progressive tax systems and reducing tax revenues essential to finance redistributive social policies and domestic infrastructure.

Some of these areas interact with one another. Notably, many investment agreements limit the capacity of countries to regulate capital flows because they include short-term flows as part of the investments to be protected. They also may allow firms to sue countries for inadequate protection of IPRs as expropriation measures—even if exceptions to such protection are adopted for health or environmental reasons—or for violating other provisions of the investment agreements, such as "fair and equitable treatment."

Several other international rules—or, again, lack of them—also may have distributive effects: trade rules, of course, but also restrictions and biases in migratory policies, lack of institutional mechanisms to restructure sovereign debt, limited capacity of countries to manage exchange rates in monetary unions, and so forth. We focus on the four families of rules because they have been the subject of significant attention in recent global debates on international rule making. Furthermore, it should be underscored that current trade negotiations are generally more about these issues than about trade as such.

International policy rules affect domestic and international inequalities through six possible channels. These channels are:

(i) The *macroeconomic* channel, which includes the effects international rules can have on the policy space of governments to adopt countercyclical macroeconomic policies to smooth capital account and commodity-price volatility: such volatility has strong distributive consequences given the diverse effects macroeconomic shocks have on different countries, and on different social groups within countries.

(ii) The *microeconomic* channel, which refers to the effects on incentives faced by particular economic agents, as well as changes in relative prices, and the effects they have on the welfare of different social groups.

(iii) The *regulatory-constraints* channel, which is created if international rules limit the willingness and capacity of governments to regulate activities that potentially may have adverse social or environmental effects because international firms are likely to sue the governments for their hypothetical losses as investors.

(iv) The *fiscal* channel, particularly the capacity to raise taxes and the functional effects the international economy can have on tax structures, particularly on direct versus indirect taxes.

(v) The *political-economy* channel, referring to the capacity of different social groups to react to and counteract international rulemaking—notably the difference in the effectiveness of such reactions when rules affect the top 1 percent (or 0.1 percent) versus the middle classes and the poor.

(vi) The *institutional* channel and, in particular, the effects that international dispute settlement can have on national judicial systems and the rule of law, including the possibility that decisions of international tribunals may subvert constitutional principles in place in countries or reverse decisions of national tribunals, including those of national constitutional or supreme courts.

The distributive effects may be understood to include not only inequalities in average per capita income across countries and income and wealth inequalities within countries, but also changes in the functional distribution of income (between wages and profits) employment opportunities, and the policy space for active social policies.

3. INTERNATIONAL RULES AND INEQUALITY

A. FOREIGN INVESTMENT RULES

Foreign investment rules are discussed from complementary economic and legal perspectives, in chapter 4 by Manuel Montes and in chapter 5 by Lise Johnson and Lisa Sachs. The essential mechanism of international cooperation in this area is the network of international investment agreements (IIAs): bilateral investment treaties (BITs) and the specific investment rules included in broader trade agreements. These agreements expose host countries to monetary penalties if legal provisions or government policies and actions are judged to be in violation of their investor-protection obligations. If there are controversies, the investor can sue the state that it deems in violation of its rights, and the associated disputes are settled by arbitration panels, which are viewed as neutral bodies of legal experts—a mechanism known as "investor-state dispute settlement" (ISDS).

ISDS is a fundamental departure from traditional practice under international law, which only allows states to sue other states, such as in the WTO state-state dispute settlement mechanism. Under human rights instruments, individuals, and sometimes corporations, can initiate claims against governments for violating their human rights. However, those seeking to challenge the government must first exhaustively pursue relief through the domestic legal system.

Furthermore, the system gives multinational enterprises (MNEs) extraordinary powers to challenge government action. As Johnson and Sachs argue, domestic jurisdictions typically restrict government exposure to litigation and liability for different types of conduct. In contrast, MNEs can bring their claims to domestic judicial systems, or they can bypass them and bring claims directly to the ISDS system.

Thus protections given to MNEs are more easily enforceable than are other rights and interests—including human rights—protected under international law. One potential consequence of such privileged access is that it will prompt governments to devote more resources to ensuring compliance with obligations regarding treatment of MNEs than to ensuring compliance with obligations owed under human rights or other treaty instruments.

This mechanism strengthens the force of the treaties' legal provisions, but it raises myriad institutional questions regarding the relation of this effectively parallel international judicial system and those that are constituted in each country under traditional democratic principles. In particular, the capacity of arbitration panels to override the highest national judicial authorities (Constitutional or Supreme Courts) becomes a major institutional problem because it may end up granting greater rights to foreign than to domestic investors, thus turning upside down the principle of "national treatment" in international trade law. Furthermore, these disputes are subject to strict secrecy and violate the principle of transparency and scrutiny by the public associated with good governance. There also may be conflicts of interests of professionals involved in arbitration. Each panel is independent of the others, and there are thousands of bilateral and multilateral treaties, so the consistency of the associated "legal doctrine" is not guaranteed.

The World Bank's International Center for Settlement of Investment Disputes (ICSID) has handled a growing number of dispute settlements, as has the United Nations Commission on International Trade Law (UNCITRAL). The size of settlements has been increasing and is particularly important in extractive industries. Most firms are American or European, and Latin American countries are the most affected. More than one-fourth of cases generate monetary compensation. A large proportion of cases found in favor of states result from a lack of jurisdiction, but 60 percent of cases based on merit have been found in favor of firms.[5]

Montes puts forward several problematic features of these arrangements. First, severe imbalances exist between rights and responsibilities because the definition of "investment" is very broad and the concept of "indirect expropriation" hypothetically generated by the effects of changes in national regulations have further expanded investors' rights. Vague treaty provisions also create grounds for many disputes, especially compared to the more rule-based regimes of international trade law, and arbitrators are able to assert their jurisdiction over a wide variety of issues, including regulatory policies on which the top national judicial authorities have already ruled. Public policy is affected not only because governments must draw on the public sector budget for the expenses associated with these disputes but also because governments, and even parliaments, are discouraged from acting on issues that may generate grounds for dispute.

In addition to distorting the business model and generating a specific "rent-seeking" behavior, which is particularly important in natural resource exploitation, two kinds of costs are generated by the system: (i) the fiscal costs of the process and the sanctions if states lose the dispute, and (ii) the perverse governance impact on regulatory policy. The latter is important for particular areas of social and environmental policy illustrated in some of the cases Montes reviews: constraints on black empowerment in South Africa (limits to affirmative action), minimum wage policies in Egypt, land reform in Zimbabwe, access to water in Cochabamba (Bolivia), and environmental regulation in NAFTA.

Furthermore, if governments want to recover their "policy space" by withdrawing from the agreements, most BITs require enforcement of these rules for an extended period after withdrawal or expiry (ten or fifteen years). In contrast to these real and potential costs, Montes suggests that these agreements have limited effects in promoting foreign direct investment (FDI), limited importance in investment decisions, and no effect on political risk premiums.

Johnson and Sachs reinforce these views in several ways. They argue that the most important rationale for investment protection is that it bars governments from discriminating against foreigners, challenging the nepotism and cronyism that elites within a country can use to concentrate market power and wealth within their countries. In this sense, IIAs are an equalizing force that promotes investment and economic growth and generates employment in recipient countries. They argue, however, that depicting IIAs as equalizers needs to be challenged on several grounds.

Arbitral tribunals have stated that actual "foreignness" is not a prerequisite for protection. Protection is sometimes granted to firms registered as foreign that are really owned by individuals or enterprises of the host state. Even when the MNE is truly foreign owned, it may not be disadvantaged because it has the same power as other companies to influence policy in specific countries—if not more. In fact, the MNE may be more connected with the political elite in the host country than are domestic firms, and it can hire highly skilled negotiators and lobbyists to ensure favorable treatment. MNEs also have the capacity to leverage their home governments to pressure host countries to provide them with favorable treatment. Finally, MNEs use their potential mobility to gain bargaining power over governments and derive benefits from their capacity to use corporate affiliates to book profits in low tax jurisdictions; engage in regulatory arbitrage; shield their assets from creditors seeking to secure payment for tax, environmental, or other liabilities; and take advantage of international tax treaties.

Indeed, Johnson and Sachs claim that the whole judicial network created by ISDS generates strong benefits for MNEs. They argue that the distribution of economic, social, and political power at the national level shape property rights in individual countries, and that international law has traditionally left the power to define the scope of property rights and allocate them among members of society to domestic jurisdictions. IIAs, however, have changed that dynamic. Rather than merely protecting property rights defined through domestic processes, they *create* new property rights in favor of MNEs that can be invoked against governments and domestic agents. This includes turning expectations into enforceable legal guarantees, such as the effective right to continue to enjoy government subsidies and to avoid paying higher taxes, to be awarded permits for activities in environmentally protected areas, to be exempted from rising social-protection standards, and to enjoy certain rates of return in public infrastructure projects, among others.

In their view, arbitral tribunals have had the power to shape and reshape the scope and nature of property rights protections through their interpretation of IIA provisions on expropriation. Following legal provisions valid at the national level, sovereign governments have the right to expropriate property in the public interest, but governments are required to compensate investors for this action. As emphasized by Montes, an additional problem with IIAs is the principle of "indirect expropriations" generated by changes in regulations that negatively affect the property's value. Through decisions on indirect expropriations, arbitral tribunals in ISDS disputes may again expand the property rights of MNEs.

The doctrine of "legitimate expectations" is particularly troublesome in this regard. An additional related threat is that unlawful or unauthorized promises can become enforceable, and government may be forced to compensate an investor or investor-owned firm for breaking an unauthorized promise. Furthermore, this may encourage improper collusion between the project proponent and those in the government that support the proposed investment—a collusive behavior forbidden in most domestic legal systems.

Furthermore, protection of the "legitimate expectations" of MNEs is particularly favorable to existing asset holders and powerful interests because the general rule adopted by tribunals is that expectations held at the time the investment is made should be protected. This includes protection against changes in legislation, court decisions, administrative actions, and shifts in policies or practices. This preference for protecting existing firms may, of course, entrench or increase inequality among firms by safeguarding the power of market incumbents.

Notably, according to Johnson and Sachs, MNEs have used IIAs to prevent legal systems from combating three of the most inequality-inducing effects that can arise from property rights systems: negative externalities, monopoly practices, and undue appropriation of gains. In the first case, MNEs have used investment protection to secure compensation for environmental laws and decisions that seek to avoid environmental externalities—an issue also raised by Montes. In the second case, they have used IIAs to protect themselves against regulations of tariffs or policies combating anticompetitive pricing in provision of public services, as well as provisions that limit IPRs. In the third case, they have combated "windfall-profits taxes" seeking to capture for the public sector a greater share of gains derived from rising commodity prices—a gain unrelated to an investor's increased efficiency.

Viewed overall, the "fair and equitable treatment" for MNEs provided by IIAs and the associated ISDS may generate unfair or inequitable impacts on others—and, indeed, on host countries as a whole. A remarkable case is the inequality they generate vis-à-vis domestic firms through the privileged access they give MNEs to procedural remedies and the protection of the expectations they had at the time an investment was made. This includes (i) unequal procedural rights for protection with respect to relations with the host state government, as well as disputes with other private parties; and (ii) unequal substantive standards of protection that strengthen the legal force of their economic rights and "expectations." This creates new property rights and privileged access to the judicial system that domestic agents lack, with potentially negative impacts on competing rights and interests held by the latter. As stated previously, this is the principle of "national treatment" upside down.

This directly generates a new form of inequality: limiting the ability of governments to increase costs through legislation or policies in different social and environmental areas, and placing limits on domestic economic regulations aimed at regulating noncompetitive markets. Environmental and social protections and land redistribution policies have been adversely affected by the domestic policy straitjackets introduced through investor protection obligations. They may even limit the capacity or costs of new tax legislation despite the exceptions included in IIAs allowing host states to maintain the autonomy to tax.[6]

In our typology of channels through which international rules can affect domestic inequality, the most important is the institutional channel, because IIAs create a parallel beneficial channel for MNEs. They also constrain policy making and have a strong capacity to influence domestic policies. In this regard, the regulatory-constraints channel and the political-economy channel are also important.

B. CAPITAL ACCOUNT RULES

Two chapters analyze the implications of capital account liberalization and associated policy rules: chapter 3, by Jonathan Ostry, Prakash Loungani, and Davide Furceri; and chapter 6, by Kevin Gallagher, Guillermo Lagarda, and Jennifer Linares.

Ostry, Loungani, and Furceri begin by analyzing the growth benefits of capital account liberalization and conclude that these benefits are small or negligible and rarely significant in statistical terms. However, this average effect hides important differences across countries: they have moderate benefits when reform episodes have not been followed by crises, but they have high costs when liberalization has led to financial collapse, which is not an uncommon phenomenon. Of the one hundred fifty episodes of capital inflows included in their database, about one-fifth have ended up in financial crises, and about half of those in strong recessions. This indicates that capital inflow surges amplify financial and macroeconomic vulnerabilities and the capacity of countries to manage them. Avoiding a succeeding crisis is, therefore, the critical issue. These vulnerabilities are also associated with the composition (not just the level) of inflows: surges associated with short-term capital flows generate stronger vulnerabilities than those in which longer-term flows (particularly foreign direct investment) play a stronger role.

Ostry, Loungani, and Furceri also present several channels through which capital account liberalization may lead to higher inequality. The most important, which is closely linked to its macroeconomic effects, is whether it leads to higher volatility and crises. When crises materialize, inequality increases. Liberalization also may have a financial access bias in favor of those who are better off—an effect that is stronger with access to international markets. In turn, international capital mobility can affect the distribution of income through its effect on the bargaining power of labor. The regression results presented suggest that capital account liberalization has typically led to an increase in the Gini coefficient of about 0.5 percent in the short term (one year after the change in liberalization), with slightly larger effects over the next couple of years. But the impact of financial openness on inequality is much larger when it is followed by a crisis.

Gallagher, Lagarda, and Linares explore these effects as well as those of capital account regulations and their links to macroeconomic stability. Their analysis is based on statistical exercises with a panel of 141 countries from 1990 to 2013. They, too, find that the effects of capital account liberalization on inequality depend heavily on macroeconomic conditions: liberalization is associated with increases in inequality when macroeconomic volatility materializes. Capital account regulations are then associated with less inequality. This can be seen in their analysis of the differential impacts of capital account liberalization on inequality during booms and busts. There are ambiguous impacts on income inequality during booms (or even positive effects), but capital account openness unambiguously exacerbates income inequality during busts.

The capacity to manage the macroeconomic effects of capital account volatility is the critical issue. The greater the financial depth of the recipient economy and the stronger its institutions, the less detrimental will be the effect of capital account liberalization on income inequality. These conditions tend to be associated with the level of development. So, adverse effects are more common in developing countries, and they are particularly severe during periods of economic contraction. The capacity to put in place adequate social-protection systems ("social safety nets") to manage the adverse social effects of economic contractions is an important factor, but the strength of these systems is strongly associated with the level of development.

Both chapters conclude that the link between economic inequality and capital account openness is associated with the macroeconomic effects of the latter. The macroeconomic volatility that capital account liberalization can generate, in particular for developing economies where capital flows are strongly procyclical, is the crucial issue. Capital account regulation or management can play a useful role in reducing the associated macroeconomic volatility.[7] Maintaining the autonomy for countries to manage such volatility is fundamental. But, as previously pointed out, although such autonomy is fully recognized in the IMF's Articles of Agreement, several investment-protection and free trade agreements, particularly those with the United States, guarantee that even short-term flows are liberalized.

In the typology of channels through which the effects of international rules can affect inequality, the macroeconomic channel is the critical one. The policy space that international agreements give countries to manage the macroeconomic effects of capital account volatility is, therefore, crucial.

C. INTELLECTUAL PROPERTY RIGHTS

Carlos Correa explores the issues associated with intellectual property rights in chapter 7. He begins by underscoring the steady increase in the protection of IPRs all over the world. In developed countries, this process was the result of domestic pressure from various industries (pharmaceutical, biotechnology, information and communications technologies, and entertainment, among others). In developing countries, protection has resulted mainly due to the pressure exercised on them by developed countries through FTAs. In Correa's view, this generates international and domestic inequalities and creates policy conflicts with other fields of international law—those that protect public health, the environment, biological diversity, food security, and access to knowledge. Furthermore, against its basic justification, the extension of IPRs often counters, rather than facilitates, the core objective of promoting innovation.

Correa proposes a taxonomy of intellectual property (IP) provisions. The first are the rules included in the WTO Agreement on Trade-Related Aspects of Intellectual Property Rights (TRIPS), which Correa refers to as "TRIPS-minimum." The second is "TRIPS-plus," which extends the terms of protection of patents, applies border measures to exports (the TRIPS agreement only requires them for imports), and protects new uses or methods/processes relating to a known product. This is the most common regime in FTAs. The third is "TRIPS-extra," which introduces issues not addressed by the WTO agreement, such as the liability of Internet service providers, the settlement of domain name disputes, data exclusivity for biological products, and the linkage between drug registration and patent protection.

In his view, implementation of the TRIPS agreement in the health area is exacerbated the lack of access to medicines, particularly in developing countries, due to higher costs of protected drugs. Contrary to its stated objectives, higher standards of IP protection do not seem to have increased technology or foreign investment flows, and they certainly have not contributed to increasing research and development on the diseases prevailing in developing countries. Large pharmaceutical companies continued to focus on commercially attractive treatments.

The TRIPS agreement allowed WTO members to introduce some measures—such as compulsory licenses and parallel imports—that may attenuate the inequalities generated by IP protections. The 2001 Doha Agreement went a step forward by establishing a specific exception to IPRs in the case of public health. This generated the expectation that the ratcheting up of IP protection would at least slow down, but this result did not materialize. Article 7 of the TRIPS agreement, proposed by developing countries, reflected the concern that granting IPRs as a tool to promote innovation could not be accompanied by an adequate transfer and dissemination of technology. It therefore set the principle that the "balance of rights and obligations" should ensure that intellectual property works "to the mutual advantage of producers and users of technological knowledge and in a manner conducive to social and economic welfare." But, again, the practical application of this principle has been limited.

FTAs also may include some flexibilities. For example, in response to concerns raised by health authorities in other countries and by nongovernmental organizations (NGOs) about the effects of IPRs on access to medicines, some FTAs signed by the United States include "side letters" or "understandings" that allude to the contracting parties' ability to protect public health. However, in contrast to this, U.S. FTAs typically require a "linkage" between patent protection and drug marketing approval, which stretches rights by allowing the patent owner to block the regulatory approval for marketing of competing generic products. This is aggravated by the "evergreening" of basic patents, which allows patenting of marginal improvements; this is commonly a result of a deficient examination of the application by the patent offices. Correa states that eliminating secondary patents could, conservatively, free up to 36 percent of new medicines for generic production. This practice could be limited if the linkage provisions applied only to active ingredients, excluding patents covering other subject matter.

The major conclusion is that strengthening IPRs in the WTO and, even more, in TRIPS-plus and TRIPS-extra agreements, is likely to aggravate current inequalities among and within countries, particularly in the latter case for developing countries.

In terms of our typology of channels through which international rules generate inequalities, the most important in this case is the microeconomic channel. The protection granted generates rents for agents whose IP is protected, allowing them to increase the prices paid by consumers. The regulatory-constraints channel may also have a role because countries will be constrained in their capacity to regulate activities that potentially have adverse social or environmental effects if those regulations are perceived by holders of IPRs as constraints on their rights.

D. TAX COMPETITION AND FISCAL ADJUSTMENT

In chapter 9, Valpy FitzGerald and Erika Siu analyze a fourth major topic: weaknesses in the principles and institutions for international tax cooperation. Global market integration tends to drive down taxes on mobile factors of production, particularly capital, and to increase taxes on less mobile factors such as labor. In the latter case, this includes ratcheting up indirect taxes, the incidence of which is also mainly borne by labor. A major issue has been the long-term trend toward lower rates for both corporate and personal income taxes (CIT and PIT, respectively) and the shift toward sales and value-added taxes.

The problem is not only the lower tax *rates* applied on profits but also, and more importantly, the lower tax *bases*. This is the result of competition among countries to attract investment to foster economic growth, and the pressure from foreign investors as well as domestic businesses that compete in international markets to obtain concessions in the form of tax holidays, tax-free zones, and acceptance of corporate-ownership structures that facilitate tax avoidance. This is mixed, particularly in the case of MNEs, with their capacity to shift profits to locations with low tax rates or tax-free offshore centers. The mix of tax competition and "base erosion" and "profit shifting"—terms widely used due to the initiative of OECD to mitigate them—has resulted in reduced corporate taxes and aggressive tax avoidance (or even evasion) by large firms.

These processes are reflected in the fact that the *effective* CIT rates—that is, the amount of tax corporations actually pay as a proportion of profits—is much lower than statutory rates. According to the World Bank's "Doing Business" data, the effective rate in OECD countries is only 13 percent, and in developing countries it averages around 16 percent. According to Reidel (2014), large MNEs transfer 30 percent or more of their income earned at high-tax affiliates to lower-tax jurisdictions.

The OECD (2015) estimates that base erosion and profit shifting cause revenue losses worldwide of $100 billion to $240 billion annually—equivalent to between 4 and 10 percent of global revenues from CIT. This may be an underestimate: IMF researchers have estimated revenue losses of approximately $200 billion, or about 1.3 percent of non-OECD countries' gross domestic product (GDP), and $400–500 billion for OECD countries, or about 1 percent of their GDP (Crivelli et al. 2015). As a proportion of tax revenues, and given developing countries' greater reliance on corporate taxes and their lower tax revenues relative to GDP, the losses for them are higher.

The costs of reduced tax revenues may be high: limited resources for social programs and infrastructure investment—in the latter case, with negative effects on economic growth. In contrast, the benefits that low-tax locations receive in terms of economic growth are generally low, as lower taxes may merely shift financial assets—and, in many cases, just the recording of where such assets are located—rather than productive capital, and may thus not lead to higher fixed-capital investment (Klemm and van Parys 2009).

According to FitzGerald and Siu, the distributive effect of these trends is clearly negative. They significantly reduce taxes on profit incomes (both CIT and PIT on dividends) and directly increase inequality, whether measured through the distribution of household income or the wage/profit split. They also may limit social spending, with equally adverse domestic distributive effects. And, as indicated, they contribute to international inequalities because the relative effects are stronger on developing countries, which depend more heavily on these taxes.

In terms of our typology, the fiscal channel plays the critical role here. FitzGerald and Siu's major conclusion is that enhanced international tax cooperation would help to reduce national income inequality as well as international inequalities; indeed, in the latter case, replacing the role of what they consider the failing system of development aid.

An interesting complement to this analysis is Ostry, Loungani, and Furceri's discussion in chapter 3 of what international rules should be in place to support fiscal adjustment—particularly in IMF programs—and the implications of debt rules introduced in international agreements, such as the Maastricht rules of the EU. The underlying macroeconomic conditions are different in these two cases: in the first case, it would involve countries facing crises; in the second case, it may involve nations that face little or no risk of a crisis.

The analysis of several episodes of fiscal consolidation provided by Ostry, Loungani, and Furceri indicates that these episodes are followed by significant drops in output and increases in inequality.[8] They thus support the IMF's policy advice—not always followed in practice—that "a case-by-case assessment of what is an appropriate pace of consolidation" is required and that fiscal policy should be more growth friendly. In this regard, they emphasize a family of fiscal policies with the potential to promote both efficiency *and* equality: taxes on activities with negative externalities paid mostly by the better-off but harmful to the poor. In turn, in countries not facing the risk of crises, they conclude that the benefits of lower debts do not generally outweigh the transitional costs associated with fiscal consolidation due to the austerity policies that may be required to reduce debt ratios.

4. IMPLICATIONS FOR GLOBAL ECONOMIC GOVERNANCE

What model for global governance might be supportive of efforts to address national and international inequalities? In relation to international inequalities, the model used after World War II is a mix of asymmetric rules that provide developing countries with a type of "positive discrimination" and special mechanisms of financing (multilateral development banks and official development assistance). Among the issues covered here, the only asymmetric rules are those included in the WTO's TRIPS agreement, which are moderate. In all four topics studied in this volume, it can be argued that existing rules may increase international inequalities because developing countries are mainly recipients of foreign investment, are subject to stronger volatility in external financing, are technologically dependent, and are more heavily reliant on corporate taxes than are developed countries.

In the case of domestic inequalities, in chapter 2 Eric Helleiner correctly argues that an important point of reference is the original design of the Bretton Woods system. The concerns about national inequalities led to an innovative model for global governance that mixed multilateral cooperation with ample policy space for countries to manage short-term macroeconomic policies, development strategies, labor standards, and social security. This "embedded liberal" model—to use the term Ruggie (1982) popularized—may be useful today for those seeking to reform global financial governance in ways that might support efforts to address national inequalities.

Embedded liberalism, in Ruggie's formulation, sought to combine strengthened multilateralism with a commitment to support interventionist economic and social policies. Rather than seeing a conflict between adequate policy space for national policies and strengthened multilateral cooperation, this model highlighted their complementarity. An interesting case Helleiner discusses extensively is that of capital controls—or capital account regulations. The two architects of the Bretton Woods system, John Maynard Keynes and Harry Dexter White, recognized that capital controls were essential to provide countries with macroeconomic policy autonomy, and in the early stages of the negotiation, they called for the cooperation of capital source and recipient countries to guarantee the effectiveness of the controls. Although this proposal ultimately was not accepted, the Bretton Woods Agreement maintained countries' autonomy to manage capital flows.

In Helleiner's view, the Bretton Woods Agreement was a product of unique circumstances: the effective role of "normative entrepreneurs," among whom Keynes and White stand out; interstate power relations; and institutional factors, which generally call for incremental rather than radical reforms.[9] The political environment today is different in many ways, but reforms have to take into account those three factors: ideas, interstate power, and institutional legacies. In the field of financial regulation, including cross-country capital flows, Helleiner suggests that the "cooperative regulatory decentralization" model is appropriate and is compatible with embedded liberalism.

In contemporary global governance debates, the relation between policy space and international cooperation should differentiate between two cases formulated in the literature as the "paradoxes" of global governance: Inge Kaul's "sovereignty paradox" and Dani Rodrik's "globalization paradox." Kaul defines the sovereignty paradox as a situation in which governments "are losing policymaking sovereignty, because they hold on to conventional strategies of realizing sovereignty, which may make them shy away from international cooperation. But, in policy fields marked by global public goods (GPG)-type challenges and interdependence, such behavior actually undermines rather than strengthens states' policymaking capacity" (2013, 34). Rodrik defines the globalization paradox as the result of the fact that "we cannot simultaneously pursue democracy, national determination, and economic globalization." This implies that "democracies have the right to protect their social arrangements, and when this right clashes with the requirements of the global economy, it is the latter that should give way." Therefore, "a thin layer of international rules that leaves substantial room for maneuver by national governments is a better globalization" (2011, xviii–xix).

As I have argued previously (Ocampo 2016), these two paradoxes apply to different domains of global governance. The first applies to areas in which there is a significant level of interdependence among countries and implies that in those cases *international institutions and rules* are essential and can be understood as cases in which sovereignty is shared by national governments. In contrast, the second is a case in which international rules should provide adequate *policy space* in a context in which the exercise of national sovereignty is still relevant, but cooperation should provide complementary mechanisms that allow national policies to be fully effective. The embedded liberalism tradition belongs predominantly to the second case but may not be incompatible with the first to the extent that national policies are still required to adapt international rules to national contexts. In both cases, international institutional reforms and new rules or a reinterpretation of existing rules could be essential.

Among the four topics discussed in this volume, the major case in which stronger international cooperation is required is in the field of taxation. This is the best case in which strong international interdependence has not been recognized, and *all* countries have therefore lost policy-making capacity.

The major form of cooperation in this area has been a network of more than three thousand bilateral tax treaties, largely aimed at avoiding double taxation. However, their capacity to correct the problem has been quite limited, leading to some cases in which they have actually facilitated the use of the tax benefits provided by both partners in the treaty—leading, in fact, to "double nontaxation." There has also been tax cooperation by major developed countries in the OECD, and in the United Nations through the Economic and Social Council (ECOSOC) Committee of Experts on International Cooperation in Tax Matters. The Global Forum on Transparency and Exchange of Information for Tax Purposes was created by the OECD in 2000 and restructured in 2009 to have an independent secretariat and allow an expanded membership. In turn, the international scandals and investigations conducted by several industrial countries that uncovered multiple examples of transfer-price abuses led the G-20 in 2012 to launch the Base Erosion and Profit Shifting (BEPS) Initiative, under the leadership of OECD.

These arrangements are, however, clearly insufficient. First, despite the significant work that it has done, the OECD is not globally representative and counts only a few emerging and no low-income countries as members. This is also true of the BEPS process, despite the fact that it has included the nine non-OECD G-20 nations. The Global Forum has a broader membership, but it is still under the OECD axis. Equally important, this loose governance structure has not been able to effectively restrain tax competition.

Several institutional reforms to enhance international tax cooperation have been put on the table throughout the years. An important one was made by the Zedillo Commission, convened by the UN in preparation for the first International Conference on Financing for Development that took place in Monterrey, Mexico, in 2002 (United Nations 2001). It proposed creation of an International Tax Organization (ITO) to surveil tax developments worldwide, take a leading role in restraining tax competition, serve as a forum for international dispute settlement on tax matters, and sponsor the sharing of information among tax authorities. A second proposal that has been on the table is to upgrade the UN Committee of Experts to an intergovernmental commission. This proposal was made by the UN Secretary General in 2004 and again by the Group of 77 and China to the Third International Conference on Financing for Development that took place in Addis Ababa in 2015. A set of complementary proposal by ICRICT (2015) includes the design of a UN Convention to combat abusive tax practices and creation of a global asset registry.[10]

Some of the new principles needed to guide this cooperation have been agreed in the BEPS process. This initiative has, first of all, adopted the principle that MNEs should be taxed "where economic activities take place and where value is created." It has decided that large MNEs have the obligation to report the revenues, profits, taxes paid, employees, and assets in each country where they do business. Such country-by-country reporting is a step toward transparency—another major objective of cooperation in this area. In addition, the BEPS process has introduced two important revisions to bilateral tax treaties: the "primary purpose test," which provides more legal authority for countries to evaluate the economic substance of income attribution; and the "permanent establishment" or economic nexus rules, which expands the ability to tax economic activity occurring through commissioner arrangements within countries' borders and potentially also through electronic commerce.

Reforms should be more ambitious. ICRICT (2015) has proposed that the world move in the long run to a system in which MNEs would be taxed as single and unified firms. This would eliminate a major problem in the existing rules, which is the appropriateness of "transfer prices" in transactions among parts of a multinational group: existing rules facilitate tax avoidance or open evasion. Global taxes would then be divided among countries through a "formulary apportionment" based on sales, employment, and resources used, among other possible factors. This system has been used to divide corporate profits at the subnational level in some federal states. In recent years, the EU also has been discussing a proposal for a system known as the Common Consolidated Corporate Tax Base, which has been approved by the European Parliament but has not yet reached the unanimous consensus of governments for full implementation. During the transition to the new system, ICRICT has proposed that leading nations could impose a global minimum corporate tax rate to stop the race to the bottom.[11]

Major institutional innovations are also required in investment agreements, in particular to reform ISDS. A clear solution to this problem would be an International Tribunal on Investment. Indeed, the Investment Court System proposed by the EU in the (now effectively suspended) negotiations of the Transatlantic Trade and Investment Partnership (TTIP) belongs to this line of recommendations.[12] A global tribunal could be set up as a formal dispute settlement mechanism within a broader Multilateral Investment Agreement, which could operate much as a similar WTO mechanism does. Indeed, in his contribution to this volume (chapter 8), Osvaldo Rosales argues that a mistake of developing countries—and, I would add, nongovernmental organizations—has been their refusal to negotiate a multilateral regime of this sort, which has made them dependent on bilateral agreements in which power relations are strongly unbalanced.

The second issue in relation to the investment rules area is the policy space for national (or in the case of Europe, regional) regulations. Rosales's analysis of the Trans-Pacific Partnership (TPP) underscores that in the investment chapter the United States agreed to expand the regulatory space reserved to states in environment, public welfare, and health, as well as in financial regulation, with temporary financial safeguards allowed in "exceptional circumstances." This was also a major area of interest of the EU in the TTIP. A related issue that links these proposals with the institutional mechanism in place is the relation between the international and national tribunals on issues associated with regulatory policies.

Following the analysis of both Johnson and Sachs (chapter 5) and Montes (chapter 4), a crucial issue is the elimination of, or severe limitations on, the principle of "indirect expropriation." This principle has generated an enormous ground for disputes in ISDS and has allowed arbitrators to assert their jurisdiction over diverse issues associated with regulatory policies. According to their analyses, the doctrine of "legitimate expectations" should be entirely eliminated, except only for explicit legal commitments made by the government or by law in the recipient country.

In the two other topics analyzed in this volume—capital account rules and IPRs—the issue is not so much the institutional mechanisms but strictly the effective policy space countries should enjoy under the current international institutional framework. The case of capital account rules is the simplest of the two cases because the IMF Articles of Agreement guarantee the autonomy of countries to regulate cross-country capital flows. In the "institutional view" on capital account management adopted by the IMF in 2012, it was agreed that full liberalization of capital flows is not an appropriate goal for all countries at all times, and that regulating (or managing) cross-border capital flows is a useful "macroprudential" instrument to guarantee macroeconomic and financial stability under certain conditions (IMF 2012). The IMF recommended that macroprudential management of capital flows be allowed in *all* bilateral and regional agreements and that they should be accepted in all future trade treaties. However, there has been no action in this field.

The major issue in this regard is the strong position of the United States in FTAs and investment agreements that there should be no limitations on cross-border capital flows. In this regard, as Rosales points out, an advance in the TPP negotiations was the acceptance by the United States of both the WTO balance of payments provisions and the IMF rules on capital account regulations. The respective provisions in the TPP would allow governments to restrict payments and transfers "in the event of serious balance of payments and external financial difficulties or threats thereof," so long as the measures would not exceed eighteen months in duration, although extension of the measure for an additional year would be allowed in exceptional circumstances.

In the case of IPRs, the crucial issue is to explore options for the implementation of the IP obligations imposed by TRIPSs and FTAs, with the aim of reducing their potential negative impact. This should include limiting the presumption of validity of patents and applying rigorous standards to examine patent applications. It should also include the more active use of provisions in the TRIPS agreement and FTAs allowing exceptions based on "public interest"—interpreting, of course, this principle in strong terms. Indeed, in the most optimistic scenario, the type of exceptions agreed for public health in the WTO in 2001 could be extended in other fields. One clear candidate would be the technologies to combat climate change. This freedom could be granted to developing countries alone, within the asymmetric principles that characterize some international agreements.

The major issue in this area has always come from the United States. The Democratic Party majority in the U.S. Congress in 2007 obtained modification of pharmaceutical-related provisions in the FTAs, which would apply to treaties signed but not yet ratified.[13] In the instructions to TPP negotiators, legislators from the Democratic Party were also able to incorporate explicit flexibilities in the chapters on IPRs and, as already pointed out, in ISDS. In any case, the result was ambiguous because the paragraphs aimed at preserving the space for public policy were accompanied by drastic provisions aimed at further protecting IPRs, which included standards of protection more demanding than that of the TRIPS in their scope for patentability of an invention, and it extended the patent terms and expanded the scope for trademarks.

Much more must be done in redesigning global institutions and rules to manage the adverse effects that some international processes and existing rules have had in terms of inequalities. This volume provides a strong analysis of several of the most important topics, as well as a set of recommendations for how to manage these issues, mixing stronger international cooperation with a redefinition of the relevant rules and greater policy space to adopt national policies to combat inequalities. However, a long road must be traveled to manage the problems that globalization and inappropriate rules have been generating.

NOTES

1. See, among others, Bourguignon and Morrison (2002), Cornia (2004), Milanovic (2005, 2011), Palma (2011, 2016), Ortiz and Cummins (2011), Stiglitz (2012), Piketty (2014), Atkinson (2015), and Bourguignon (2015). See also Palma (2017), which was a background paper for this project.

2. These results hold even when standard growth determinants are included, such as physical and human capital as well as external shocks, the quality of institutions, and measures of openness to trade.

3. See Ocampo and Parra (2007) and the analysis of the heterogeneity of developing countries in Alonso (2016).

4. See, among other IMF contributions, Ostry et al. (2014).

5. See a detailed analysis of these issues in UNCTAD (2015).

6. The only restriction is that any tax changes must be nondiscriminatory in nature—meeting the criteria of national treatment and the most favored nation rule.

7. There is an extensive literature on this subject. For a recent survey and analysis of the effects of capital account regulations, see Erten and Ocampo (2017).

8. Specifically, a fiscal adjustment of about 1 percentage point of GDP on average is followed by a 2 percentage point drop in output at the peak (two years after the consolidation episode) and by a 1.5 percent increase in the Gini coefficient in the same year as the consolidation episode and by more than 3 percent two years after.

9. In the Bretton Woods Agreement, in Helleiner's view, they built on the several institutions that had been put in place in inter-American relations during World War II.

10. They also include the proposal that the UN Global Compact and the OECD Guidelines for MNEs recognize that the obligation to pay fair taxes is a preeminent corporate social responsibility.

11. Reforms of the transfer pricing rules could be useful—a topic on which significant work has been done by the OECD. There also could be a broader use of the profit-split method already used in the OECD guidelines, which combines company profits from groups of transactions (revenues and expenses) and apportions them among jurisdictions.

12. See, in this regard, http://trade.ec.europa.eu/doclib/docs/2015/january/tradoc_153018.pdf.

13. According to the summary provided by Rosales, the proposed changes included limiting granting marketing exclusivity in some cases to a period contemporaneous with that obtained in the United States; eliminating provision for patent term extensions based on approval delay; eliminating the express linkage between patents and marketing approval; and incorporating express provision for use of compulsory licensing notwithstanding existing marketing exclusivity.

REFERENCES

Alonso, José Antonio. 2016. "Beyond Aid: Reshaping the Development Cooperation System." In *Global Governance and Development*, ed. José Antonio Ocampo, 101–35. New York: Oxford University Press.

Atkinson, Anthony. 2015. *Inequality: What Can Be Done?*. Cambridge, MA: Harvard University Press.

Bourguignon, François. 2015. *The Globalization of Inequality*. Princeton, NJ: Princeton University Press.

Bourguignon, François, and Christian Morrison. 2002. "Inequality Among World Citizens: 1820–1992." *American Economic Review* 92 (4): 727–44.

Chenery, Hollis, Montek Ahluwalia, C. L. G. Bell, John H. Duloy, and Richard Jolly, eds. 1974. *Redistribution with Growth*. New York: Oxford University Press.

Cornia, Giovanni Andrea, ed. 2004. *Inequality, Growth, and Poverty in an Era of Liberalization and Globalization*. Oxford: Oxford University Press/United Nations University, World Institute for Development Economics Research.

Crivelli, Ernesto, Ruud De Mooij, and Michael Keen, eds. 2015. "Base Erosion, Profit Shifting and Developing Countries." IMF Working Paper WP/15/118, May.

Erten, Bilge, and José Antonio Ocampo. 2017. "Macroeconomic Effects of Capital Account Regulations." *IMF Economic Review* 65 (2): 193–240.

ICRICT (Independent Commission for the Reform of International Corporate Taxation). 2015. "Declaration." https://www.icrict.com/icrict-documentsthe-declaration.

ILO (International Labour Organization). 1976. *Employment, Growth and Basic Needs: A One-World Problem.* Geneva: ILO.

IMF (International Monetary Fund). 2012. "The Liberalization and Management of Capital Flows: An Institutional View." Washington, DC: International Monetary Fund.

Kaul, Inge. 2013. "Meeting Global Challenges: Assessing Governance Readiness." In *The Governance Report 2013: Sovereignty, Fiscal Policy, Innovations, Trade-Offs, Indicators,* Hertie School of Governance, 33–58. Oxford: Oxford University Press.

Klemm, Alexander, and Stefan van Parys. 2009. "Empirical Evidence on the Effects of Tax Incentives." IMF Working Paper WP/09/136, July.

Milanovic, Branko. 2005. *Worlds Apart: Global and International Inequality, 1950–2000.* Princeton, NJ: Princeton University Press.

——. 2011. *The Haves and Have-Nots: A Brief and Idiosyncratic History of Global Inequality.* New York: Basic Books.

Ocampo, José Antonio. 2016. "Global Economic and Social Governance and the United Nations System." In *Global Governance and Development,* ed. José Antonio Ocampo, 3–31. New York: Oxford University Press.

Ocampo, José Antonio, and Mariángela Parra. 2007. "The Dual Divergence: Growth Successes and Collapses in the Developing World Since 1980." In *Economic Growth with Equity: Challenges for Latin America,* ed. Ricardo Ffrench-Davis and José Luis Machinea, 61–92. Houndmills, UK: Palgrave Macmillan and ECLAC.

OECD (Organization for Economic Cooperation and Development). 2015. "Countering Harmful Tax Practices More Effectively, Taking Into Account Transparency and Substance, Action 5—2015 Final Report." OECD/G20 Base Erosion and Profit Shifting Project.

Ortiz, Isabel, and Matthew Cummins. 2011. "Global Inequality: Beyond the Bottom Billion: A Rapid Review of Income Distribution in 141 Countries." UNICEF Social and Economic Policy Working Paper, April (rev. July).

Ostry, Jonathan D., Andrew Berg, and Charalambos G. Tsangarides. 2014. "Redistribution, Inequality, and Growth." IMF Staff Discussion Note, SDN/14/02, February.

Palma, José Gabriel. 2011. "Homogeneous Middles vs. Heterogeneous Tails, and the End of the 'Inverted-U': The Share of the Rich Is What It's All About." *Development and Change* 42 (1): 87–153.

——. 2016. "Do Nations Just Get the Inequality They Deserve? The 'Palma Ratio' Re-examined." In *Inequality and Growth: Patterns and Policy,* vol. 2: *Regions and Regularities,* ed. Kaushik Basu and Joseph E. Stiglitz, 35–93. Houndmills, UK: Palgrave Macmillan.

——. 2017. "Does the Broad Spectrum of Inequality Across the World in the Current Era of Neo-Liberal Globalization Reflect a Wide Diversity of Fundamentals, or

Just a Multiplicity of Political Settlements and Market Failures?." Working Paper. Initiative for Policy Dialogue. http://policydialogue.org/files/publications/papers /Palma-Intl-Rules.pdf.

Piketty, Thomas. 2014. *Capital in the Twenty-First Century*. Cambridge, MA: Belknap Press of Harvard University Press.

Reidel, Nadine. 2014. "Quantifying International Tax Avoidance: A Review of the Academic Literature." ETPF Policy Paper No. 2. London: European Tax Policy Forum.

Rodrik, Dani. 2011. *The Globalization Paradox: Democracy and the Future of the World Economy*. New York: Norton.

Ruggie, John. 1982. "International Regimes, Transactions and Change: Embedded Liberalism in the Postwar Economic Order." *International Organization* 36: 379–415.

Stiglitz, Joseph E. 2012. *The Price of Inequality*. New York: Norton.

UNCTAD (United Nations Conference on Trade and Development). 2015. "World Investment Report: Reforming International Investment Governance." Geneva: UNCTAD.

United Nations. 2001. "Report of the High-Level Panel on Financing for Development." *Zedillo Report*. New York: United Nations.

——. 2017. *World Economic and Social Survey: Reflecting on Seventy Years of Development Policy Analysis*. New York: United Nations.

CHAPTER 2

National Inequalities and the Political Economy of Global Financial Reform

Eric Helleiner

Other chapters in this volume examine how international rules contribute to national economic inequalities. Some of them also offer recommendations for global governance reform that could counterbalance the negative impacts existing international rules may have on national inequalities. Building on their insights, in this chapter I explore two political economy questions related to the reform process, with a special focus on global financial governance: What model for global financial governance can support efforts to address national equalities? What political variables drive and shape the process of global financial reform?

It is often forgotten that the key architects of the Bretton Woods system also worried about national inequalities and that their proposals for global financial reform were explicitly designed with these concerns in mind. Examining the origins of the postwar global financial order provides a useful framework for answering these questions. I begin with a brief overview of that history. The Bretton Woods architects linked national inequality concerns to an innovative "autonomy-reinforcing" model of global financial reform that sought to strengthen multilateral cooperation in ways that bolstered national policy space. This "embedded liberal" model may be useful today for reforming global financial governance in ways that address national inequalities.

I then analyze how the Bretton Woods discussions help us understand how global financial reform takes place and explore the role of key political cal variables—ideas, power and interests, and institutional legacies—in shaping the reform process in the early 1940s. Although the world has changed in many ways since that time, these variables remain relevant to the prospects for reviving an autonomy-reinforcing model of global financial governance today. In the final section of the chapter, I suggest that those seeking this kind of reform need to strategize accordingly.

BRETTON WOODS PLANNING AS A PRECEDENT

The Bretton Woods negotiations are often portrayed as very technical discussions about international money and finance. It is important to recall that the negotiators placed these discussions in the context of broader social concerns, including concerns about economic inequality. Some of these concerns focused on intercountry inequality, notably the growing gap in living standards between industrialized and nonindustrialized countries (Helleiner 2014a). Equally important, however, were their concerns about intracountry inequality.

Policy makers from the United States, the dominant power in the negotiations, were particularly interested in this issue. The domestic inequalities associated with the Gilded Age in the United States during the late-nineteenth and early-twentieth centuries had triggered a growing political backlash that culminated in Franklin Roosevelt's New Deal of the 1930s. A core goal of the New Deal was to provide greater economic security to low-income Americans as well as to impose new taxes and other constraints on the country's wealthy elite, particularly the financial elite. Many of the U.S. officials involved in the Bretton Woods negotiations were committed to these New Deal values, and their proposals for the postwar international financial order reflected these values.

Roosevelt himself set the tone with his famous "Four Freedoms" speech in January 1941 in which he committed to promote "freedom from want" everywhere in the world as a postwar goal. As Elizabeth Borgwardt highlights, Roosevelt's commitment to this idea stemmed from his desire to "internationalize the New Deal" and its commitment to provide all citizens with greater economic security (2005, 3). The promise of "freedom from want" was then embedded in the Atlantic Charter that Roosevelt and British Prime Minister Winston Churchill announced in August 1941, a document widely recognized as the first official statement of the Anglo-American goals for the postwar world.

This idea found its way into the UN's founding charter in 1945, whose preamble noted that the peoples of the UN are determined to promote "better standards of life in larger freedom." Article 25 of the Universal Declaration of Human Rights, adopted by the UN General Assembly in 1948, reiterated the idea with greater precision: "Everyone has the right to a standard of living adequate for the health and well-being of himself and of his family, including food, clothing, housing and medical care and necessary social services, and the right to security in the event of unemployment, sickness, disability, widowhood, old age or other lack of livelihood in circumstances beyond his control."

When U.S. Treasury Secretary Henry Morgenthau presented the first draft plans for the postwar global financial system to Roosevelt in the spring of 1942, he invoked the U.S. president's broad goals. As Morgenthau put it, the plans were designed to create "a New Deal in international economics" (U.S. State Department 1963, 172). Like Morgenthau, the Treasury official leading the detailed drafting of these plans, Harry Dexter White, was also an "ardent New Dealer" and he too referred to Roosevelt's goals in his early drafts (Van Dormael 1978, 42). In White's words, the new international fund being proposed was designed to facilitate "the attainment of the economic objectives of the Atlantic charter," and member countries of his proposed international bank would be required to "subscribe publicly to the 'Magna Carta of the United Nations' " that set forth "the ideal of freedom for which most of the peoples are fighting the aggressor nations and hope they will be able to attain and believe they are defending." This latter provision, noted White, "would make clear to the peoples everywhere that these new instrumentalities which are being developed go far beyond usual commercial considerations and considerations of economic self-interest" (quoted in Helleiner 2014a, 121).

Two years later at the Bretton Woods conference itself, Morgenthau continued to prominently highlight Roosevelt's goal of addressing poverty in all countries of the world as a driving force behind the negotiations. As he put it in his opening speech, one of the core goals of the meeting was to establish "a satisfactory standard of living for all the people of all the countries on this earth." He justified this objective in the following way: "Prosperity, like peace, is indivisible. We cannot afford to have it scattered here or there among the fortunate or to enjoy it at the expense of others. Poverty, wherever it exists, is menacing to us all and undermines the well-being of each of us" (U.S. State Department 1948, 81). The last sentence about the dangers of poverty was similar to a statement the International Labor Organization (ILO) had endorsed at a meeting two months earlier stating that "poverty anywhere constitutes a danger to prosperity everywhere" (quoted in Alcalde 1987, 141). At the end of that ILO meeting, Roosevelt had gone out of his way to praise that statement, noting that

"this principle is a guide to all of our international economic deliberations" (Roosevelt 1944, 1).

New Deal rhetoric about constraining elite behavior featured less
prominently in the U.S. plans for the postwar order than this goal of
addressing poverty, but it was still present.[1] In his Four Freedoms speech,
Roosevelt (1941) spoke of "the ending of special privilege for the few" as
one of the key foundations of "a healthy and strong democracy." As he
put it, this was one of "the simple, the basic things that must never be
lost sight of in the turmoil and unbelievable complexity of our modern
world." He continued: "The inner and abiding strength of our economic
and political systems is dependent upon the degree to which they fulfill
these expectations."

When discussing the Bretton Woods proposals, Morgenthau sometimes invoked New Deal ideas about constraining the power of private
financial elites. For example, in his final speech at the Bretton Woods
conference, Morgenthau noted that the new international institutions
being proposed by the conference would "limit the control which certain private bankers have in the past exercised over international finance"
(U.S. State Department 1948, 1118). Afterward, he also boasted that one
of his objectives in the Bretton Woods negotiations was "to move the
financial center of the world from London and Wall Street to the United
States Treasury, and to create a new concept between nations in international finance" (quoted in Gardner 1980, 76). Another U.S. official
involved in Bretton Woods planning, Adolf Berle, had advocated earlier
in 1941 for public international development lending on the grounds that
it would mark "the beginning of a system in which finance is the servant
of exchange and development" (quoted in Helleiner 2014a, 50). When
proposing cooperative provisions to control capital movements (described
below), White also noted that this would mean "less freedom for owners
of liquid capital," restrictions he justified on the ground that they "would
be exercised in the interests of the people" (Horsefield 1969, 67).

The broad goals of the New Dealers were echoed by policy makers
from Britain, the other major power that played a significant role in the
Bretton Woods negotiations. When Britain's foreign minister, Anthony
Eden, outlined Britain's postwar goals in May 1941, he echoed Roosevelt's
commitment to improved living conditions for the poor in the postwar
world. As he put it, "social security must be the first objective of our
domestic policy after the war, and social security will be our policy abroad
no less than at home" (quoted in Broad 1955, 154). Eden explicitly drew a

parallel between this commitment to "social security" and Roosevelt's idea of "freedom from want."

Eden's words drew directly on the thinking of John Maynard Keynes, the lead official developing Britain's postwar international financial plans. Although Keynes did not share the more populist anti-elite sentiments of some American New Dealers, Jonathan Kirshner reminds us that he was a critic—for economic, political, and philosophical reasons—of the large national disparities of income and wealth that existed within Britain and other industrialized countries during his time (1999, 319). In his first reflections on postwar planning in late 1940, Keynes developed the ideas that Eden subsequently invoked: "Mr. Bevin said recently that social security must be the first object of our domestic policy after the war. And social security for the peoples of all the European countries will be our policy abroad not less than at home" (quoted in Helleiner 2014a, 209).

Keynes's reference to the ideas of trade unionist and Labour politician Ernest Bevin was important. Bevin had emerged as an influential member of Churchill's inner War Cabinet, and he had been arguing in the fall of 1940 that postwar international economic plans must prioritize social security for all citizens. As he put it in a private letter at the time:

> It seems necessary to look for a binding form of peace not in the Customs Union or economic groups, although these will emerge, but in those matters in which all human beings, irrespective of nationality, have a common interest. These are security against poverty, care in sickness and trouble, protection against injury, provision for old age. . . . In short, international policy should be based not on the increase and safeguarding of the total trade and income of individual countries, but on the provision by international cooperation of the needs of human individuals. (quoted in Bullock 1967, 201–2)

Bevin subsequently successfully pushed for the inclusion in the Atlantic charter of a commitment to "the fullest collaboration between all nations in the economic field, with the object of securing for all improved labor standards, economic advancement, and social security" (quoted in Borgwardt 2005, 304). Roosevelt welcomed the language because he felt it reinforced his idea of "freedom from want." Indeed, when developing his Four Freedoms speech, Roosevelt had been following discussions in the British press about the need to defeat Hitlerism with an economic bill of rights that established minimum standards for housing, food, education, and medical care—as well as free speech, free press, and free worship (Rosenman 1952, 265).

Support within Britain for these ideas was widespread in expert circles. For example, in June 1941, prominent British economists associated with the Royal Institute of International Affairs urged that postwar international economic plans be judged according to the following standard: "The release of all peoples from poverty and its evil consequences" (quoted in Helleiner 2014a, 213). The popular reaction in Britain to the Beveridge Report of late 1942 only reinforced British official support for the goal of building a postwar international order that strengthened social security at home. That report had explicitly translated the aspirations of the Atlantic charter into specific domestic recommendations for "a Plan for Social Security designed to abolish physical want, by ensuring for all citizens at all times a subsistence income and the means of meeting exceptional expenditure at birth, marriage and death."[2]

In addition to prioritizing social security, British officials also followed their U.S. colleagues in occasionally referencing the need to constrain elite behavior in postwar international financial plans. Keynes's discussion in April 1942 of the need for postwar capital controls provides one example: "Surely in the post-war years there is hardly a country in which we ought not to expect keen political discussions affecting the position of the wealthier classes and the treatment of private property. If so, there will be a number of people constantly taking fright because they think that the degree of leftism in one country looks for the time being likely to be greater than somewhere else" (Keynes 1980, 149). Like White, Keynes believed that these kinds of private flows needed to be constrained to allow governments to better serve national goals.

Although the Americans and the British played the lead role in the Bretton Woods negotiations, policy makers from other countries were also deeply involved, and many of them shared the U.S. and British concerns about national inequalities. In Canada, for example, the financial official Robert Bryce explicitly invoked U.S. ideas when writing about postwar international economic plans in December 1941:

We must achieve freedom from want, as Roosevelt said, "everywhere in the world." . . . It does not take a political expert to forecast that following an Allied victory, many nations will embark upon "New Deals." Quite apart from the development of socialism itself, the social temper seems sure to require forthright and vigorous action to provide work and security under all circumstances. (1941, 2)

His colleague Louis Rasminsky was even more blunt in May 1942:

> This is in fact a revolutionary war and the object of economic policy after the war will not be to make the institutions of a capitalist or semi-capitalist society work with a minimum of friction but to make sure that . . . the fruits of production are widely distributed. . . . This point of view [must be] kept constantly in the foreground. (quoted in Helleiner 2006, 76–77)

NATIONAL INEQUALITIES AND THE EMBEDDED LIBERAL MODEL

What kind of model of global economic governance did the Bretton Woods negotiators propose to address their concerns about national inequalities? In a famous article, John Ruggie (1982) described the model as one that sought to combine strengthened liberal multilateralism with a commitment to support interventionist economic practices that had become influential across the world since the 1930s. He coined the phrase "embedded liberalism" to describe the vision underlying this model.

The innovative nature of this embedded liberal model deserves underlining. The liberal multilateral dimensions of the Bretton Woods regime signaled a sharp break from the closed economic blocs and the conflictual international economic relations of the 1930s. But they also represented a significant departure from the liberal international financial regime of the pre-1930s period. The latter had been characterized by informal "rules of the game" and a kind of networked financial governance involving central banks and private financiers. The Bretton Woods architects established a stronger, more legalized multilateral "constitution" for the postwar international financial system under which all countries committed to maintain stable exchange rates and current account convertibility.

They also created two new public intergovernmental financial institutions—the International Monetary Fund (IMF) and the International Bank for Reconstruction and Development (IBRD)—tasked with promoting international financial cooperation, upholding rules and responsibilities of membership, providing public short-term balance-of-payments finance, and mobilizing long-term reconstruction and development lending. The institutions, designed to be open to all members of the United Nations, were novel in their design.[3] The only existing international financial institution at the time was the Bank for International Settlements (BIS), a Swiss-chartered bank that acted more as an informal "club" of central bankers not directly accountable to governments and whose founding members in 1930 included just six central banks and one private U.S. banking group.

These strengthened multilateral features of global financial governance were predicated on what Ruggie calls "domestic interventionism" (1982, 393). In contemporary language, national governments were to be granted greater "policy space" than they had under the gold standard so they could intervene in their domestic economies in ways that had become popular since the 1930s. This commitment to policy space was closely linked to the goals outlined in the previous section. Governments needed greater policy autonomy because they were, in Ruggie's words, "assuming much more direct responsibility for domestic social security and economic stability . . . demands for social protection were very nearly universal, coming from all sides of the political spectrum and from all ranks of the social hierarchy (with the possible exception of orthodox financial circles)" (388).

In what ways would greater policy space enable governments to guarantee "social security" or "freedom from want"? Ruggie himself highlights a key macroeconomic channel. Although countries at Bretton Woods committed to stable exchange rates and current account convertibility, their domestic economies would be cushioned "against the strictures of the balance of payments" by multilateral rules allowing adjustable exchange rates and capital controls as well as by the IMF's provision of short-term balance of payments support (395). Under the gold standard, the burden of adjustment to changing balance-of-payments conditions often fell disproportionately on the poor in the form of wage adjustments, unemployment, or cutbacks to government spending. The Bretton Woods order provided governments with greater policy autonomy to insulate their citizens from external shocks and to pursue macroeconomic policies aimed at domestic objectives, including equity-oriented ones.

Both Keynes and White also discussed how capital controls could enhance government policy autonomy in other relevant ways. For example, in discussing the need for capital controls in his first plans of early 1942, White highlighted the difficulties that could be posed by capital outflows initiated by a "desire to evade the impact of new taxes or burdens of social legislation" (Horsefield 1969, 67). In September 1941, Keynes expressed similar concerns when explaining why capital movements needed to be regulated after the war:

> Social changes affecting the position of the wealth-owning class are likely to occur or (what is worse in the present condition) to be threatened in many countries. The whereabouts of "the better 'ole" will shift with the speed of the magic carpet. Loose funds may sweep round the world disorganizing all steady business. (1980, 30–31)

If greater national policy space was needed to pursue equity-oriented goals, strengthened multilateral cooperation was also critically important to reinforce this space. The significance of the IMF's provision of short-term loans has already been noted. Because of the controversies surrounding the IMF's tough and intrusive lending conditionality in more recent times, it is important to reiterate that the IMF's lending role was originally designed to bolster policy autonomy rather than to undermine it (and no provision for conditionality was included in its original Articles of Agreement). Although Keynes hoped for a larger, more generous, and more ambitious fund, both he and White agreed on this core idea. The priority assigned to policy autonomy was also apparent in the IMF's rules for approving changes to exchange rates, which stated that the fund "shall not object to a proposed change because of the domestic social or political policies of the member proposing the change."[4]

The IBRD was also designed to boost the capacity of countries that were either devastated by the war or simply poor to raise the living standards of their citizens. It would do this by mobilizing long-term capital for their reconstruction and development. This goal was aimed partly at raising incomes in these countries as a whole, thereby reducing inter-country disparities. But the IBRD's mandate also spoke to intracountry inequalities, linking back to Roosevelt's concern that all citizens of all countries have "freedom from want." It was hoped that the encouragement of flows of long-term capital would help strengthen the capacity of national governments to eliminate poverty within their borders. In the words of the IBRD's charter, the encouragement of international investment was designed to assist in raising "the standard of living and conditions of labor" in member countries (article 1(iii)).

Both Keynes and White also saw multilateral cooperation between countries exporting capital and those importing it as critically important for buttressing the effectiveness of national capital controls. Because this proposal is less well known, it deserves more explanation. Keynes first discussed this idea in his 1941 drafts of postwar international financial plans, in which he called for a "uniform multilateral agreement by which movements of capital can be controlled *at both ends*" (1980, 52). In White's first drafts in early 1942, he echoed Keynes's idea, noting that "without the cooperation of other countries such control [of capital flows] is difficult, expensive and subject to considerable evasion." He added: "The consequence of cooperation in this matter among the member governments would give each government much greater measure of control in carrying out its monetary and tax policies" (quoted in Horsefield 1969, 66–67).

White's proposals in this area were more specific than those of Keynes. Initially, White proposed that all members of his international fund would be required to help enforce the capital controls of other member countries in ambitious ways:

> Each country agrees (a) not to accept or permit deposits or investments from any member country except with the permission of that country, and (b) to make available to the government of any member country at its request all property in form of deposits, investments, securities, safety deposit vault contents, of the nationals of member countries. (1942, 10)

In a subsequent draft a few months later, White explicitly noted the distributional impact of this proposal (using the language partially quoted above):

> Such an increase in the effectiveness of control means, however, less freedom for owners of liquid capital. It would constitute another restriction on the property rights of the 5 or 10 percent of persons in foreign countries who have enough wealth or income to keep or invest some of it abroad, but a restriction that presumably would be exercised in the interests of the people—at least so far as the government is competent to judge that interest. (quoted in Horsefield 1969, 67)

In mid-1943, White scaled back these ambitious ideas somewhat, making cooperation mandatory only if the IMF requested it and requiring governments to make "information" available about foreign-owned property instead of the property itself (Horsefield 1969, 96).

These proposals for cooperative controls were popular beyond the United States and Britain. For example, when Canada and China each developed plans for the postwar international financial order in mid-1943, they both included provisions in this area similar to those of White (Horsefield 1969, 118; Helleiner 2014a, 195). Around the same time, Mexican officials also told White that "it would be very helpful to Mexico to have international cooperation in the control of capital movements across their borders, should circumstances arise requiring control."[5]

But White's proposals were strongly opposed by the U.S. financial community, which succeeded in watering them down considerably. The final IMF Articles of Agreement *permitted* cooperation between countries to control capital movements but *required* cooperation only in one very limited way: contracts that were contrary to the exchange controls of other member countries had to be "unenforceable" in the territories of any member.[6] The failure of this initiative to establish strong cooperative controls—and of subsequent efforts to implement such cooperation—contributed to the difficulties governments encountered in their efforts to control capital flows in the postwar years (Helleiner 1994).

TOWARD AUTONOMY-REINFORCING GLOBAL
FINANCIAL GOVERNANCE TODAY?

The discussions about cooperative controls and public international lending reveal that Keynes and White both saw a complementary relationship between strengthening the national policy space and bolstering multilateral cooperation. Their stance has important contemporary relevance.

Debates about how best to address rising national inequalities in the context of today's global economy often present two stark alternatives. On one side is the "globalist" position favoring stronger global economic governance because the nation-state is seen as too small and ineffective to address global systemic causes of growing national inequalities. On the other side is a more "nationalist" stance favoring stronger national economic controls on the grounds that the global economy and existing global economic governance arrangements are contributing to growing national inequalities or constraining the policy space that is needed to address them.

The Bretton Woods architects rejected the binary nature of this debate. From their perspective, strengthened multilateral cooperation was a tool for bolstering the national policy space needed to address national inequalities. In other words, stronger global economic governance was not seen in opposition to national autonomy but rather complementary and reinforcing of it.

The distinctiveness of this position is that it highlights the need to differentiate between different kinds of global economic governance. In the contemporary context, global economic governance is usually depicted as undermining national autonomy. But the Bretton Woods vision suggests that it need not be. As Dani Rodrik (2011) has noted, the Bretton Woods variety of multilateralism was more compatible with national policy space than the kind of global economic governance that has characterized the more recent age of globalization.

Rodrik himself suggests the term "shallow" multilateralism to refer to the Bretton Woods variety (2011, xvii). That description fits the trade arrangements embodied within the weak General Agreement on Tariffs and Trade (GATT) in the early postwar years. It may, however, be less useful as a description of some of the ambitious financial ideas of the

Bretton Woods architects, such as cooperative capital controls that, if they had been implemented, would have involved quite "deep" forms of cooperation. An alternative label for the Bretton Woods multilateral vision might be autonomy-reinforcing global economic governance.

This variety of global economic governance is as important, if not more so, as it was at the time of Bretton Woods. Recent debates about capital controls provide one example of its significance. Since the 2008 financial crisis, support for capital controls has grown in international public policy circles, including within the IMF (Gallagher 2014; Grabel 2015). In their chapter in this volume, Kevin Gallagher, Guillermo Lagarda, and Jennifer Linares show how concerns about rising national inequalities provide one of the new rationales for capital controls. But supporters of capital controls also often are acutely aware of a problem noted by the Bretton Woods architects—the difficulties in making national capital controls effective. Indeed, this problem is even more acute in today's integrated global economy than it was at the time of Bretton Woods.

In this context, it is not entirely surprising to see renewed interest in the Bretton Woods ideas about controls "at both ends." For example, some IMF staff have recently called attention to Keynes's and White's proposals for cooperation as a tool for enhancing the effectiveness of capital controls. As Ostry, Ghosh, and Korinek put it:

> Both Keynes and White firmly held that rules for managing capital flows would be much more effective if movements of capital "could be controlled at both ends" than if a patchwork of unilateral policies ruled the day. . . . Global financial integration has progressed a long way in six decades, but multilateral oversight of both source and recipient countries to assist in the management of capital flow volatility remains a worthy objective, and one likely to be essential to safeguard the stability of the international monetary system. (2012, 22)

This new IMF interest in cooperative control mechanisms provides an important illustration of how the national policy space could be reinforced—rather than undermined—by stronger global cooperation. It also demonstrates how the content of global economic governance can serve very different purposes. Not so long ago, in the mid- to late-1990s, IMF management pushed—unsuccessfully in the end—for stronger global rules to promote financial liberalization among all IMF members (Abdelal 2007). The goals of that earlier initiative were very different from those underlying the new IMF staff interest in cooperative controls.

The former initiative sought a kind of "autonomy-constraining" form of global economic governance, whereas the latter is advocating an "autonomy-reinforcing" variety. In both cases, multilateral practices would be strengthened and deepened, but their purposes are quite different.

Although the new IMF work on cooperative controls has not yet generated specific international reform initiatives, the idea of cooperative controls has *already* been implemented in limited ways in some contexts. International efforts to clamp down on illicit capital outflows from developing countries via the World Bank's Stolen Asset Recovery program and other multilateral initiatives have been used to curtail international financial flows linked to money laundering, terrorist finance, tax evasion, corruption, and bribery. In these various cases, governments have sought to contain undesirable financial flows through complex multilateral cooperative arrangements that involve the very provisions Keynes and White discussed in the early 1940s: information-sharing, blocking flows, and repatriating assets.

Effective unilateral controls are often difficult to establish, and cooperative mechanisms are critically important to bolster the national policy space of the countries concerned. Cooperation is particularly important for states that have weak administrative capacities to enforce controls. These initiatives demonstrate how new efforts to protect national policy space from illicit financial flows are associated with, and necessitate, the construction of stronger multilateral practices with new autonomy-reinforcing purposes.

Many of these initiatives also are directly relevant to addressing the issue of national inequality. Financial flows linked to tax evasion or illicit capital flight are major contributors to worsening national inequality. As Keynes and White suggested, these capital flows are often associated with the protection or augmentation of the wealth of the rich. Equally important, they can undermine the position of the poor by triggering public services cutbacks (in the case of tax evasion) or broader national economic troubles that affect them disproportionately (in the case of capital flight from poorer countries).

White invoked the special problems capital flight posed for poorer countries when justifying capital controls in his early 1942 drafts of the Bretton Woods agreements:

> Less hectic and less dramatic yet in the case of some countries during some stages of their development capable in the long run of even greater harm, is the steady drain of capital from a country that needs the capital

but is unable for one reason or another to offer sufficient monetary return to keep its capital at home. (quoted in Helleiner 2014a, 110)

The prospects for, and problems caused by, that kind of "steady drain" of capital from poorer countries have become much more acute today with the proliferation of tax havens.

For these reasons, it is important not to assume that strengthening global economic governance in the current era will necessarily under-mine national policy autonomy. This point has important implications for the choices within Rodrik's well-known globalization paradox that "[w]e cannot simultaneously pursue democracy, national determination, and economic globalization" (2011, xviii). Rodrik is critical of those who favor "global governance" as a solution to the paradox, a solution that he suggests reflects their willingness to abandon the nation-state and reject the "Bretton Woods" solution of embedded liberalism, which prioritized national policy space. But contemporary efforts to regulate financial flows highlight how the prioritization of national policy space often requires strengthened global governance to be effective.

The details of Rodrik's preferred global financial order also seem to point to this conclusion. Although such an order would prioritize national policy space, Rodrik argues that it "would certainly involve an improved IMF with increased resources." It would also include the impo-sition of a new, "small global tax on financial transactions" that "would generate tens of billions of dollars to address global challenges." In addi-tion, Rodrik highlights the need for a new international financial charter "focused on encouraging financial transparency, promoting consultation and information sharing among national regulators, and placing limits on jurisdictions (such as financial safe havens) that export financial instabil-ity" (2011, 2264). All of these reforms would involve strengthened and new kinds of multilateral cooperation.

Thomas Piketty's proposals to address rising national inequalities raise the same issue in the other direction. Piketty calls for a "progressive global tax on capital" as well as strengthened "international financial transpar-ency" and information-sharing to support this tax initiative (2014, 471, 515). Piketty contrasts this "global" reform program with more "defen-sive" and "nationalist" policies associated with trade protectionism and capital controls (516). But the binary contrast he draws between global-oriented proposals and more defensive, nationalist ones is overdrawn. After all, his proposals are designed to protect and boost the redistributive capacity of what he calls the national "social state." Intensified global cooperation, in other words, is serving the defensive and nationalist goal of protecting and strengthening policy space.

The embedded liberal model of global financial governance first developed by the Bretton Woods architects thus has considerable contemporary relevance. At its core, this model seeks to address national inequalities by strengthening forms of multilateral cooperation that can boost the policy space of national governments to pursue equity-oriented goals. This may include forms identified during the Bretton Woods negotiations, such as cooperative capital controls or the provision of various kinds of lending. But it also may include other kinds of multilateral cooperation highlighted by Rodrik and Piketty, such as initiatives to introduce a global financial transactions tax, efforts to enhance international financial transparency and information-sharing, and plans to constrain jurisdictions that "export financial instability."

One further example of autonomy-reinforcing cooperation involves initiatives to strengthen the administrative capacity of poorer states. For example, as part of building the new embedded liberal order during the 1940s, U.S. officials prioritized providing technical assistance to poorer countries designed to strengthen their institutional capacity to protect their policy autonomy. Assistance focused on establishing new central banks, consolidating national currencies, new legislation supporting capital controls and adjustable exchange rates, and strengthening research capacity. These U.S. officials explained how different their advice was from the more orthodox advice offered by earlier U.S. "money doctors" who had urged policies that constrained policy autonomy, such as adherence to the gold standard (Helleiner 2014a). The contrast highlighted once again how international cooperation can serve either to reinforce policy autonomy or to undermine it.

WHAT SHAPED GLOBAL FINANCIAL REFORM?

A study of the origins of Bretton Woods is useful for highlighting how past policy makers linked concerns about national inequalities with this new embedded liberal model of global financial reform. But the historical perspective also provides insights into some of the political variables that drive and shape the process of global financial reform. The Bretton Woods negotiations are widely seen as the most ambitious initiative to reform global financial governance that has ever been undertaken. What made this initiative possible?

To begin with, ideas mattered. Ruggie highlights how the shared commitment to the new embedded liberal vision among Anglo-American officials helped to facilitate the success of the negotiations. Their sense of shared social purpose extended beyond the general embedded liberal vision to many of the more technocratic ideas about how to implement it, such as the need for capital controls, adjustable exchange rate pegs, and public international lending. More recent research has shown that support for these ideas also was widespread among officials from many of the other forty-two governments involved in the negotiations (Helleiner 2014a).

The ideational consensus among the Bretton Woods negotiators was a product of some unique circumstances. The Bretton Woods plans were developed among military allies fighting a momentous war. This wartime context encouraged forging a sense of ambitious common purpose. Indeed, the early proposals of both White and Keynes had the explicit propaganda purpose of outlining an attractive alternative to the public German proposals for a "New Order" in international economic relations. This role was evident at the end of the Bretton Woods conference itself when Morgenthau told the delegates:

> We must offer this [the Bretton Woods agreements] to the men in the armies and on the sea and in the air. We must offer them some hope that there is something to look forward to a little better than in the past and I like to think that Bretton Woods is the hope in somewhat concrete form. (U.S. State Department 1948, 1126)

The severity of the Great Depression also played an important role in undermining the legitimacy of old policy paradigms in global financial governance and created an opening for a new common vision. That opening was effectively filled by some remarkable "normative entrepreneurs," and Keynes and White stand out for their intellectual agency during the Bretton Woods negotiations. As John Ikenberry (1992) has noted, these entrepreneurs promoted their new embedded liberal vision through the cultivation of a transnational expert coalition of supporters. The highly technical nature of global financial issues gave this "transnational epistemic community" considerable autonomy to shape the outcomes of the negotiations.

The Bretton Woods negotiations were shaped not just by this commitment to shared ideas but also by power and interests. The fact that the

United States was such a dominant power at the time was very important to the success of the negotiations. The United States was able to throw its weight around to secure agreements, and other states were willing to defer to many of its preferences because they recognized that the United States would emerge from the war as the key banker to the world. In addition, America's preeminent economic position provided U.S. officials with a strong interest and an incentive to assume the lead role in rebuilding a more open and stable global economy that would benefit its economy and leading businesses. Recognizing the benefits they might gain, many of those businesses (with the exception of the New York financial community) also supported the Bretton Woods negotiations and outcomes.

Although power was asymmetrically distributed at the time, U.S. officials recognized the importance of cultivating the support of other key powers. Britain was particularly significant, and its power provided Keynes with many opportunities to shape outcomes both before and during the 1944 conference. Some less powerful countries also boosted their influence in the negotiations through coalition-building. Particularly important were Latin American governments, which made up nineteen of the forty-four governments represented at the Bretton Woods conference. Because the conference made decisions with a one-country one-vote rule, they were able to flex their muscle by voting as a bloc (Helleiner 2014a, chap. 6, 157–72).

The final key political variable that helps to explain the success of the Bretton Woods negotiations is an institutional one. Historically, global governance is rarely redesigned in a "big bang" fashion. Instead, successful reforms to global governance are usually incremental, building directly on previous institutional innovations and legacies that have shaped political preferences and provided precedents, templates, and opportunities to enable further reform (Fioretos 2012; Fioretos, Falleti, and Sheingate 2016). The Bretton Woods agreements were no exception to this pattern.

Although often portrayed as a dramatic process in which the global financial order was transformed *de novo*, the Bretton Woods negotiations actually built carefully on a set of incremental institutional innovations that predated the formal negotiations. One was the 1936 Tripartite Accord between Britain, France, and the United States that established the precedent of a new kind of multilateral financial cooperation that endorsed adjustable exchange-rate pegs. But more important was a set of institutional innovations designed in the inter-American context of the late 1930s (Helleiner 2016).

These innovations emerged from a shift in U.S. policy toward Latin America that was associated with Roosevelt's Good Neighbor policy. The policy had initially been focused on the idea of renouncing U.S. military intervention in the region. In the late 1930s, however, U.S. officials increasingly embraced a more active idea of pioneering a new kind of financial partnership with Latin American countries that was designed to promote their economic development. The motivations for this shift in U.S. policy included a complex mix of economic goals, strategic fears of growing German influence in Latin America, and New Deal idealism.

The new financial partnership included bilateral public lending programs to Latin American governments for both short-term currency stabilization and long-term development purposes. These programs anticipated the lending functions of the IMF and IBRD, and they helped to set a key precedent for the U.S. plans of the Bretton Woods institutions. In 1939–40, U.S. officials went one step further to design (in cooperation with Latin American governments) a new Inter-American Bank (IAB) that could offer these kinds of loans through a public multilateral institutional setting. The IAB combined the lending functions of the future Bretton Woods institutions into one body, and its governance structures anticipated core features of those institutions. U.S. deliberations surrounding the IAB's design also discussed issues such as capital flight from poorer countries, which was addressed in the Bretton Woods plans. Although congressional opposition prevented the IAB's ratification, its design served as a kind of "first draft" for White's Bretton Woods plans of early 1942 (Oliver 1975, 99).[7] White had, in fact, been at the center of drafting the IAB as well as other U.S. public lending initiatives in the late 1930s.

The Bretton Woods negotiations thus involved less innovation than is sometimes suggested. Success built directly on an institutional prehistory of incremental innovations that set the stage for the Bretton Woods reforms. These institutional legacies generated not just precedents and templates for reform but also new experiences and relationships, which shaped preferences and built support for the subsequent Bretton Woods negotiations. For example, the new U.S. public lending programs to Latin America in the late 1930s benefited U.S. exporters and internationally oriented manufacturing firms in ways that contributed to a widening of domestic political support for a more internationalist U.S. foreign economic policy. White's extensive involvement in Latin America in the late 1930s also built relationships with Latin American officials that helped him later cultivate support in that region for the Bretton Woods proposals (Helleiner 2016).

This brief historical analysis highlights how the reform of global financial governance in the early 1940s was shaped by a unique combination of factors. The political environment today is different in many ways, but each of the core political variables revealed by the Bretton Woods history—ideas, power and interests, and institutional legacies—remains relevant in determining the prospects for reform today. Those seeking to construct a more embedded liberal model of global financial governance can strategize accordingly.

In the ideational realm, contemporary reformers should benefit from the fact that national inequalities have already become an issue of major concern in countries around the world, with politicians of many political stripes promising—often with quite populist rhetoric—to address the trend. The emerging consensus on the need for action was confirmed in 2015 when world leaders endorsed the UN's new Sustainable Development Goals (SDGs). Included in this endorsement was SDG 10, which called for inequality to be reduced not just "among countries" but also "within" them.

Equally important is the fact that SDG 10 outlines a target that appears to link the commitment to reduce national inequality to the cause of global financial reform: "Improve regulation and monitoring of global financial markets and institutions and strengthen implementation of such regulations."[8] The next political step is to translate this vague wording into a more specific vision for global financial reform that can attract wide support, particularly among the technocratic experts who dominate policy making in the global financial sphere.

The Bretton Woods experience calls attention to the important role to be played in this process by normative entrepreneurs with a capacity and talent for building transnational expert coalitions. In the early 1940s, that role was assumed by national policy makers such as Keynes and White. But a much wider range of groups participate actively in expert debates about global financial reform today, including officials in international organizations, scholars outside official circles, think tanks, and other nongovernmental groups. Intellectual leaders from these various groups can play key roles in advancing detailed global financial reform agendas linked to the broader cause of addressing national inequalities.

The Bretton Woods history also highlights the importance of power and interests. The global economic power of the United States has diminished since the time of the Bretton Woods negotiations, but it remains the key power in the world financial system due to the international importance of its financial markets and the dollar as well as to its influence inside key institutions of global financial governance. U.S. preferences and interests today will be of crucial importance for global financial reform along more embedded liberal lines.

Concerns about national inequality trends have assumed high political salience in the United States in the current age. The key task for reformers is to mobilize that salience into support for transformations in global financial governance. A recent example of how U.S. power might support change of this kind is the landmark 2014 multilateral tax agreement among over fifty jurisdictions for automatic information-sharing related to foreign-earned capital income. As Lukas Hakelberg (2016) explains, this breakthrough in international tax cooperation was made possible because the United States threatened to deny access to its markets and clearing systems to noncomplying jurisdictions. U.S. authorities were encouraged to flex their international power in this way by growing domestic distributional concerns about "fairness" in taxation.

The election of Donald Trump as U.S. president in 2016 is widely seen as a setback for multilateral economic cooperation because of his nationalistic "America First" rhetoric and priorities. But this common wisdom may too readily accept the dichotomy criticized earlier in this paper between globalists and nationalists. The Trump administration certainly appears to be skeptical of global economic governance that constrains U.S. policy autonomy. Less clear, however, is its view toward multilateral economic cooperation that is autonomy-reinforcing. If that kind of cooperation helps Trump administration officials bolster U.S. policy autonomy, they might be less inclined to dismiss it.

Prominent analysts have speculated that the Trump administration might consider capital controls as part of its prioritization of American policy autonomy. As Benjamin Cohen (2016) puts it, "if protectionism is really on his agenda, then we must assume that capital controls are, too." Both Daniel Drezner (2016) and Nouriel Roubini (2017) have speculated that capital controls might be seen by Trump administration officials as a way to fend off dollar-strengthening capital inflows generated by a U.S. policy mix of expansionary fiscal policy and monetary tightening. If controls were imposed for that purpose, the Trump administration might quickly recognize that their effectiveness could be enhanced through cooperation with capital-sending countries.

Lobbying U.S. policy makers is critically important for reformers, but the Bretton Woods negotiations also showed the influence of lesser powers in global financial reform. The growing nationalist populist movements across Europe—responding partly to national inequality trends—might lead governments in that region to support more autonomy-reinforcing reforms to global financial governance. The BRICS countries (Brazil, Russia, India, China, and South Africa) may also be a particularly important constituency to cultivate. They are emerging powers that place a priority on protecting policy autonomy. Their potential role in promoting a more embedded liberal model of global financial governance was evident in their recent push for the IMF to become more supportive of capital controls. As Kevin Gallagher (2014) has shown, the BRICS played a key role in securing a moderate shift in 2012 in the official IMF position by using their growing diplomatic influence and by allying with normative entrepreneurs who developed new intellectually powerful rationales for capital controls.

China has also emerged as a key player for those seeking to boost the policy space of poorer countries through the provision of development finance. China has enormous lending capacity as the world's largest creditor, and Chinese leadership has already displayed a keen interest in supporting development abroad through growing bilateral lending and support for the creation of new multilateral development banks such as the Asian Infrastructure Investment Bank and the New Development Bank. Chinese President Xi Jinping (2017) has been explicit in outlining his concerns about the "uneven development space" in poor countries as well as the persistence of extreme poverty in the world. Echoing Roosevelt in the early 1940s, Xi (2017) noted his views about the latter in a prominent speech to the World Economic Forum in early 2017: "700 million people in the world are still living in extreme poverty. For many families, to have warm houses, enough food and secure jobs is still a distant dream. This is the biggest challenge facing the world today."

Although it is possible to identify how power and interests might align to support reforms aimed at creating a more embedded liberal model of global financial governance, the difficulties should not be understated. We now lived in a much more multipolar world than existed at the time of the Bretton Woods negotiations. Forging international cooperation among states with divergent interests is more difficult today. The recent experience of uneven efforts to reform global financial governance in the wake of the 2008 crisis provides ample evidence of the complexities involved (Helleiner 2014b; Helleiner, Pagliari, and Spagna 2018)

The post-2008 experience also highlights how reforms will generate opposition from powerful private interests who gain from the status quo. At the time of Bretton Woods, the New York financial community fought hard against construction of the embedded liberal model of global financial governance. They succeeded in diluting some of the more ambitious proposals, but U.S. supporters of the Bretton Woods goals successfully mobilized a wide coalition—including many leading business interests—to secure passage of the Bretton Woods agreements (Gardner 1980). In the contemporary period, those private interests in the United States and elsewhere who derive enormous benefits from the existing global financial order may have more power to block these kinds of reforms. Construction of broad-based coalitions to counteract the influence of these interests is a key political task for reformers today.

The significance of institutional legacies in the Bretton Woods negotiations also contains important lessons for contemporary reformers. In contrast to the 1940s, reformers today may benefit from being able to draw upon existing international financial institutions that could support new patterns of financial cooperation. Their task need not be institution-building but rather simply converting established international bodies to take on new roles more supportive of embedded liberal values. As historical institutionalist scholars have shown, this strategy of "conversion" is a common mechanism by which transformations in global governance have taken place in the past (Fioretos 2012; Fioretos et al. 2016).

Some officials in existing international financial institutions already seem quite open to the idea of seeing their institutions converted in this way. As noted earlier, some IMF staff have been reviving Keynes's and White's ideas about cooperative capital controls and promoting the IMF's potential role in fostering this kind of cooperation. Since the 2008 financial crisis, regulators working within the new Financial Stability Board (FSB) have begun to support international regulatory principles that endorse greater national policy space. One example is their acceptance of the widespread turn toward host country rules and subsidiarization in bank regulation. Another is their recognition that new derivatives clearinghouses are likely to be increasingly governed by location rules, which require trades to be cleared locally. These changes signal a "cooperative regulatory decentralization" trend that is compatible with a more embedded liberal model of autonomy-reinforcing global financial governance (Helleiner and Pagliari 2011).

Because of its unique governance structure and mandate, the FSB might play a particularly useful role in an embedded liberal model of global financial governance. Although it has a formal charter, the FSB was established as a "network of networks" rather than as a powerful international institution.[9] It has few staff and no formal power to challenge the policy autonomy of its members. Its effectiveness rests primarily on its ability to mobilize transgovernmental networks of financial officials to develop and promote voluntary international regulatory standards and to foster transparency, consultation, information-sharing, and capacity-building. These tasks echo those Rodrik prioritized for his preferred model of global financial governance. The FSB has even shown willingness to take on another role that Rodrik mentions: threatening nonmember jurisdictions, such as offshore financial centers, with penalties if they refuse to abide by minimum international principles (Helleiner and Paglairi 2011).

The Bretton Woods experience contains one final strategic lesson for reformers: the need for patience. Some advocates for change invoke the Bretton Woods negotiations as evidence that global financial governance can be quickly and radically designed if only policy makers embrace the appropriate ambition and creativity. It is important, however, to remember that even the Bretton Woods negotiators did not redesign global financial governance from scratch. Their initiatives built carefully upon past institutional innovations in incremental ways. Global financial reform is rarely a product of just one set of decisive negotiations or of a momentous historical moment. Longer and more incremental processes of institutional change are the norm.

CONCLUSION

Other chapters in this volume show how international economic rules are contributing to rising national inequalities. A key implication of their argument is that efforts to address rising national inequalities should be focused on governance reforms not just at the domestic level but also at the international level. To date, however, policy debates have devoted much more attention to the former than the latter.

In this chapter, I have sought to advance the debate on the international side of a reform program to address national inequalities, with a specific focus on global financial governance. I have taken a historical perspective for a simple reason: ours is not the first generation to be interested in how national inequalities might be addressed through global financial reform. This issue was front and center at the time of the creation of the Bretton Woods financial order as well. Two important political economy lessons can be learned from this historical precedent for contemporary advocates of change.

The first concerns the "constitutional" question of how global financial governance might be reformed to support efforts to address national equalities. The Bretton Woods architects suggested an "embedded liberal" model that remains relevant today. In this model, liberal multilateral cooperation is strengthened to bolster national policy space. Rather than seeing a conflict between expanded policy space and strengthened multilateral cooperation, this model highlights their complementarity. At the core of the original Bretton Woods model was the view that the domestic policy space needed to tackle national inequalities required strong multilateral cooperation in the regulation of capital movements, the provision of international liquidity, the mobilization of long-term lending, and capacity-building. An updated version of this model might add cooperation with other purposes such as taxing financial transactions globally, tracking illicit flows, strengthening international financial transparency and information-sharing, supporting host country bank regulation and location rules for derivatives clearinghouses, and constraining lightly regulated offshore jurisdictions.

Second, the study of Bretton Woods reveals the importance of some key political variables that shape the process of global financial reform: ideas, power and interests, and institutional legacies. Each can help inform the strategies of those seeking to revive an embedded liberal model of global financial governance. In the ideational realm, normative entrepreneurs must generate a specific vision of reform and build transnational coalitions of technocratic experts to back it. Reform will advance only if key powers and interests can be mobilized behind it. Reformers must work diligently to cultivate the conversion of existing international financial institutions to the purposes they favor. Finally, reformers need to keep in mind one more lesson: the reform of global financial governance along more embedded liberal lines is likely to be a slow and incremental process.

NOTES

For their helpful comments, I thank Jonathan Kirshner and José Antonio Ocampo. I am also grateful to the Social Sciences and Humanities Research Council of Canada for helping to finance some of the research in this paper.

1. The targets supporting the UN Sustainable Development Goals to reduce inequality are also more heavily focused on improving the relative position of the poor than on constraining elites.

2. "Social Insurance and Allied Services: Summary of Report by Sir William Beveridge (17/11/1942)," 1, London School of Economic Archives, BEV 8/46.

3. It is sometimes forgotten that the formal title of the Bretton Woods conference was the "United Nations Monetary and Financial Conference."

4. Article 4 section 5(f) of the IMF's Articles of Agreement.

5. Quotation is a U.S. summary of the views expressed by Mexican officials in 'Memorandum of a Meeting on the International Stabilization Fund in Mr. White's Office, May 25, 1943, 1943," 2, U.S. National Archives, Record Group 56, box 20, file D4-27, Intra-Treasury Memoranda of Harry Dexter White, 1934–45.

6. Article 8 section 2(b) of the IMF Articles of Agreement.

7. See also chapter 2 in Helleiner 2014a.

8. Target 10(5) of SDG 10, https://sustainabledevelopment.un.org/sdg10.

9. Porter (2007, 127) used the phrase "network of networks" to describe the FSB's predecessor: the Financial Stability Forum (FSF). The FSB's governance retained the core model of the FSF.

REFERENCES

Abdelal, Rawi. 2007. *Capital Rules: The Construction of Global Finance.* Cambridge, MA: Harvard University Press.

Alcalde, Javier Gonzalo. 1987. *The Idea of Third World Development: Emerging Perspectives in the United States and Britain, 1900–1950.* New York: University Press of America.

Borgwardt, Elizabeth. 2005. *A New Deal for the World: America's Vision for Human Rights.* Cambridge, MA: Belknap Press for Harvard University Press.

Broad, Lewis. 1955. *Sir Antony Eden: The Chronicles of a Career.* London: Hutchinson.

Bryce, R. B. 1941. "Basic Issues in Post-War International Economic Relations." National Archives of Canada, Record Group 19, vol. 3977 E-3-1-2, November.

Bullock, Alan. 1967. *The Life and Times of Ernest Bevin*, vol. 2: *Minister of Labour, 1940–1945.* London: Heinemann.

Cohen, Benjamin. 2016. "Will the Dollar Be Trumped?" Project Syndicate. November23.https://www.project-syndicate.org/commentary/trump-dollar-longer-term-value-by-benjamin-j--cohen-2016-11.

Drezner, Daniel. 2016. "How a Trump Administration Could Lead to Trade and Capital Controls." November 17. https://www.washingtonpost.com/posteverything/wp/2016/11/17/how-a-trump-administration-could-lead-to-trade-and-capital-controls/?utm_term=.7f583be5b969.

Fioretos, Orfeo. 2012. "Historical Institutionalism in International Relations." *International Organization* 65 (2): 367–99.

Fioretos, Orfeo, Tulia G. Falleti, and Adam Sheingate, eds. 2016. *The Oxford Handbook of Historical Institutionalism.* New York: Oxford University Press.

Gallagher, Kevin. 2014. *Ruling Capital: Emerging Markets and the Re-regulation of Cross-Border Finance.* Ithaca, NY: Cornell University Press.

Gardner, Richard. 1980. *Sterling Dollar Diplomacy in Current Perspective.* New York: Columbia University Press.

Grabel, Ilene. 2015. "The Rebranding of Capital Controls in an Era of Productive Incoherence." *Review of International Political Economy* 22 (1): 7–43.

Hackleberg. Lukas. 2016. Coercion in International Tax Cooperation: Identifying the Prerequisites for Sanctions Threat by a Great Power. *Review of International Political Economy* 23 (2): 511–41.

Helleiner, Eric. 1994. *States and the Reemergence of Global Finance: From Bretton Woods to the 1990s.* Ithaca, NY: Cornell University Press.

Helleiner, Eric. 2006. *Towards a North American Monetary Union? The Politics and History of Canada's Exchange Rate Regime.* Montreal, Canada: McGill-Queen's University Press.

Helleiner, Eric. 2014a. *Forgotten Foundations of Bretton Woods: International Development and the Making of the Postwar Order.* Ithaca, NY: Cornell University Press.

Helleiner, Eric. 2014b. *The Status Quo Crisis: Global Financial Governance After the 2008 Meltdown.* Oxford: Oxford University Press.

Helleiner, Eric. 2016. "Incremental Origins of Bretton Woods." In *The Oxford Handbook of Historical Institutionalism,* ed. Orfeo Fioretos, Tulia G. Falleti, and Adam Sheingate, 627–41. New York: Oxford University Press.

Helleiner, Eric, and Stefano Pagliari. 2011. "The End of an Era in International Financial Regulation? A Post-Crisis Research Agenda." *International Organization* 65 (Winter): 169–200.

Helleiner, Eric, Stefano Pagliari, and Irene Spagna, eds. 2018. *Governing the World's Biggest Market: The Politics of Derivatives Regulation After the 2008 Crisis.* Oxford: Oxford University Press.

Horsefield, J. Keith. 1969. *The International Monetary Fund 1945–1965: Twenty Years of International Monetary Cooperation,* vol. 1. Washington, DC: International Monetary Fund.

Ikenberry, John. 1992. "A World Economy Restored: Expert Consensus and the Anglo-American Postwar Settlement." *International Organization* 46 (1): 289–321.

Keynes, John Maynard. 1980. *The Collected Writings of John Maynard Keynes,* vol. 25, ed. Donald Moggridge. London: MacMillan, 1980.

Kirshner, Jonathan. 1999. "Keynes, Capital Mobility and the Crisis of Embedded Liberalism." *Review of International Political Economy* 6 (3): 313–37.

Oliver, Robert. 1975. *International Economic Co-operation and the World Bank.* London: Macmillan.

Ostry, Jonathan, Atish Ghosh, and Anton Korinek. 2012. "Multilateral Aspects of Managing the Capital Account." IMF Staff Discussion Note, SDN/12/10, September 7. Washington, DC: International Monetary Fund.

Piketty, Thomas. 2014. *Capital in the Twenty First Century,* trans. Arthur Goldhammer. Cambridge, MA: Belknap Press.

Porter, Tony. 2007. "Compromises of Embedded Knowledge." In *Global Liberalism and Political Order,* ed. Stephen Bernstein and Louis Pauly, 109–33. Albany: SUNY Press.

Rodrik, Dani. 2011. *The Globalization Paradox: Democracy and the Future of the World Economy.* New York: Norton.

Roosevelt, Franklin. 1941. "The Four Freedoms." State of the Union Address, January 6. http://voicesofdemocracy.umd.edu/fdr-the-four-freedoms-speech-text/.

Roosevelt, Franklin. 1944. "Address to an International Labor Conference, May 17, 1944." In *The American Presidency Project*, Gerhard Peters and John T. Woolley. http://www.presidency.ucsb.edu/ws/?pid=16509.

Rosenman, Samuel. 1952. *Working with Roosevelt*. New York: Harper & Brothers.

Roubini, Nouriel. 2017. "The End of Trump's Market Honeymoon." February 2. https://www.project-syndicate.org/commentary/trump-market-honeymoon-over-by-nouriel-roubini-2017-02.

Ruggie, John. 1982. "International Regimes, Transactions and Change: Embedded Liberalism in the Postwar Economic Order." *International Organization* 36 (2): 379–415.

United Nations. 1945. "Charter of the United Nations." http://www.un.org/en/charter-united-nations/index.html.

United Nations General Assembly. 1948. "Universal Declaration of Human Rights." http://www.un.org/en/universal-declaration-human-rights/index.html.

U.S. State Department. 1948. *Proceedings and Documents of the United Nations Monetary and Financial Conference, Bretton Woods, New Hampshire, July 1–22, 1944.* Washington, DC: U.S. Government Printing Office.

U.S. State Department. 1963. Foreign Relations of the United States: Diplomatic Papers, 1942, vol. 1: General; the British Commonwealth; the Far East. Washington, DC: U.S. Government Printing Office.

Van Dormael, Armand. 1978. *Bretton Woods: Birth of a Monetary System*. London: Macmillan.

White, Harry Dexter. 1942. "Suggested Plan for a United Nations Stabilization Fund and a United Nations Bank." U.S. National Archives, Record Group 56, box 44, January. General Records of the Department of the Treasury, Office of the Assistant Secretary for International Affairs, Records of the Bretton Woods Agreements, 1938–46.

Xi Jinping. 2017. President Xi's speech to Davos in full, January 17. https://www.weforum.org/agenda/2017/01/full-text-of-xi-jinping-keynote-at-the-world-economic-forum.

CHAPTER 3

Are New Economic Policy Rules Desirable to Mitigate Rising National Inequalities?

Jonathan D. Ostry, Prakash Loungani, and Davide Furceri

1. INTRODUCTION

The pursuit of free markets has commanded a consensus among policy makers for more than three decades. Since the 1980s, countries have been increasingly introducing competition in various spheres of economic activity, as illustrated in figure 3.1. At the same time, globalization is expanding thanks to the ease of moving funds across borders and the declining role of the state—represented by the share of government expenditure to GDP.

The motivation for these policies—many of which are key aspects of the Washington Consensus—has been to deliver strong growth and macroeconomic stability. Indeed, there is much to cheer about the substantial benefits generated by these policies. Global growth increased in the 1990s and was fairly robust, in particular in populous countries such as China and India, before the onset of the Great Recession. As a result, between-country inequality has declined, and millions have been rescued from abject poverty. The Millennium Development Goal of reduction in absolute poverty was met five years ahead of schedule. Output volatility has steadily declined, and inflation has been tamed not only in advanced economies but in many developing economies as well.

These substantial benefits have not been equally shared, however (figure 3.2). Median incomes have stagnated in the United States and in many other advanced economies; the labor share of income has steadily declined in many countries; and within-country inequality has increased in almost all advanced economies and in several emerging markets. We argue that greater attention must be paid to the distributional

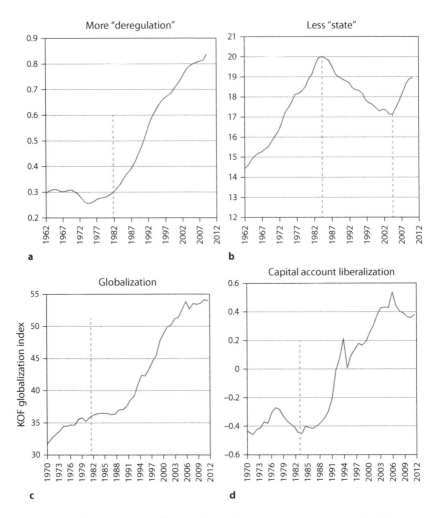

Figure 3.1 The evolution of free market policies. (*a*) Composite index of policies to increase competition and to deregulate. Index takes values between 0 and 1. The median value across countries is shown. The index is smoothed using a five-year moving average. *Source*: Ostry et al. (2016). (*b*) Government expenditures as a share of GDP (including health and education). The median value across countries is shown. Data is smoothed using a five-year moving average. *Source*: Feenstra, Inklaar, and Timmer (2015). (*c*) The KOF globalization index measures the extent to which a country is globalized in three dimensions: economic, social, and political. The index ranges from 0–100, and larger values indicate more globalization. *Source*: Dreher (2006). (*d*) Chinn-Ito index for 1970–2014. The index takes values between −1.89 (most restrictive) and 2.39 (most open). The mean value across countries is shown. *Source*: Chinn and Ito (2006).

consequences of many economic policies and the global rules of the road underpinning them. The reasons are fourfold.

First, excessive levels of inequality are detrimental not only for social and moral reasons but also for growth and efficiency. Although the relation between inequality and growth can be complex and varies depending on countries' initial positions and characteristics, higher levels of inequality are associated, on average, with lower and less durable growth. Hence, even from the perspective of the goal of fostering growth, attention to inequality is necessary. Second, high levels of inequality may lead to latent social conflicts that ultimately translate into political backlash against the pursuit of free market polices, including globalization. Third, the fear that redistribution would have an adverse impact on growth is not supported in the data—on average, implementing policies to reduce excessive inequality tend to support growth (by reducing inequality) rather than retard growth. Fourth, many of the adverse distributional developments arise from policy choices made by governments. They are not, as

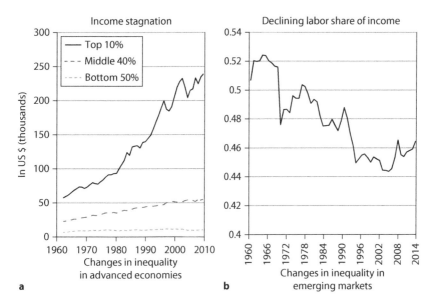

a   b

Figure 3.2   Indicators of within-country inequality in advanced economies (*a*) and emerging markets (*b*). Changes in the Gini coefficient between the latest year and 1990, authors' calculation based on data from Solt (2009). *Source*: Authors' calculation based on data from U.S. Bureau of Economic Analysis (2017), The World Wealth and Income Database.

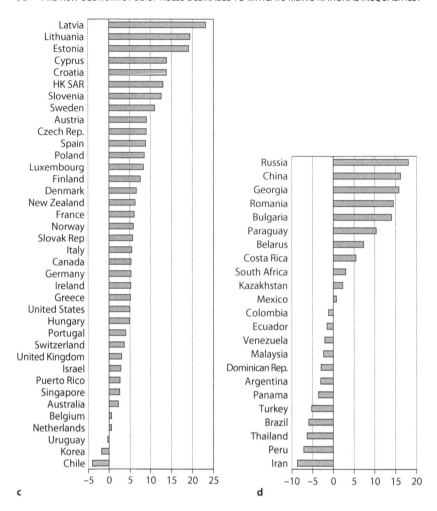

Figure 3.2 (*continued*)   Changes in the Gini coefficient between the latest year and 1990 in advanced economies (*c*) and emerging markets (*d*), authors' calculation based on data from Solt (2009). *Source:* Authors' calculation based on Labor Share of Income in Sustainable Development Goals Indicators from UN Statistics Division (2016). The mean value across countries is shown.

sometimes argued, exclusively due to technological developments and other global trends beyond the control of governments.

For these reasons, we suggest a course correction in the rules of the road—actual or perceived—that have governed economic policy making across much of the world. The pursuit of market-friendly policies is needed and desirable to ensure an increase in average living standards.

But the distributional consequences of these policies should be recognized and addressed ex ante, through better policy design with aggregate and distributional effects in mind, and ex post, through redistribution.

To achieve this course correction, it is important to understand the equity-efficiency trade-offs posed by a number of economic policies. In this chapter, we focus on two policies: capital account liberalization and fiscal consolidation. We chose these two policies for the following reasons. First, they are both important determinants of inequality, even after controlling for the effects of a number other determinants. Second, the growth benefits of these policies are often uncertain and depend on policy design and country-specific characteristics.

The structure of the chapter is as follows. Section 2 reviews a number of economic policies at the center of the Washington Consensus and presents evidence on the links between growth, inequality, and redistribution. Section 3 describes the efficiency and equity effects of capital account liberalization. Section 4 discusses efficiency-equity trade-offs associated with excessive fiscal discipline. The last section discusses the policy implications of improving the rules of the road.

2. GROWTH, INEQUALITY, AND REDISTRIBUTION

THE RULES OF THE ROAD

The notion that economists should worry about growth more than about its distribution has a long tradition. Schumpeter noted that the benefits of growth could be expected to trickle down to even the poorest: "The capitalist achievement does not typically consist in providing more silk stockings for queens but in bringing them within reach of factory girls" (1942, 67). The importance of attention to growth is stated by Lucas in a famous quote:

> Is there some action a government of India could take that would lead the Indian economy to grow like Indonesia's? If so, what, exactly? The consequences for human welfare involved in questions like these are simply staggering: Once one starts to think about them, it is hard to think about anything else. (1988, 5)

Lucas's work launched an intensive inquiry into the determinants of growth. Although academic debates rage to this day, by 1988 policy makers had converged on the broad policy ingredients they felt were needed to foster growth. The consensus was summarized by Williamson (1990) and rested on the triad of (i) macroeconomic discipline, particularly fiscal discipline; (ii) structural reforms, particularly deregulation of markets and privatization; (iii) and globalization, liberalization of trade and inward foreign direct investment. Broader capital account liberalization was not part of Williamson's list, but it became an important pursuit of policy makers in subsequent decades.

Along with the emphasis on growth, the consensus view in macroeconomics cautioned against worrying too much about redistribution. Lucas, for instance, states: "Of the tendencies that are harmful to sound economics, the most seductive, and in my opinion the most poisonous, is to focus on questions of distribution" (2004, 20).

There are two reasons for this disregard of distribution. First, it is assumed that markets work well for the most part and give people just rewards for their work. Overruling the judgment of markets is thus unfair and unnecessary. Second, efforts to redistribute may themselves undercut growth. Even if inequality is considered undesirable for some reason, using taxes and transfers to lower it may be the wrong remedy. The negative effect of redistributive policies is the central theme of Arthur Okun's famous 1975 book on the trade-offs between efficiency and equity and on the efficiency "leaks" that efforts to reduce inequality engender.

COURSE CORRECTION

We advocate for a course correction for two reasons: (i) inequality is an important determinant of growth and must be addressed if the ultimate goal is growth; and (ii) fears about the adverse growth effects of redistribution are misplaced.

We use two econometric approaches to explain our position. First, we follow the literature and examine the determinants of medium-term growth using standard panel regressions. Specifically, we ask how average growth over a five-year period depends on a variety of lagged indicators, including the level of income, the quality of institutions, and, especially important in our setting, the level of inequality and extent of redistributive transfers. Second, we examine whether the duration of growth periods is related to the initial level of inequality and to redistribution. Looking at growth periods is important because in many economies—and in developing countries in particular—average incomes do not typically grow steadily for decades. Periods of rapid growth are followed by collapses and sometimes by stagnation. As emphasized by Pritchett (2000), to understand growth it is important to explain why some countries are able to keep growing for long periods of time and others stop growing after just a few years.

We measure the duration of "growth periods" starting when growth takes off (the "upbreak") and ending when growth slackens (the "downbreak"). To examine trends, the minimum length of a growth period is set at five years. Both upbreaks and downbreaks are quite common and are fairly evenly spread across regions and decades. Latin America and Africa, two regions in which countries have the most difficulty sustaining growth, have plenty of growth periods. The real problem seems to be their inability to sustain growth over long periods. For example, almost all growth periods in industrial countries and emerging Asian countries last ten years or more, but this is true for only about two-thirds of Latin American and African countries.

The measure of inequality is the Gini coefficient from the Standardized World Income Inequality Database (Solt 2009). A constraint on previous studies on inequality and growth has been the lack of data on both net and market inequality measures on a comparable basis for a large number of countries. Solt (2009) represents the best effort so far to address these problems, combining information from available surveys to infer comparable series for net and market inequality for the largest possible number of countries and years. Redistribution is defined as the difference between the market and the net inequality series.

We begin by investigating the relationship between inequality and growth. The first panel of figure 3.3 shows the scatter plots of net inequality against growth for the subsequent ten years.

The second panel shows the scatter plots of net inequality at the start of a growth period against the duration of that period. Figure 3.3 illustrates a strong negative relation between the level of net inequality and growth in income per capita over the subsequent period. Similarly, higher levels of inequality are associated with shorter periods of sustained growth.

What do the data tell us about the relation between redistribution and growth? Figure 3.4 presents scatter plots of growth (medium-term growth or growth-period duration) against the initial level of redistribution. There is no significant relation between redistribution and growth (left panel), and the relation between the duration of growth and redistribution is slightly negative (right panel).

This evidence suggests that inequality and redistribution are not bad for growth, but it is important to go beyond a simple correlation. First, other factors drive growth—such as human capital, investment, population growth, and openness—and may be related to inequality. Second, inequality and redistribution are interrelated. Third, growth may affect inequality.

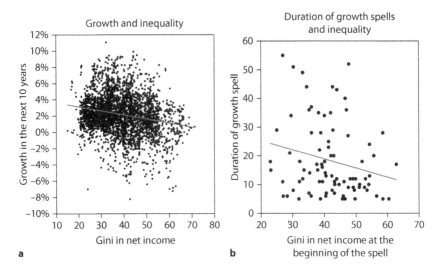

Figure 3.3   Inequality and growth. (*a*) Simple correlations between growth in the next ten years, and the average net income inequality and transfers for a sample. *Source*: Ostry, Berg, and Tsangarides (2014). (*b*) Simple correlation between length of growth periods and the average net income inequality and transfers during the period. Periods that end in-sample are included; minimum period length is five years. *Source*: Ostry, Berg, and Tsangarides (2014).

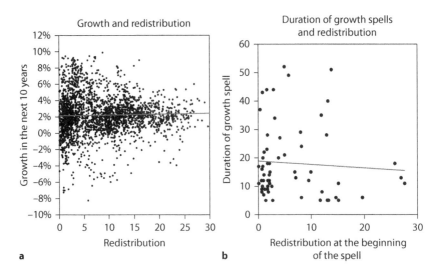

Figure 3.4   Redistribution and growth. (*a*) Simple correlations between growth in the next ten years and the average net income inequality and transfers for a sample. *Source*: Ostry, Berg, and Tsangarides (2014). (*b*) Simple correlation between length of growth periods and the average net income inequality and transfers during the period. Periods that end in-sample are included; minimum period length is five years. *Source*: Ostry, Berg, and Tsangarides (2014).

To address these issues, we used a panel framework in which medium-term growth (growth period duration) is regressed against the initial level of inequality and redistribution and a standard set of growth covariates. Endogeneity is addressed using system-GMM, in which potentially endogenous right-hand side variables are "instrumented" using appropriate lagged values and first differences.[1]

Regression results bear out these preliminary indications from the data. Table 3.1 shows the results of regressions of average growth over a five-year period on the level of inequality, the extent of redistributive transfers, and the variables commonly included in growth regressions. The baseline framework assumes that growth depends on initial income, net inequality, and redistribution. We find that higher inequality decreases growth.

Table 3.1   Baseline Results: Impact of Net Inequality and Redistribution on Growth

	Dependent Variable: Growth Rate of Per Capita GDP			
	Baseline	Baseline + controls		
	(1)	(2)	(3)	(4)
Log (initial income)	-0.0069^{**}	-0.0081^{**}	-0.0140^{***}	-0.0135^{***}
	(0.0034)	(0.0035)	(0.0037)	(0.0046)
Net inequality	-0.1435^{***}	-0.0914^{***}	-0.0739^{***}	-0.1057^{**}
	(0.0444)	(0.0336)	(0.0266)	(0.0492)
Redistribution	0.0046	0.0258	0.0109	0.0530
	(0.0492)	(0.0516)	(0.0428)	(0.0494)
Log (investment)		0.0241^{***}	0.0250^{***}	0.0076
		(0.0077)	(0.0084)	(0.0125)
Log (population growth)		-0.0159	-0.0215	-0.0084
		(0.0182)	(0.0174)	(0.0160)
Log (total education)			0.0206^{***}	0.0164^{*}
			(0.0073)	(0.0099)
Large negative terms of trade shock				-0.0424^{***}
				(0.0158)
Political institutions				-0.0011
				(0.0008)
Openness				0.0001
				(0.0001)
Debt liabilities				-0.0002^{**}
				(0.0001)
Constant	0.1262^{***}	0.0718	0.0965^{**}	0.1687^{***}
	(0.0389)	(0.0456)	(0.0389)	(0.0573)
Number of observations	828	828	751	558

1/ System GMM estimation. Robust standard errors are in brackets where *, **, and *** indicate statistical significance at the 10, 5, and 1 percent levels, respectively.

Source: Ostry, Berg, and Tsangarides (2014).

Quantitatively, an increase in net Gini from 37 (such as in the United States in 2005) to 42 (such as in Gabon in 2005) decreases growth on average by 0.5 percentage point; that is, from 5 percent to 4.5 percent per year, holding redistribution and initial income constant. Redistribution, in contrast, has virtually no effect on growth. These results continue to hold when standard growth determinants such as physical and human capital are included as well as factors such as external shocks, the quality of institutions, and measures of openness to trade. The literature suggests that a given increase in inequality may be more harmful for growth if the level of inequality is already high. However, we find little evidence of such nonlinearities, nor do we find evidence of such nonlinear effects of redistribution on growth.[2]

Table 3.2 presents results for the duration of growth. Again, the baseline specification relates the duration of growth periods—that is, the hazard of a growth period ending—to initial income at the start of the period, and inequality and redistribution during the period. Inequality has a statistically significant negative relationship with the duration of growth periods. When redistribution is already high (above the 75th percentile), further redistribution is indeed harmful to growth, as Okun conjectured. When it is below that level, however, there is no evidence that further redistribution has any effect on growth. As in table 3.1, inequality retains its statistical significance despite the inclusion of many more possible determinants.

In summary, there is a direct economic cost to inequality in terms of lower and less durable growth. Hence, even if growth is the primary goal, inequality cannot be ignored. The results are also inconsistent with the view of a trade-off between redistribution and growth. If there were such a trade-off, redistribution should have a negative impact on growth stronger than that of net inequality. Rather than a trade-off, the average result across the sample is a win-win for both (figure 3.5): redistribution has an overall pro-growth effect (third bar), counting both the negative direct effects of inequality (first bar) and the positive direct effects of redistribution (second bar).

3. EFFICIENCY-EQUITY TRADE-OFFS: CAPITAL ACCOUNT LIBERALIZATION

MACROECONOMIC BENEFITS

Economic theory states that capital account liberalization fosters economic efficiency, enabling the international capital market to channel

Table 3.2 Baseline Results: Impact of Net Inequality and Redistribution on Growth Periods

	Dependent Variable: Risk That the Growth Period Will End			
	Baseline	Baseline + controls		
	(1)	(2)	(3)	(4)
Net Inequality	1.060**	1.050*	1.060**	1.074**
	(0.0266)	(0.0266)	(0.0291)	(0.0314)
Redistribution x Top 25th	1.098***	1.099***	1.055	0.990
percentile	(0.0322)	(0.0329)	(0.0378)	(0.0567)
Redistribution x Bottom	0.987	0.961	0.971	0.938
75th percentile	(0.0690)	(0.0735)	(0.0695)	(0.0734)
Log (initial income)	1.024	1.026	1.077*	1.216***
	(0.0318)	(0.0318)	(0.0413)	(0.0844)
Log (investment)		3.050**		
		(1.7293)		
Log (population growth)		1.201		
		(1.7085)		
Log (total education)			0.694	0.845
			(0.2705)	(0.4260)
Large negative global			1.391	1.153
interest rate shock			(0.6620)	(0.5945)
Large negative terms of			2.719**	3.198**
trade shock			(1.1700)	(1.4887)
Political institutions				0.924*
				(0.0398)
Openness				0.990
				(0.0066)
Debt liabilities				1.001
				(0.0027)
Number of observations	640	640	609	549
Number of total spells/number of complete spells	62/28	62/28	55/23	49/20

Note: The table reports results using the baseline sample and an estimation of a proportional hazard model with time-varying covariates, which relates the probability that a growth period will end to a variety of economic and political variables. A hazard ratio of 0.9 means that a unit change in the regressor decreases the expected time of duration by 10 percent; a hazard ratio of 1 means there is no effect; and a ratio of 1.1 means it increases expected duration by 10 percent. We tested the probability that the true hazard ratio equals 1, and statistical significance at the 10, 5, and 1 percent level is indicated by *, **, ***, respectively.

Source: Ostry, Berg, and Tsangarides (2014).

world savings to their most productive uses around the globe. Developing countries with little capital can borrow to finance investment to promote their economic growth without requiring sharp increases in their own saving. All of this should contribute to higher growth. At the same time, there is a general consensus that greater openness to foreign financial flows is a driver of increased financial and economic volatility in many countries, raising crisis vulnerabilities.

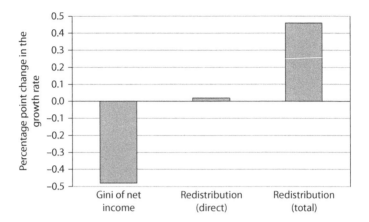

Figure 3.5   The effect of inequality and redistribution on growth. For each variable, the height of the column shows the increase in the five-year average real per capita income growth associated with an increase in that variable from the 50th to the 60th percentile, with other variables at the 50th percentile. The calculation of the total effect of redistribution assumes that redistribution has no effect on market inequality. *Source*: Ostry, Berg, and Tsangarides (2014).

From an empirical point of view, it has been difficult to prove that financial openness benefits growth. Indeed, on average, the growth benefits of capital account liberalization have been small to negligible and are rarely statistically significant (see Eichengreen 2001; Prasad et al. 2003; Rodrik and Subramanian 2009). However, these average effects mask important differences across countries, episodes, and type of financial flows. First, growth benefits tend to be larger for foreign direct investment (FDI) flows than for portfolio and debt flows (Dell'Ariccia et al. 2008; Kose et al. 2009; Ostry, Spilimbergo, and Prati 2009). Second, positive growth effects are found for capital account liberalization episodes in countries with strong financial institutions (which presumably would have lowered the odds that capital-flow surges ended up in crises).

We revisit this empirical evidence in this section, first, by documenting the frequency of crises following episodes of capital inflow surges—episodes of very large net inflows (in the top 30th percentile of both the country-specific and full sample distribution of net flows, in percent of GDP). Then we examine the consequences for growth that crises have had on capital account liberalization.

CRISES AND VOLATILITY

Capital inflow surges amplify financial and macroeconomic vulnerabilities. The former centers around excess credit growth (including in foreign currencies), excessive leverage, and asset price growth. The latter centers on the exchange rate (currency overvaluation), inflation, and overheating. The extent of these vulnerabilities depends on the composition (not just the level) of inflows during the surge phase: vulnerabilities are more problematic when the surge is dominated by shorter-term carry-trade flows rather than, say, by foreign direct investment. Some surges end in a return to normal times—a dignified end that does not involve a crisis. Other surges end in a full-blown crisis—a banking crisis, a currency crisis, or what may be called a growth crisis, a period of exceptionally bad growth performance. The cost of these crises include foregone output, loss of jobs, and increased welfare needs. To understand these issues, we examined the end of surges in a sample of fifty-three emerging-market countries from 1980 to 2014 (figure 3.6). We classified the episodes according to whether they ended in a crash or a soft landing and associated the outcome with shifts in global conditions, domestic factors, and policy responses over the surge episode.

The methodology, discussed more fully in Ghosh, Ostry, and Qureshi (2016), produced 150 episodes of surges in capital inflows. About 20 percent of the time the surges ended in a financial crisis, and, of those, 50 percent were associated with large output declines (first panel). Surges and crashes have many drivers, but increased capital account openness consistently figures as a risk factor—it raises the probability of a surge and of a crash after the surge (second panel). The nature of financial openness—in particular the role of structural measures designed to improve the benefit-risk composition of flows—was also a salient factor in our analysis, with a safer composition of flows associated with a lower risk of crash landings.

GROWTH BENEFITS

To examine the growth benefits associated with capital account openness, we used the Chinn-Ito index (Chinn and Ito 2008) to measure a country's degree of capital account openness based on the tabulation of restrictions on cross-border financial transactions reported in the IMF's Annual Report on Exchange Arrangements and Exchange Restrictions (AREAER) database. The index ranges from about –2 (more restricted capital account) to 2.5 (less restricted). The score of the capital account

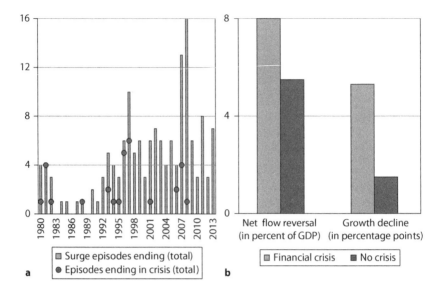

Figure 3.6   Capital surges and financial crisis. (*a*) Total number of surges end-ing in a given year and those that end in a financial crisis. (*b*) Comparison of capital flow reversal and growth between surges that end in a crisis and those that do not. The analysis is based on data for fifty-three emerging-market econo-mies from 1980 to 2014. *Source*: Ghosh, Ostry, and Qureshi (2016).

openness index varies greatly between income groups, with increased restrictions typically recorded in low-income and lower-middle-income countries. Capital account openness increased in all income groups, with a more significant rise occurring at the beginning of the 1990s.

To increase the likelihood of capturing deliberate policy attempts at liberalization, we only considered cases in which the annual change in the capital account liberalization index exceeded the average annual change over all observations by two standard deviations. This criterion identi-fied 224 episodes of liberalization, with the majority of them occurring during the last two decades. In particular, the largest number of episodes occurred during the 1990s among middle-income countries.

The impact of liberalization on growth and inequality was estimated by tracing the response of GDP in the aftermath of these episodes. Two specifications were used. The first examined the average response of GDP to capital account liberalization.[3] The second assessed variations in responses across episodes depending on whether they ended in crises.[4]

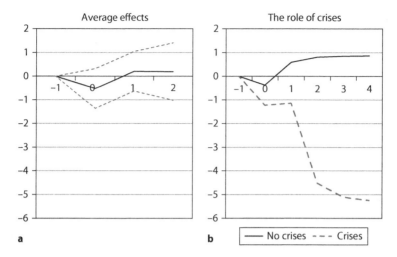

Figure 3.7   Capital account liberalization and growth. Estimated impact on growth and market Gini following a capital account liberalization episode. Liberalization is measured using the Chinn-Ito Index. Estimates are based on an autoregressive distributed lag model. The horizontal scale is in years before or after the episode. The vertical scale shows percent change. *Source*: **Ostry, Loungani, and Furceri (2016).**

Figure 3.7a presents the impulse response functions from the estimated regressions along with the associated one-standard-error confidence bands (dotted lines). The estimates show that liberalization has little impact on output (confirming the results of previous studies). This average effect, however, masks important differences. Although capital account liberalization has led to moderate output benefits when reform episodes have not been followed by crises, liberalization followed by crises have led to significant output contractions (figure 3.7b).

DISTRIBUTIONAL CONSEQUENCES

The impact of technology and trade on inequality has been studied extensively, but much less attention has been paid to the impact on inequality of opening capital markets to foreign entry and competition. Furceri and Loungani (2018) discuss several channels through which capital account liberalization may lead to increased inequality.

First, where financial institutions are weak and access to credit is not inclusive, liberalization may bias financial access in favor of those who are well-off, thereby increasing inequality. Second, capital account openness may affect the distribution of income through its effect on the bargaining power of labor. If capital account liberalization represents a credible threat to reallocate production abroad, it may lead to an increase in the profit-wage ratio and to a decrease in the labor share of income (Harrison 2002). Third, as discussed above, capital account liberalization may lead to increased volatility and crises, which tend to increase inequality (de Haan and Sturm 2016).

To estimate the distributional consequences of capital account liberalization, we ran a regression similar to the one in figure 3.7, using the Gini coefficient as the dependent variable. Figure 3.8 shows the response of the Gini coefficient to capital account liberalization episodes and the associated 90 percent confidence bands (left panel). The results suggest that capital account liberalization has typically led to an increase in the Gini coefficient of about 0.5 percent in the short term (one year after the change in liberalization), with slightly larger effects over the next couple

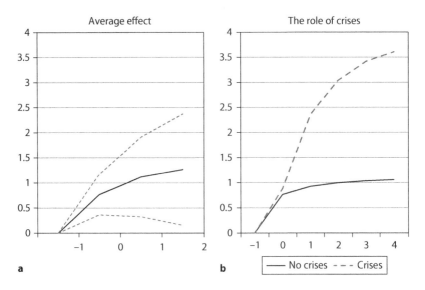

Figure 3.8   Capital account liberalization and inequality. Estimated impact on growth and market Gini following a capital account liberalization episode. Liberalization is measured using the Chinn-Ito Index. Estimates are based on an autoregressive distributed lag model. The horizontal scale is in years before or after the episode. The vertical scale shows percent change.
Source: Ostry, Loungani, and Furceri (2016).

of years. In addition, the results show that the effect of financial globaliza-tion on inequality varies markedly depending on whether or not a crisis follows. The impact of financial openness on inequality is much larger when followed by a crisis (right panel).

In summary, capital account liberalization has been associated with limited growth benefits but with significant distributional consequences. Designing liberalization in a way that does not compromise macroeco-nomic stability and limits the risk of crises is key to enhancing its macro-economic benefits while mitigating its distributional consequences.

4. EFFICIENCY-EQUITY EFFECTS OF FISCAL CONSOLIDATION

Along with increased competition through various means—such as open-ing up to foreign capital—an important standard has been curbs on the size of the state. Privatization of some government functions is one way to achieve this. Another is to control government spending through limits on the size on fiscal deficits and on the ability of governments to accumu-late debt. The economic history of recent decades offers many examples of such limits, such as a debt limit of 60 percent on GDP required for countries to join the euro area (the so-called Maastricht criteria).

Fiscal prudence is an important prerequisite for achieving macro-economic stability and creating fiscal space when it is needed; that is, in periods of recessions. A key question is, "How much fiscal prudence should governments try to pursue?" Governments facing market pres-sure may have few options other than consolidation to avoid or mitigate the effects of a crisis. But for countries that face little or no risk of a crisis, the answer is far from obvious. It requires examining whether the benefits of lower debt—in terms of reduced recourse to distortive taxation and the greater insurance value of low debt in terms of being able to respond to future adverse shocks and avoid sovereign crises—outweigh the tran-sitional costs associated with fiscal consolidation such as higher taxes or reduced spending during the consolidation phase. Because the benefits from low public debt are reaped in perpetuity, it is tempting to conclude that incurring some short-term pain during consolidation today is a price worth paying. But is it?

One issue is determining an appropriate medium-run public debt target from a normative standpoint. Economic theory provides many answers—from ever-rising public debt levels (emphasized when govern-ments find it difficult to commit and time-consistency problems loom

large) to aiming for a large stock of net assets (negative debt) out of a pre-
cautionary saving motive (saving for the inevitable rainy day). Of course,
optimal public debt targets are often associated with institutionally
enshrined levels (such as the 60 percent of GDP under the Maastricht
Treaty or the 90 percent of GDP threshold discussed in Reinhart and
Rogoff 2010), but it is difficult to know on what basis these ratios are
normatively justified.

In our work on this topic, we have considered the situation of countries with ample fiscal space; that is, countries in which the risk of an
imminent sovereign crisis is remote. They may have significant amounts
of public debt, but their track record of paying down those debts—of
acting responsibly as discussed in Mendoza and Ostry (2007)—gives
them wide latitude not to be overly concerned when an adverse debt
shock occurs (say, the need to bail out the financial system after a major
financial crisis). How should such "green-zone" countries respond to an
unfavorable public debt shock?[5] Should they pay down the debt, acquiring insurance against future sovereign crises and laying a stronger foundation for more robust medium-run growth? Should they instead use
the opportunity of very low borrowing costs to further ramp up debt?
Or should they simply live with their additional debts, allowing future
growth to organically reduce the increase in the debt ratio?

We developed a theoretical framework biased in favor of consolidation but found that the right thing from a welfare standpoint is simply to
live with the debt, allowing debt ratios to decline organically as a result
of growth. The optimal, welfare-maximizing debt path following a debt
shock is essentially parallel to the original (preshock) path. Although debt
is bad for growth due to the distortive taxes needed to service the debt,
the burden of the debt is a sunk cost. Temporarily distorting the economy
by raising taxes today in order to permanently lower them tomorrow only
adds to this burden.

This might be worth doing if the crisis-insurance benefit were substantial. But we found that the probability of a crisis is relatively flat in the
level of debt for green-zone countries. The insurance value of consolidation for such countries is rather small, but the additional distortive cost
from consolidation is substantial and increases sharply with the extent
and speed of consolidation. For example, moving from a debt ratio of
120 percent of GDP to 100 percent of GDP over a few years buys you
very little in terms of reduced crisis risk (Baldacci et al. 2011), but it
incurs a much larger distortionary welfare cost (Ostry et al. 2010, 2015).

Faced with a choice between living with the higher debt, allowing the debt ratio to decline organically through economic growth, or deliberately running budgetary surpluses to reduce the debt, governments with ample fiscal space do better by living with the debt.

SHORT-RUN TRADE-OFF

Beyond these medium-run considerations, fiscal consolidation has short-run macroeconomic and distributional effects. To document these, we relied on the fiscal consolidation episodes identified by Guajardo, Leigh, and Pescatori (2014) for a sample of seventeen OECD countries from 1978 to 2009.[6] There were a total of 173 episodes, and the magnitude of consolidation ranged from 0.1 percent to about 5 percent of GDP, with an average of about 1 percent of GDP. The measure of consolidation was based on a narrative approach and focused on *policy* actions taken by governments with the intent of reducing the budget deficit. In previous studies, fiscal consolidation has been measured by successful budget *outcomes* (for example, Alesina and Ardagna 2010); however, budget outcomes are an imperfect measure of policy intent (IMF 2010). The measure of distributional outcomes is the net Gini coefficient.

We adopted the same specification used in the previous section to trace the impacts of fiscal consolidation on output and inequality. Figure 3.9 shows the estimated impulse-response function and the associated one-standard-error bands. The horizontal axis measures years after the beginning of the episode of fiscal consolidation.

The results reported in the first panel of the figure suggest that fiscal consolidation episodes have been followed by a significant drop in output—about 2 percent two years after the consolidation episode. The notion that fiscal consolidations can be expansionary (that is, raise output and employment), championed by Alesina (2010) among others, finds little support in the data. Moreover, the results suggest not only that income falls but that it falls more for those who were worse-off before the consolidation episode. In particular, inequality (represented by the Gini coefficient) rises by about 1.5 percent during the consolidation event and by more than 3 percent two years later.

To summarize, embarking on fiscal consolidation to reduce debt is painful, but it should be considered only by countries with a weak track record and when markets attach a high probability of a debt crisis. For countries with a strong fiscal track record and a low probability of crisis,

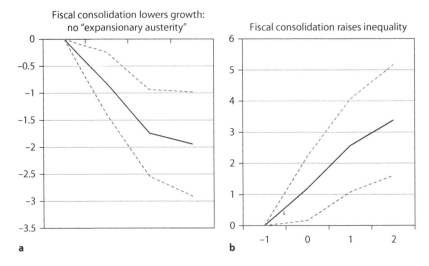

Figure 3.9   The effect of fiscal consolidation on output and inequality. Estimated impact on growth and market Gini following an episode of fiscal consolidation. Episodes are based on the narrative approach and use an autoregressive distributed lag model. The horizontal scale is in years before or after the episode. The vertical scale shows percent change. *Source*: Ostry, Loungani, and Furceri (2016).

reducing the level of debt sharply may be less effective than letting the debt decline organically through higher economic growth.

5. CONCLUSIONS

The field of macroeconomics was born in the aftermath of the Great Depression of the 1930s, when aggregate incomes fell by 25 percent in some countries. Avoiding such a decline through the use of monetary and fiscal policies became the central policy concern of macroeconomists. In the 1980s, the study of cross-country differences in average incomes became a second important topic of investigation. Over the past three decades, a consensus has emerged that a triad of policies— (i) macroeconomic discipline, (ii) structural reforms to free up markets, and (iii) the global spread of markets through free trade and movement of capital and labor—can deliver growth in average incomes and help cross-country convergence in average incomes. Other than a concern with reducing poverty, distributional concerns have been largely ignored in this consensus.

Macroeconomics is in the midst of a third wave, and this consensus is being challenged. Distributional outcomes are now being studied side-by-side with aggregate outcomes (Stiglitz, Sen, and Fitoussi 2009; Jones and Klenow 2016). Our chapter contributes to this endeavor with several important results. First, inequality is detrimental to growth, so its study is important even if one's interest is solely in aggregate outcomes. Second, redistribution has not been harmful to growth, obviating worries that redressing inequality would itself hurt aggregate outcomes. Third, most economic policies pose efficiency-equity trade-offs, as documented by Ostry et al. (2018) for structural policies, Ball et al. (2013) for fiscal policies, and Furceri, Loungani, and Zdzienicka (2018) for monetary policies.

The focus of this chapter is on understanding the efficiency-equity trade-offs posed by policies to liberalize international capital flows and fiscal consolidation. We chose these two policies for a number of reasons. First, they are both important determinants of inequality, even after controlling for the effects of a number other determinants. The fact that trade generates winners and losers has been long recognized, but the equity impacts of financial globalization have attracted much less scrutiny.

Second, the efficiency benefits claimed for these policies often have been overstated. In the case of financial openness, some capital flows such as foreign direct investment do appear to confer the benefits claimed for them. But for others, particularly short-term capital flows, the benefits to growth are difficult to reap whereas the risks of greater volatility and crises loom large. In the case of fiscal consolidation, the short-run costs of lower output and higher unemployment have been underplayed, and the desirability for many countries to simply live with high debt-to-GDP ratios is only now beginning to be acknowledged. These findings pose a dilemma for proponents of the consensus: "Why support them if there are few efficiency benefits but palpable equity costs?"[7]

Third, both capital account liberalization and fiscal policies are important areas of IMF policy advice, which has been changing in light of the evidence. Among policy makers today, there is increased acceptance of capital controls to mitigate financial stability and macroeconomic risks associated with capital flows (especially short-term carry-trade flows). Capital controls are not the only tools available, but they may be the best option when borrowing from abroad is the source of an unsustainable credit boom (Ostry et al. 2012). The IMF also recognizes that capital flow liberalization is generally more beneficial and less risky for countries that have reached certain thresholds of financial and institutional development, and that full liberalization may not be the appropriate end goal for many countries.

On fiscal policy, the IMF's policy advice has been to support "a case-by-case assessment of what is an appropriate pace of consolidation" and to emphasize the need "to make fiscal policy more growth-friendly" (Lipton 2013). In 2010, the institution's then-chief economist Olivier Blanchard said: "What is needed in many advanced economies is a credible medium-term fiscal consolidation, not a fiscal noose today" (IMF 2010). In October 2013, the IMF's managing director Christine Lagarde applauded the decision by the U.S. Congress to raise the country's debt ceiling. On the pace of U.S. fiscal consolidation, Lagarde advised: "We say slow down because the point is not to contract the economy by slashing spending brutally now as recovery is picking up" (Howell 2013). For the euro area, the IMF has advocated that "those with fiscal space should use it to support investment" (IMF 2015).

Recent events have prompted concerns about a reversal of globalization. Such a reversal would negate the great benefits that freer trade has engendered, as we noted at the outset. At the same time, the problems with questionable efficiency benefits and sizable equity costs from some policies will not go away if we do not acknowledge them. In particular, the evidence on the economic damage from inequality implies that policy makers should design policies to enhance their benefits and mitigate their distributional costs. For example, fostering financial inclusion safely and enhancing the resilience of the financial system are important preconditions to garner the benefits of financial globalization in terms of growth and equality. Likewise, the design of fiscal consolidation could be done in a way that minimizes the impact on low-income groups and preserves productive spending.

Nevertheless, some distributional consequences of policies would have to be remedied ex post. Equality-enhancing interventions could help growth. Several studies (Bénabou 2000, 2002; Kneller, Bleaney, and Gemmell 1999) point out that some categories of government spending—for example, public investments in infrastructure, spending on health and education, and social insurance provision—may be both pro-growth and pro-equality. We should not jump to the conclusion that the treatment for inequality may be worse for growth than the disease itself: win-win policies have the potential to promote efficiency *and* equality. Examples could include taxes on activities with negative externalities paid mostly by the better-off but harmful to the poor (such as, perhaps, excessive risk-taking in the financial sector), cash transfers aimed at encouraging better attendance at primary schools in developing countries, or spending on public capital and education that benefits the poor.

Since the Great Recession, much attention has been given to *macrofinancial linkages* and, more recently, to fears of *secular stagnation* in growth. Broadly speaking, we point out that just as much attention needs to be devoted to *macrodistributional linkages* and to the *secular exclusion* of large parts of the population from the benefits of increased growth.

NOTES

This chapter draws on a number of our recent papers, including Ostry, Berg, and Kothari (2017), Ostry, Loungani, and Furceri (2016), Ghosh et al. (2016), Furceri and Loungani (2015), Ostry et al. (2015), and Ostry et al. (2012). Views expressed are those of the authors and should not be ascribed to the IMF.

1. The technique appropriately accounts for both the cross-sectional and time-series variations in the data. A concern with sGMM estimation is that sensitivity to slight variations in instrumentation strategy, and a proliferation of instruments, may reflect problems of weak or invalid instruments. With respect to validity, Hansen tests for overidentifying restrictions and the first- and second-order residual autocorrelation tests confirm the validity of the instruments. Robustness checks were also undertaken to confirm robustness of the results to small variations in instrumentation strategy. With respect to instrument strength, where the concern is that inference may be unreliable even in large samples if instruments are weak, the literature as it applies to sGMM is still evolving, complicated by the fact that tests applied to instrumental variable estimation do not extend to the case of GMM; the application of weak-instrument robust methods to sGMM is lacking; and the use of projection methods to construct weak instrument robust confidence intervals costs power as the number of endogenous variables increases. Full consideration of potentially weak instruments makes inference challenging in the sGMM context. Nevertheless, using a variety of approaches and considering the implications of potentially weak instruments, the robustness checks we have carried out suggest that inequality remains harmful to growth and that redistribution has insignificant effects on growth.

2. The results are robust to different samples of countries. We found that higher inequality is bad for growth for both OECD and non-OECD countries, and that the effect is greater in OECD than in non-OECD countries.

3. In particular, we used an autoregressive distributed lag (ARDL) specification, as in Romer and Romer (2010) and several others:

$$g_{it} = a_i + \sum_{j=1}^{l} \beta_j g_{i,t-j} + \sum_{j=0}^{l} \delta_j \Delta Kaopen_{i,t-j} + \gamma T_t + \varepsilon_{it},$$

where g is either the growth rate of real GDP or the growth in the Gini coefficient, $\Delta Kaopen$ is the change in the capital account liberalization index, a_i are country fixed effects, and T is a time trend. The equation is estimated using OLS on an unbalanced panel of annual observations from 1970 to 2010 for 149 advanced and developing economies. The number of lags is 2, but the results are robust to the choice of alternate lag lengths. We derived the impulse response functions (IRFs) from an autoregressive distributed lag specification. The results are robust when controlling for liberalization in other areas and instrumental variables approaches.

4. We augmented the baseline specification with an interaction term of the change in capital account liberalization and a dummy variable indicating whether the change in the index was followed by the occurrence of a financial crisis (as identified in Laeven and Valencia 2010) over a time horizon of five years:

$$g_{it} = a_i + \sum_{j=1}^{l}\beta_j g_{i,t-j} + \sum_{j=0}^{l}\delta_j \Delta Kaopen_{i,t-j} + \sum_{j=0}^{l}\theta_j \Delta Kaopen_{i,t-j}^{no-crisis} + \gamma T_t + \varepsilon_{it}$$

5. Moody's identifies a group of countries as green-zone on the basis of the methodology in Ostry et al. (2010).

6. The economies are Australia, Austria, Belgium, Canada, Denmark, Finland, France, Germany, Ireland, Italy, Japan, Netherlands, Portugal, Spain, Sweden, the United Kingdom, and the United States.

7. In ongoing work, we document an important interaction between the two policies: capital account liberalization disciplines the conduct of domestic fiscal policy and leads to greater fiscal consolidation.

REFERENCES

Alesina, Alberto. 2010. "Fiscal Adjustments: Lessons from Recent History." Prepared for the Ecofin Meeting in Madrid, April 15.
Alesina, Alberto, and Silvia Ardagna. 2010. "Large Changes in Fiscal Policy: Taxes Versus Spending." *Tax Policy and the Economy* 24 (1): 35–68. https://doi.org/10.1086/649828.
Baldacci, Emanuele, Iva Petrova, Nazim Belhocine, Gabriela Dobrescu, and Samah Mazraani. 2011. "Assessing Fiscal Stress." IMF Working Paper WP/11/100. Washington, DC: International Monetary Fund.
Ball, Laurence M., Davide Furceri, Daniel Leigh, and Prakash Loungani. 2013. "The Distributional Effects of Fiscal Consolidation." IMF Working Paper WP/13/151. https://doi.org/10.5089/9781475551945.001.
Bénabou, Roland. 2000. "Unequal Societies: Income Distribution and the Social Contract." *American Economic Review* 90 (1): 96–129. https://doi.org/10.1257/aer.90.1.96.
———. 2002. "Tax and Education Policy in a Heterogeneous-Agent Economy: What Levels of Redistribution Maximize Growth and Efficiency?" *Econometrica* 70 (2): 481–517. https://doi.org/10.1111/1468-0262.00293.
Chinn, Menzie D., and Hiro Ito. 2006. "What Matters for Financial Development? Capital Controls, Institutions, and Interactions." *Journal of Development Economics* 81 (1): 163–92. https://doi.org/10.1016/j.jdeveco.2005.05.010.

——. 2008. "A New Measure of Financial Openness." *Journal of Comparative Policy Analysis* 10 (3): 309–22.

de Haan, Jakob, and Jan-Egbert Sturm. 2016. "Finance and Income Inequality: A Review and New Evidence." CESifo Working Paper Series 6079, CESifo Group Munich.

Dell'Ariccia, Giovanni, Paolo Mauro, André Faria, Jonathan Ostry, Julian Di Giovanni, Martin Schindler, M. Kose, and Marco Terrones. 2008. "Reaping the Benefits of Financial Globalization." IMF Occasional Papers. https://doi .org/10.5089/9781589067486.084.

Dreher, Axel, Noel Gaston, and Pim Martens. 2008. "The Measurement of Globalisation." *Measuring Globalisation*: 25–74. https://doi.org/10.1007/978-0 -387-74069-0_3.

Eichengreen, B. 2001. "Capital Account Liberalization: What Do Cross-Country Studies Tell Us?" *The World Bank Economic Review* 15 (3): 341–65. https://doi .org/10.1093/wber/15.3.341.

Feenstra, Robert C., Robert Inklaar, and Marcel P. Timmer. 2015. "The Next Genera-tion of the Penn World Table." *American Economic Review* 105 (10): 3150–82.

Furceri, Davide, and Prakash Loungani. 2018. "The Distributional Effects of Capital Account Liberlization." *Journal of Development Economics* 130 (C), 127–144

Furceri, Davide, Prakash Loungani, and Aleksandra Zdzienicka. 2018. "The Effects of Monetary Policy Shocks on Inequality." *Journal of International Money and Finance* 85 (C), 168–86.

Ghosh, Atish R., Jonathan D. Ostry, and Mahvash S. Qureshi. 2016. "When Do Capital Inflow Surges End in Tears?" *American Economic Review* 106 (5): 581–85. https://doi.org/10.1257/aer.p20161015.

Guajardo, Jaime, Daniel Leigh, and Andrea Pescatori. 2014. "Expansionary Austerity? International Evidence." *Journal of the European Economic Association* 12: 949–68. https://doi.org/ 10.1111/jeea.12083.

Harrison, Ann. 2002. "Has Globalization Eroded Labor's Share? Some Cross-Country Evidence." Columbia Business School (revised September 2012, MPRA Paper 39649, University Library of Munich, Germany).

Howell, Tom. 2013. "IMF Chief: U.S. Dance with the Debt Limit Is 'Very, Very Con-cerning'." *The Washington Times*, October 13, 2013. http://www.washingtontimes .com/news/2013/oct/13/imf-chief-us-dance-debt-limit-very-very-concerning/.

International Monetary Fund (IMF). 2010. "IMF Survey: IMF Urges Action to Tackle Unemployment, Create Jobs." IMF Survey. https://www.imf.org/en/News /Articles/2015/09/28/04/53/sonew090910a.

——. 2015. "Euro Area Policies: 2015 Article IV Consultation-Press Release; Staff Report; and Statement by the Executive Director." https://www.imf.org/external /pubs/cat/longres.aspx?sk=43126.0.

Jones, Charles I., and Peter J. Klenow. 2016. "Beyond GDP? Welfare Across Countries and Time." *American Economic Review* 106 (9): 2426–57. https://doi.org/10.1257 /aer.20110236.

Kneller, Richard, Michael F. Bleaney, and Norman Gemmell. 1999. "Fiscal Policy and Growth: Evidence from OECD Countries." *Journal of Public Economics* 74 (2): 171–90. https://doi.org/10.1016/s0047-2727(99)00022-5.

Kose, Ayhan, Eswar Prasad, Kenneth Rogoff, and Shang-Jin Wei. 2009. "Financial Globalization: A Reappraisal." *Panoeconomicus* 56 (2): 143–97. https://doi.org /10.2298/pan0902143k.

Laeven, Luc, and Fabian Valencia. 2010. "Resolution of Banking Crises: The Good, the Bad, and the Ugly." IMF Working Paper WP/10/146. Washington, DC: International Monetary Fund.

Lipton, David. 2013. "Bellwether Europe 2013 Speech by David Lipton, First Deputy Managing Director, International Monetary Fund." http://www.imf.org/external /np/speeches/2013/042513.htm.

Lucas, Robert E. 1988. "On the Mechanics of Economic Development." *Journal of Monetary Economics* 22 (1): 3–42.

——. 2004. "The Industrial Revolution: Past and Future." *The Region* (2003 Annual Report of the Federal Reserve Bank of Minneapolis): 5–20.

Mendoza, Enrique, and Jonathan Ostry. 2007. "International Evidence on Fiscal Solvency: Is Fiscal Policy 'Responsible'?" NBER Working Papers 12947. https://doi .org/10.3386/w12947.

Okun, Arthur M. 1975. *Equality and Efficiency, the Big Tradeoff.* Washington, DC: Brookings Institution.

Ostry, Jonathan, Andrew Berg, and Siddharth Kothari. 2018. "Growth-Equity Tradeoffs in Structural Reforms?" IMF Working Paper WP/18/5, January.

Ostry, Jonathan, Andrew Berg, and Charalambos Tsangarides. 2014. "Redistribution, Inequality, and Growth." IMF Staff Discussion Notes 14/02. https://doi .org/10.5089/9781484352076.006.

Ostry, Jonathan, Atish Ghosh, Jun Kim, and Mahvash Qureshi. 2010. "Fiscal Space." IMF Staff Position Notes 2010/11. Washington, DC: International Monetary Fund.

Ostry, Jonathan, Atish Ghosh, Marcos Chamon, and Mahvash S. Qureshi. 2012. "Tools for Managing Financial-Stability Risks from Capital Inflows." *Journal of International Economics* 88 (2): 407–21.

Ostry, Jonathan, Atish Ghosh, and Raphael Espinoza. 2015. "When Should Public Debt Be Reduced?" IMF Staff Discussion Notes 15/10. https://doi.org/10.5089 /9781498379205.006.

Ostry, Jonathan D., Prakash Loungani, and Davide Furceri. 2016. "Neoliberalism: Oversold?" *Finance & Development* 53, no. 2 (June): 38–41.

Ostry, Jonathan, Antonio Spilimbergo, and Alessandro Prati, 2009. "Structural Reforms and Economic Performance in Advanced and Developing Countries," IMF Occasional Papers 268. Washington, DC: International Monetary Fund.

Prasad, Eswar, Kenneth Rogoff, Shang-Jin Wei, and Ayhan Kose. 2003. "Effects of Financial Globalization on Developing Countries; Some New Evidence." IMF Occasional Papers 220. Washington, DC: International Monetary Fund.

Pritchett, L. 2000. "Understanding Patterns of Economic Growth: Searching for Hills Among Plateaus, Mountains, and Plains." *The World Bank Economic Review* 14 (2): 221–50. https://doi.org/10.1093/wber/14.2.221.

Reinhart, Carmen M., and Kenneth S. Rogoff. 2010. "Growth in a Time of Debt." *American Economic Review* 100 (2): 573–78.

Rodrik, Dani, and Arvind Subramanian. 2009. "Why Did Financial Globalization Disappoint?" *IMF Staff Papers* 56 (1): 112–38. https://doi.org/10.1057/imfsp .2008.29.

Romer, Christina D., and David H. Romer. 2010. "The Macroeconomic Effects of Tax Changes: Estimates Based on a New Measure of Fiscal Shocks." *American Economic Review* 100 (3): 763–801.

Schumpeter, Joseph A. 1942. *Capitalism, Socialism, and Democracy.* London: G. Allen & Unwin.

Solt, Frederick. 2009. "Standardizing the World Income Inequality Database." *Social Science Quarterly* 90 (2): 231–42. https://doi.org/10.1111/j.1540-6237.2009.00614.x.

Stiglitz, Joseph E., Amartya Sen, and Jean-Paul Fitoussi. 2009. "Report by the Commission on the Measurement of Economic Performance and Social Progress." Paris. http://www.stiglitzsen-fitoussi.fr/en/index.htm.

United Nations Statistics Division. 2016. "Sustainable Development Goals Indicators" [Labour share of GDP, comprising wages and social protection transfers]. http://data.un.org/Data.aspx?q=labor+share&d=SDGs&f=series%3aSL_EMP _GTOTL#SDGs.

U.S. Bureau of Economic Analysis. 2017. "Real Gross Domestic Product Per Capita." A939RX0Q048SBEA. Federal Reserve Bank of St. Louis. https://fred.stlouisfed .org/series/A939RX0Q048SBEA.

Williamson, John. 1990. "What Washington Means by Policy Reform." *Latin American Adjustment: How Much Has Happened?*, 7–20. Washington, DC: Peterson Institute for International Economics.

CHAPTER 4

The Impact of Foreign Investor Protections on Domestic Inequality

Manuel F. Montes

1. INTRODUCTION

A prominent element of international economic governance is the provision of legal protections to foreign investors as codified in international investment agreements (IIas). In this essay, I explore how these investment protections undermine the capabilities of host governments, particularly in developing countries, to reduce essential aspects of domestic inequality.

My main argument is that foreign investor protections obstruct government policies to contain domestic inequality even though there is no direct evidence that these investor protections increase domestic inequality (see section 6). These protections impose a regulatory and policy chill in the domestic sphere, which may prove congenial to the interests of a local elite. Global data suggest that inequality between countries has been decreasing whereas inequality within countries is increasing (Lakner and Milanovic 2016). However, the policy challenges involved in these two arenas are very different, and the "smaller" source of inequality may require equal or greater attention in order to reduce overall inequality (Memiş 2013). It has been suggested that treaty-enforced investor protections originating from international rules may act as obstructions, limiting government efforts to reduce domestic inequality.

Bilateral investment treaties (BITs) and investment chapters in free trade agreements between developed and developing countries are the two forms of IIas. In these agreements, states promise that foreign investors will be protected from arbitrary and unfair treatment—in terms of both process and policy actions—by the host government. The current dominant form of these BITs[1] exposes host countries to litigation costs and monetary penalties should their policies and actions be judged to be in violation of their investor-protection obligations.

These treaties between sovereign states have been promoted by Western governments based on the argument that providing strong commercial protections to foreign investors will increase the flow of investment into developing countries (Montes 2015). In section 3, I present evidence showing that states are heavily disadvantaged in the operation of BITs, and survey evidence suggests that their existence is not a key factor in private decisions on where to invest. The continuing prevalence of BITs can be seen as a key partial replacement for the previous colonial treaties of friendship, commerce, and freedom of navigation. Because the system does not impose countervailing obligations on investors, it is relatively "costless" to private parties but has clear upside benefits for them.

The rationale for investor protection is the view that courts in developing and non-Western countries are relatively underdeveloped and "too biased, too slow and sometimes too corrupt" (CEO/TNI 2012, 11) to provide a fair and independent dispute-settlement system for foreign investors in case of conflicts with the host state. These treaties provide that these disputes will be decided by a "neutral" body of legal experts meant to act independently in arbitration panels. The most prominent convenor of arbitration panels for these treaties is the International Center for Settlement of Investment Disputes (ICSID), hosted by the World Bank.

2. KEY GOVERNANCE FEATURES OF INVESTMENT TREATIES

There are 3,304 known IIAs in existence today (UN Conference on Trade and Development [UNCTAD] 2016, 101). Many treaties are, by their own provisions, secret, so it is possible only to approximate the total number of treaties.

The BIT system framework is imported from the commercial contractual and dispute-resolution system among private parties. Because one side of the system involves the public sector of a host country, it is especially open to being associated with a violation of the governance principle of transparency. In most BITs, the contractual obligations are all on the side of the host country and the liable party is a state—not a private entity—which has built-in accountability to its own citizens. The secrecy provisions of almost all treaties can prevent government officials from publicly disclosing the country's obligations to foreign investors.

These treaties also require that disputes arising between investors and the state, including the process of dispute resolution and any awards granted, be subject to strict secrecy. Such secrecy is a standard feature of commercial contracts and their dispute resolution. Currently only 608 investor-state dispute-settlement (ISDS) cases are known, but the actual number is likely to be higher because most IIAs allow for fully confidential arbitration (UNCTAD 2015, 112).

The international system of dispute resolution in the BIT system is extremely powerful and is unique in the existing (Westphalian) system of states. Unlike other international mechanisms, it allows private parties to sue states directly and obtain compensation. In the World Trade Organization (WTO), for example, only states can sue states (although the dispute often involves some aggrieved private company). Under BITs, ISDS exposes states to enormous monetary penalties to be paid to the aggrieved investor. It is estimated that 450 cases were processed in 2011. "In 2009/2010, 151 investment arbitration cases involved corporations demanding at least US$100 million from states" (CEO/TNI 2012, 7).

Four interrelated features of the BIT system are particularly problematical from a governance point of view:

1. **Severe imbalances in rights and responsibilities** are present in the provisions of the investment treaties, including broad definitions of what is investment and who is an investor, free transfer of capital, right to establishment, national treatment and most favored nation clauses, fair and equitable treatment, protection from direct and indirect expropriation, and prohibition of performance requirements (Bernasconi-Osterwalder et al. 2011). These provisions characterize investors' rights and ignore investors' responsibilities. A short list of government obligations under BITs include the following:

- Fair and equitable treatment (FET);
- Compensation in the case of direct or indirect expropriation;
- National treatment, or treatment no less favorable than that given to domestic investors;
- Most favored nation (MFN) treatment, or treatment no less favorable than that given to investors from third countries;
- Freedom from so-called performance requirements as a condition of entry or operation, such as requirements to transfer technology, to export a certain percentage of production, to purchase inputs domestically, or to undertake research and development;

- Free transfer of capital, guaranteeing that investors can freely move assets in and out of the country;
- A blanket obligation, known as an "umbrella clause," that the host state respect any legal or contractual obligations it may have to the investor; and
- The right to bring arbitration claims against host governments. (Bernasconi-Osterwalder et al. 2011, 11)

Not all BITs contain these obligations, but the list is consistent with the existing U.S. model treaty.

In the prevailing models of these treaties and in the overwhelming majority of actual treaties, provisions recognizing the need to uphold host states' regulatory authority are not present. Khor (2014) briefly summarizes the most problematic imbalances in the BIT provisions:

- The definition and scope of "investment" is very broad; it covers all kinds of assets including portfolio investment, credit, derivatives, contracts, intellectual property rights (IPRs), and expectations of future gains and profits. Legal cases can arise if an investor feels aggrieved about how any of these "investments" are affected.
- National treatment. The foreign investor has the right to be treated similar to or better than local investors. The foreign investor can claim to be discriminated against if the local investor is given preference or any other advantage.
- Fair and equitable treatment. This has been interpreted by some tribunals as the investor having a stable legal and business framework or predictable investment environment for the life of the investment. Investors have sued on the grounds of nonrenewal or change in terms of the license or contract, and changes in policies or regulations (including economic, health, or environment measures) that the investor claims will reduce its future profits. The claims for unfair treatment are "practically limitless" in scope, according to a study by the UN Conference on Trade and Development (UNCTAD 2014). Most ISDS cases are brought under this clause.
- Expropriation. This includes direct expropriation such as a government takeover of a property, and indirect expropriation, in which tribunals have ruled in favor of investors that claimed losses due to changes to existing or introduction of new government policies or regulations.
- "Survival clause." It is difficult to withdraw from state obligations in a BIT. Most BITs have a default renewal feature: if no party to a BIT gives notice of withdrawal upon expiry, the BIT is deemed to roll over

and continue, usually for another similar period. If a country wishes to withdraw from or not renew the BIT upon expiry, the host government is required to provide the investor with protections for a period of years after termination. Most BITS include a provision that the rules remain in force for an extended period (in many cases ten or fifteen years) after withdrawal or expiry. The import of this legal provision is extremely important because it is the key obstacle to global reform of the system. A multilateral treaty on investment will not extinguish existing BIT obligations nor terminate the survival clauses.

2. **Vague treaty provisions** create broad grounds for disputes, especially compared to the more rule-based regimes of international trade law (Roberts 2014) and allow for expansive interpretation of provisions by arbitrators. The rise of a systemic bias in favor of the investors in the resolution of disputes under investment treaty law[2] is consistent with the increase in the volume of these disputes, creating the opportunity for the expansion of this kind of practice among the network of arbitrators involved. Interpreted or created obligations from arbitral rulings are often in conflict with the original intent of the states that negotiated the treaty. Arbitrators have asserted jurisdiction over a wide scope of issues, including regulatory policies on which national constitutional courts have already ruled, which means that the international investor-protection system can override the highest judicial authorities in a national system. The way the arbitration system has operated so far generates deep concerns with regard to democratic governance and accountability.

3. **Conflicts of interest** stem from the monopolization by a cabal and the impertinent expertise among the professionals involved in the ISDS mechanism. The network of arbitrators is dominated by private lawyers, with a shared background and expertise most often from commercial law (CEO/TNI 2012). They participate in the revolving door among the roles of arbitrators, counsellors, and expert witnesses for parties involved in disputes. Until 2011, fifteen arbitrators had decided 55 percent of the known disputes, 64 percent of the disputes involving claims higher than $100 million, and 75 percent of the cases involving claims higher than $4 billion (CEO/TNI 2012, 38). Arbitrators have sat in judgment over cases involving companies in which they have a conflict of interest because of their membership on the board of a holding company.[3]

4. **Chilling effect on public policy**. Both the cost of litigation and monetary penalties in the event of an adverse arbitral judgment have a

direct chilling effect on a sitting government that must draw on the general public budget for these expenses. Claims or threats by investors to bring forward a claim against a particular state are increasingly being used to stop new legislation from being adopted or applied, thus creating an ex ante chilling effect on regulatory policy making.[4] The built-in lack of transparency and disclosure over ISDS procedures limits the space for public participation and accountability as well as the possibility of shaming private companies for their predatory or antiregulatory actions.

To avoid the regulatory chilling effect, foreign investors must accept domestic policy changes, including new environmental regulations, that could have a material effect on their operations, as long as they apply, for example, to all similar enterprises. Foreign investors have won awards on environmental policies that apply to all local companies. The impotence of the carve out for changes in tax policy preventing arbitral actions, which exist in most investment treaties, is an illustration of the limits of such an approach (Uribe and Montes 2017).

3. THE STATISTICS OF DEFECTIVE GOVERNANCE

What is the impact of the deeply flawed investor-protection system? In theory, the costs of such a system would be borne anywhere foreign investment occurs. Developing countries now absorb about half of foreign-investment flows, so one would expect that the costs of the system would be equally borne by developed and developing countries. However, the costs are borne in much greater proportion in developing countries because most foreign investors still come from developed countries, and their investments in other developed countries occur without the protection of a BIT.

This is changing with the EU-Canada Comprehensive Economic and Trade Agreement (CETA), which was signed October 30, 2016,[5] and the proposed EU-U.S. Transatlantic Trade and Investment Partnership (TTIP) agreement. Both will have "NAFTA-style" investor protections enforceable through arbitral procedures.[6] In CETA, an investment treaty among developed countries, Canada and the European Union introduced an International Court System (ICS) with extensive changes in arbitral procedures. These proposed changes in the ISDS procedures are meant to reduce issues of arbitrary and inconsistent interpretation, conflicts of interest, and the enormous costs of litigation in the current practice of ISDS. However, these procedural changes, applicable in CETA, if implemented,[7] and in future treaties if they incorporate some form of ICS, do not alter the fact that the matter being adjudicated is one in which only one party, the state, has obligations to the other party. The private sector and many practitioners of international law have expressed criticisms of these governance changes on multiple grounds, including that they do not necessarily improve the legitimacy and efficiency of the system (Koeth 2016, 12).

Currently the bulk of treaty-protected foreign investment occurs in developing countries, and this discussion focuses on the costs borne by developing countries from this governance system. Developing countries now are the destination for 55 percent of foreign-investment inflows (UNCTAD 2016, 1). In 2014, total foreign-investment flows declined due to a sharp decline of foreign investment into developed economies in the midst of the continuing global economic crisis. (All the data used in this section, unless as otherwise noted, is as of the end of 2014, the most complete ICSID data available.)

Among the top ten hosts of foreign investment, five are developing countries (figure 4.1).

Figure 4.2 summarizes the long-term trends in IIAs. There is a noticeable tapering off in the number of new BITs, and the cumulative pattern exhibits a negative first derivative. This is partly driven by the loss of "targets"—many countries that could accede to BITs already have them—and partly due to the declining interest and changes in developing country approaches to investor protection. This is discussed in more detail in the final section. Figure 4.2 reflects only the number of cases, not the size of populations or economies subject to BITs. If the proposed "mega-regional" arrangements come to pass, such as the TransPacific Partnership (TPP) and TTIP agreements, both with NAFTA-style investor protections, millions of people will be introduced to the disciplines and rigors of BITs. However, the U.S. administration inaugurated in January 2017 has withdrawn from the TPP and could withdraw from further negotiations in TTIP. The delegations in Geneva are considering the possibility of commencing discussions on investment facilitation that could import investor protections into WTO disciplines.

In contrast to the clear tapering off of new BITs, the number of (known) ISDS cases continues to escalate (figure 4.3). ICSID is the dominant arena for known cases and is the forum most frequently mentioned in known IIAs.[8] Parties can choose other venues to settle their disputes, including private arbitration services or facilities provided by the International Chamber of Commerce and other international bodies.

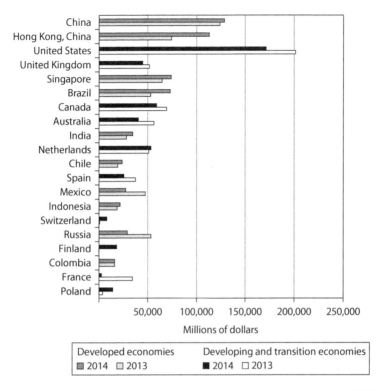

Figure 4.1 Top foreign direct investment hosts: Ranking and amount of FDI, 2013–14. *Source*: UNCTAD (2015), figure I.3.

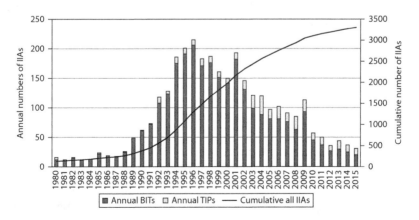

Figure 4.2 Annual additions of IIAs and cumulative number. *Source*: UNCTAD 2016, figure III.3.

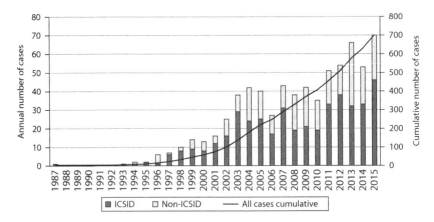

Figure 4.3   Known ISDS cases, annual and cumulative. *Source*: UNCTAD 2016, figure III.4.

In 2014, "of the 42 new known disputes, 33 were filed with the International Centre for Settlement of Investment Disputes (ICSID) . . . , 6 under the arbitration rules of UNCITRAL, 2 under the arbitration rules of the Stockholm Chamber of Commerce (SCC) and 1 under those of the International Chamber of Commerce" (UNCTAD 2015, 114). The ICSID Convention, which established ICSID in 1966, is a multilateral "treaty formulated by the Executive Directors of the World Bank to further the Bank's objective of *promoting* international investment" by providing "for settlement of disputes by conciliation, arbitration or fact-finding" (ICSID 2016). ICSID does not conduct arbitration or conciliation proceedings itself, but it offers institutional and procedural support to conciliation commissions, tribunals, and other committees that conduct such matters.

Settlements are mainly monetary penalties payable to (mostly private) enterprises. Not only have the number of cases been increasing but the size of arbitral awards decided by ISDS tribunals also have been increasing. In 2014, three awards amounting to US$ 50 billion were decided against Russia in cases brought by Yukos oil company majority shareholders. In the same year, an ICSID tribunal ordered Venezuela to pay US$ 1.6 billion, which includes compounded interest at the rate of 3.5 percent, as compensation to Exxon Mobil. In October 2012, Ecuador was ordered to pay to the U.S.-based Occidental Petroleum Corporation US$ 1.7 billion plus interest for having canceled its operating contract in 2006. In March 2010, Ecuador had lost another oil-related case, this one brought by Chevron for approximately US$ 700 million. These two awards combined are the equivalent to approximately 3.3 percent of that nation's gross domestic product (GDP) (Anderson and Perez-Rocha 2013). In 2014, an ICSID tribunal awarded the mining company Gold Reserve US$ 713 million plus arbitration costs against Venezuela (Mohamadieh and Uribe 2016).

The potentially high cost to the host government of compensatory damages provides investors with protection from arbitrary expropriation. (In the case of Yukos, the aggrieved parties are Russian nationals round-tripping as foreign investors.) The actual practice of the awards, however, raises the question of the expansive manner in which the panels determine the grounds of "arbitrary expropriation," the size of the awards, including punitive elements and the fact that in a majority of cases of expropriation claims are based on the nonrenewal of already expiring contracts.

The incidence of disputes in the extractive sectors is noteworthy. In the matter of poverty, inequality, environmental degradation, impact on health, and the treatment of indigenous populations, extractive industries are particularly pertinent. Figure 4.4 indicates that sub-Saharan Africa,

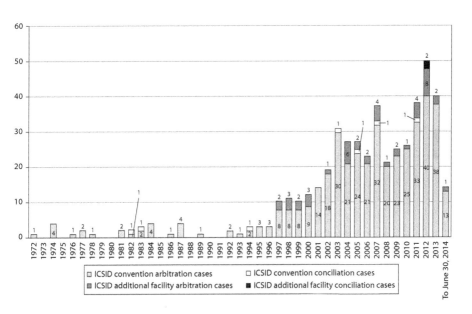

Figure 4.4   Geographic distribution of all ISDS cases registered under the ICSID convention and additional facility rules, by location of state party.
Source: Mohamadieh and Uribe (2016), graph 1.

South America, and Eastern Europe and Central Asia, where foreign investment in extractive industries are prominent, have the largest proportion of ICSID disputes.

The states that have been subject to the greatest number of suits are shown in figure 4.5. Argentina has fielded the highest number of suits, twenty of which are under the Argentina-United States BIT (UNCTAD 2015, 114). Four of the eleven respondent states are in Latin America.

The most frequent home state of claimants is the United States (figure 4.6), followed by three large European economies. Overall, U.S. and EU investors together account for 75 percent of the global number of ISDS claims (UNCTAD 2014).

An overall characterization of the outcomes of arbitral judgments is stymied by the secrecy obligations of parties to the system. Many compilations rely only on ICSID reports, which do not include all disputes, and documentation about the nature of the case *and* of the awards is often a matter of guesswork or indirect reference from government documents or academic papers. UNCTAD reports that at the end of 2015, the number of "concluded cases" was 444. Of these, 36 percent were decided in favor of respondent states and all claims were either dismissed on jurisdictional grounds or on their merits. In 2 percent of the cases, tribunals found a breach of treaty obligations but no monetary compensation was awarded to the investor. Nine percent of the cases were discontinued for reasons

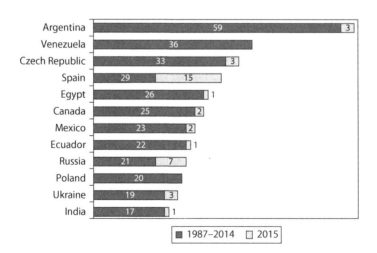

Figure 4.5   Most frequent respondent states, total at the end of 2014.
Source: UNCTAD (2016), figure III.5.

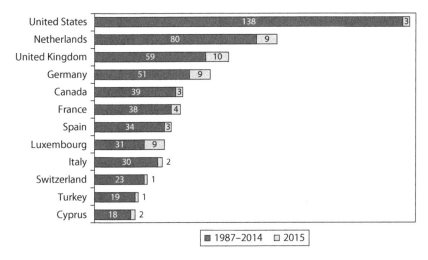

Figure 4.6   Most frequent home states of claimants, total at the end of 2014.
Source: UNCTAD (2016), table III.6.

other than settlement. Twenty-six percent were "settled," most likely generating a monetary award in favor of the investor, although the terms of settlement often remain confidential. Twenty-seven percent of the cases were decided in favor of the investor (2016, 107). Because the state is the bearer of all the obligations in a standard BIT, adding those decided in favor of the investor to those settled provides a total of 55 percent of cases in which investors prevailed in ISDS proceedings.

A specific uncertainty about the category of "settled" cases is the extent to which these would have involved monetary payments by respondent states to investors. Information on the nature of the settlements is not readily available, and settled cases could include withdrawals on the part of the investor, perhaps because of the high cost of the legal process, but this is unlikely. It is more likely that respondent states have settled these cases to minimize their losses due to the prohibitive costs of the legal process.[9] Among the known BIT cases, the Organisation for Co-operation and Development (OECD) found that legal and arbitration costs averaged over US$ 8 million, with some exceeding US$ 30 million; this compares unfavorably with the average cost of the antitrust litigation process in the United States of US$ 194,000 (CEO/TNI 2012). The Philippine government "spent US$ 58 million to defend two cases against German airport operator Fraport—the equivalent of the salaries of 12,500 teachers for 1 year, vaccination for 3.8 million children against diseases such as TB, diphtheria, tetanus, and polio; or the building of 2 new airports" (15).

The BIT regime provides an alternative path to financial profits for internationally active private actors through settlements and awards from states in millions of dollars. This distorts the business model of foreign investors, and it works to the disadvantage of host countries seeking investments to meet development objectives.

Of the 144 cases with outcomes in favor of the state, almost half (71 cases) were dismissed by the tribunals for lack of jurisdiction (UNCTAD 2015, 116). The stage in which tribunals decide that they have jurisdiction is critical from the point of view of host countries. Even in this stage, litigation and process costs are already being incurred by countries.

UNCTAD provides a breakdown of the outcomes of cases decided only on merit, which could indicate possible biases in the arbitral process. UNCTAD (2015) found that 60 percent of the cases were decided in favor of the investor, and 40 percent in favor the state. Because in BITs all of the obligations are to the account of the state, ISDS already has a built-in bias toward awards for investors. The fact that an enormous proportion of judgments end in favor of the investor suggests many things, including (i) inadequate quality and impartiality in the ISDS process despite its cost, (ii) encouragement of an alternative business model oriented toward obtaining profits from the "deep pockets" of government bodies, and (iii) use of the dispute system as a tool to influence state policy, a tool not available to indigenous investors. Knowing which of these possibilities, if any, apply to specific cases requires more detailed information than is publicly available.

In understanding outcomes from the ISDS system, it is also important to recognize the differences among host countries in their susceptibility to dispute actions. The United States is an important host country and has a greater capacity to absorb the fiscal cost of investment disputes than do developing countries. It is an important destination of outward investment from developing countries (though in absolute amounts the scale of investments is tiny) and contracting businesses. It can be argued that these investors and contractors would take greater care before initiating a dispute action against the United States, even if federal, state, and city policies continually change and have an impact on the expected profits of the foreign investors.[10]

The outcomes of the arbitral system suggest that two kinds of costs are generated by the system: (i) the fiscal costs of the process and (ii) the perverse governance impact on regulatory policy and the business model for enterprises operating internationally. The fiscal costs derive from the process and the possibility that states are paying damages at a scale beyond the actual costs borne by investors. The second kind of costs includes the chilling effect on public regulatory policy, encouraging an international business model based on exploiting the public finances of developing countries, and the corruption of the arbitration process.

Under a different worldview, and remembering that ICSID's stated goal is the promotion of foreign investment, the costly outcomes of the foreign-investor protection system can be justified. This *Weltanschauung*[11] would look upon the system as a necessary evil to elicit foreign-investment flows into developing countries, investments that otherwise would not occur at the levels observed. Only a tiny number of studies confirm this supposition. In these studies, it takes heroic efforts by researchers sympathetic to BITs to find weak positive effects (see Sauvant and Sachs, 2009, for an example of such a study). Most of the research indicates that the necessary evil of BITs has no positive impact on the scale of foreign-investment flows into developing countries.

Detailed research based on firm-level surveys indicates that the existence of BITs is not important in corporate investment decisions. In fact, some surveys indicate that legal departments of U.S. companies might not be aware of their existence or the kinds of provisions available in BITs (Skovgaard Poulsen 2011, 163). In a survey of general counsels of the top 200 of the Fortune 500 firms, Yackee found "a low level of familiarity with BITs, a pessimistic view of their ability to protect against adverse host state actions, and a low level of influence over FDI decisions" (2010, 429). Only about 20 percent of respondents indicated familiarity with BITs above "medium" (on a scale of none to high), and all respondents indicate that nonlawyer chief executives were not very familiar with BITs. Only about 5 percent of the general counsels considered BITs to be "very important" to a "typical FDI decision" (430).

There is no evidence that the existence of BITs reduces the cost of political risk insurance. Interviews with officials of the Multilateral Investment Guarantee Agency (MIGA) and executives in private insurers suggest that BITs are not a factor in setting these rates (Skovgaard Poulsen 2010).

Real-world evidence also suggests that BITs are not an important component in corporate investment decisions. Brazil has no BITs in force and has been a favored destination of foreign investment (ranking seventh as a national destination globally). South Africa's publicly announced decision to withdraw from a BITs-enforced investor-protection system in 2011 has had no noticeable impact on the scale of investment inflows and investor interest (although existing investors, supported by diplomatic pressure from their home countries, have publicly expressed objections to the new policy). After the end of apartheid in 1994, South Africa, just like the former communist countries in that era, rapidly agreed to numerous BITs with OECD countries to attract foreign investment. And China enjoyed large foreign-investment inflows before it began signing BITs, offering investors only domestic protection under a communist judicial system.

4. CONSTRAINING SOCIAL POLICY AGAINST INEQUALITY

Inequality has many dimensions beyond income, including access to productive assets, secure livelihoods and family incomes, a healthy environment, clean water, and affordable social services such as health care. Investors have successfully made it costly for states to undertake social policy to reform various dimensions of inequality. This section reviews some of these cases.

HINDERING BLACK ECONOMIC EMPOWERMENT POLICIES IN SOUTH AFRICA

Upon taking office in 1994, the African National Congress (ANC) instituted a set of measures toward the redistribution of assets and opportunities. The ANC said these policies were needed to resolve the economic disparities created by apartheid policies that had favored white business owners. These policies were to be implemented across government departments.

South Africa's Department of Mining and Energy implemented a set of policies to meet social, labor, and development objectives as set out in a broad-based socioeconomic empowerment mining charter. The legislation required mining companies to divest themselves of a portion of their assets to increase indigenous ownership. In *Foresti v. South Africa* (2010), a group of investors sued South Africa, claiming that its black economic empowerment legislation violated the terms of investment-protection treaties concluded by South Africa with Italy and Luxembourg. The individual investors, all Italian nationals, sued for violations of protections contained in the Italy–South Africa investment treaty. The case was settled on terms favorable to the claimants, and South Africa agreed to substantially reduce the ownership share required for divestment by the claimants.

This illustrates how an investment treaty lawsuit can affect implementation of affirmative action and other human rights measures. It raises the prospect that governments will be deterred from adopting such measures due to the risk of investor claims. Some analysts also questioned whether this settlement could lead other investors in South Africa, who previously accepted the requirements for divestment, to demand a watering-down of the requirements to match the treatment received by the foreign claimants in this case (van Harten 2011b).

UNDERCUTTING NATIONAL MINIMUM WAGE POLICIES

After the downfall of the Mubarak regime, in June 2012 the new Morsi government in Egypt raised the national minimum wage. In *Veolia v. Egypt* (2015), the French company Veolia sued the national government for breach of protections under the France-Egypt BIT, claiming that changes in domestic labor laws would affect its expected profit. This case is still pending.[12]

Veolia had a concession with the City of Alexandria for waste management beginning in 2001. The fifteen-year contract was terminated in 2011. Veolia claimed that the France-Egypt BIT shielded the concessionaire from the financial implications of these legal changes (Peterson 2012).The dates associated with the case are quite interesting. The case was registered on June 25, 2012, and the Morsi government took office on June 30, 2012. No doubt the termination of the existing contract in 2011 was a consideration in the complaint. The termination of an existing contract has been a ground for many other cases. If the trigger for the complaint was the contract termination, the case also illustrates that national governments can be held liable for compensation for damages stemming from the actions of local governments.

UNDERMINING LAND REFORM

Land reform had been part of the revolutionary program in Zimbabwe, but the process had been allowed a longer transition. When it was implemented, the policy collided with the country's obligations under some investment treaties. The *Border Timbers Limited and others v. Zimbabwe* (2010) and the *Bernhard von Pezold and others v. Zimbabwe* (2015) are two cases challenging Zimbabwe's land reform policies.

In the *Border Timbers* case, investors sought compensation on the grounds that Zimbabwe expropriated the claimants' large agricultural estates. Investors claimed that they had been targeted as part of the state's well-known land reform process (Bastin 2013).

This case also illustrates the question of representation in arbitration procedures, which are not codified and over which sitting arbitral panels have practically absolute control. An NGO and several Zimbabwean indigenous communities sought permission jointly to participate as *amici curiae* in the proceedings. In particular, they sought to file a joint written submission, to access key case materials, and to attend the oral hearings and reply to questions posed by the tribunal. The tribunal rejected applications by nondisputing parties to participate as amici curiae (*Border Timbers Limited and others v. Zimbabwe* 2010).

Judgment in *Bernhard von Pezold and others v. Zimbabwe* was rendered by the tribunal on July 28, 2015, but the Republic of Zimbabwe requested annulment procedures, which are still pending. In *Border Timbers Limited v. Zimbabwe*, the award was rendered by the tribunal on July 28, 2015, and annulment proceedings, requested by the respondent, are currently pending. No information is available on the content of the judgments, but given the request for annulment by the respondent government, the awards most likely favored the investors. That the investors obtained a judgment of "restitution and damages" against Zimbabwe is indirectly confirmed on the partnership's website by Matthew Coleman, of counsel for the investors, saying that this is standard practice (Steptoe 2016).

DESTABILIZING THE PUBLIC PROVISION OF ESSENTIAL SERVICES (WATER)

In this justly famous case, *Bechtel v. Bolivia* (2002), the Bolivian city of Cochabamba was forced to reverse the privatization of water services to a consortium that included the foreign company Bechtel within one year of awarding it in response to consumer complaints and mass actions about high prices and loss of access. The aggrieved consortium initiated a US$ 50 million case against Bolivia at ICSID, arguing not only would cancellation of the contract result in write-offs of about US$ 1 million in costs so far incurred by the consortium but also loss of future profits.

In August 2003, more than three hundred organizations from forty-three countries, including Bolivia, sent an International Citizens Petition to the tribunal demanding that the case be transparent and open to citizen participation. The ICSID tribunal rejected the petition. However, the case proved extremely controversial in public and destructive to the image of the claimants. In 2006, one year after an ICSID panel accepted jurisdiction of the case, the main shareholders of the consortium agreed to settle the case for a symbolic sum of 2 bolivianos ($0.30). The Bolivian

government saved further litigation costs but had to concede that plaintiffs were on the right side of the law.

On January 6, 2016, TransCanada announced that it was filing an
investor-state suit against the U.S. government under NAFTA, seeking
US$ 15 billion in damages, for its decision to cancel the company's
Keystone XL project. This case is at an early stage, but there are many
other examples of regulatory chill. In *Metalclad v. Mexico* (2000),
brought under NAFTA chapter 11, the city of Guadalcázar decided
to convert the area of operation of the investor (a U.S. waste disposal
company) to an ecological reserve. The ICSID award against Mexico of
US$ 16.7 million payable within forty-five days from the date of the
award, following which interest would "accrue on the unpaid award or
any unpaid part thereof at the rate of 6 percent compounded monthly"
(para. 131), addressed two issues (Mohamadieh and Montes 2014, 11).

1. The sequence of events that cumulatively denied the company a
permit to operate a hazardous waste disposal: The tribunal stated that
"expropriation under NAFTA includes not only open, deliberate, and
acknowledged takings of property, such as outright seizure or formal or
obligatory transfer of title in favour of the host State, but also covert or
incidental interference with the use of property which has the effect of
depriving the owner, in whole or in significant part, of the use or reasonably-
to-be-expected economic benefit of property even if not necessarily to the
obvious benefit of the host state" (*Metalclad v. Mexico* 2000, para. 103).
2. A subnational (state) level act that converted the area of operation of
the investor to an ecological reserve: The tribunal stated that the "tribunal
need not decide or consider the motivation of intent of the adoption of the
Ecological Decree" (para. 111). Thus the tribunal explicitly decided that the
purpose of the measure was not important.

The phrase "reasonably-to-be-expected benefit" has since featured in
many cases. The power of interpretation by arbitral tribunals under BITs
appears to include the authority to weigh government actions against the
"legitimate expectations" of the investor. In *Bilcon of Delaware et al. v.
Canada* (2015), a tribunal accepted jurisdiction and determined liability on the part of Canada on the ground that rejection of the investor's
project by the province of Nova Scotia because it failed the standard

environmental impact assessment violated the investor's legitimate expectations created by the investment-promotion activities and promises of the Canadian province publicly broadcast in television advertisements.

5. REFORMING THE SYSTEM

Enforcement of state obligations under BITs has been used by investors to obstruct social and environmental policies. In South Africa, in particular, the settlement with investors in the black empowerment case proved unpalatable to the government and was the occasion for rethinking its approach to investor protection. The government has embarked on a publicly announced program of withdrawing from its BITs and relocating its investor-protection system in domestic law.

Other undesirable features of BITs have also provoked reform efforts. In India, for example, recent dispute-settlement defeats that subvert or circumvent the country's judicial system have been a key motivation (Dar 2015). In February 2012, India's Supreme Court invalidated 122 grants of licenses on the 2G telecommunications spectrum on the grounds that the awards had not followed the correct procedures and were tainted by corruption. Domestic adjudication of this case went all the way to the supreme court, which ruled the allocation "unconstitutional and arbitrary" on public interest grounds and resulted in a prison sentence for the minister of Communications and Information Technology. Nevertheless, the cancellation of the spectrum awards has triggered investor disputes based on claims of indirect appropriation and the violation of fair and equitable treatment.

Brazil has signed fourteen treaties, none of which have been ratified by the legislature, and has now embarked on designing its own model treaty based explicitly on investment promotion instead of investor protection (under the preferred title of Agreement on Cooperation and Facilitation of Investments). The specific elements of the Brazilian approach continue to evolve as it negotiates treaties sequentially with other developing countries,[13] but the new approach eliminates investor-state dispute resolution. The Brazilian approach involves constant state-to-state involvement over investment projects from the early stages to the settlement of disputes if they cannot be avoided. There is no guarantee that social objectives for reducing inequality will be incorporated in the resulting treaties. However, to the extent that this approach requires active state involvement and that policies against inequality are a responsibility of the state, the Brazilian approach is a step in the right direction.

In the developed world, recent efforts at reform may apply to future treaties, but not to existing treaties. The EU-Canada CETA of October 2016 provides (i) expanded definitions of the concepts of greatest contention in ISDS, including "indirect expropriation" and "fair and equal treatment;" (ii) explicit general exceptions recognizing the right of the state to regulate on the grounds of public health, the environment, public order, and morality; and (iii) a preamble that explains that the purpose of the agreement is not just the protection of the rights of investors but also to achieve social objectives such as the respect for human rights and realizing sustainable development (Koeth 2016). These changes go some way toward reducing the imbalance in rights that tie the hands of a state interested in reducing domestic inequality.

That language in investment treaties currently being negotiated have to explicitly recognize the right of the state to regulate reflects the intolerable imbalance in current practice. The right to regulate is a basic element of sovereignty under international law, reflecting both the power and the responsibility of the state in discharging *Salus populi suprema lex esto* (the well-being of the people is the highest law). This right has not been granted by investment agreements because the main purpose of investment treaties is to attract foreign investment and to protect foreign investors from acts considered injurious to them. In upholding this purpose, arbitral tribunals have ruled that states have lost their soverign right to regulate for the good of their people.

In recent years, strong diplomatic trends have leaned toward incorporating NAFTA-style investor protections in proposed mega-regional agreements and possibly lodging such a regime in a multilateral manner in the WTO. The United States was active in initiating free trade negotiations, notably the TransPacific Partnership (TPP) among twelve economies in the Pacific Rim and the Trans-Atlantic Trade and Investment Partnership (TTIP) between the United States and the European Union. However, on January 23, 2017, an executive order from the president directed the U.S. Trade Representative to "withdraw the United States as a signatory to the Trans-Pacific Partnership (TPP)" and "to permanently withdraw the United States from TPP negotiations" (Whitehouse. gov 2017). This new U.S. administration seems likely to end its assertive leadership in mega-regional agreements that can be highly advantageous for its international corporations.

With some relatively minor adjustments, investor-state dispute enforcement for investor protection is part of the TPP, and a NAFTA-style ISDS is an important feature of the proposed TTIP. The contents and underlying philosophy of both TPP and TTIP are comparable in principle, so it is likely that the United States will withdraw from the TTIP as well. Should the TTIP become reality, however, European governments would find themselves newly subjected to investor protections for U.S. investors interfering with their social and environmental policies. Due to the volume of investments from the United States compared to those from developing countries and the more litigious character of U.S. investors, TTIP has the potential to increase the global populations whose governments will confront obstacles to their policies to reduce inequality. The precedent presented by CETA suggests that should the EU be involved in future investment treaty negotiations, it will seek to incorporate the ICS for investment disputes, which is an attempt to improve the process without eliminating the imbalance of obligations in investment treaties.

6. INTERNATIONAL GOVERNANCE AND DOMESTIC INEQUALITY

There are many dimensions of domestic inequality beyond income distribution, including gender, racial and other ascriptive inequities, differential skills, and regional imbalances. BITs can have an impact on domestic inequality through multiple channels. One set of channels is the impact of foreign investment on domestic growth, employment, and incomes. Another set of channels is the impact of BITs on fiscal health that affects both public policy and public resources for social programs.

IMPACT OF BITS THROUGH FOREIGN INVESTMENT

Studies on foreign investment suggest that BITs generally worsen domestic inequality. There are many well-rehearsed conduits supporting this effect. For example, foreign-investment projects tend to use more advanced technology and rely on skilled workers in the domestic economy. Basu and Guariglia (2007) found that foreign investment increases inequality in a dual economy model: increased growth through investment tends to reduce the weight of agriculture (where incomes and productivity are lower) in the economy.

However, there is only weak evidence that BITs have a positive impact on foreign investment. So BITs cannot be strongly implicated as a driver for increased inequality. The evidence that BITs have a negative impact on domestic inequality in developing countries through its impact on investment is weak and, possibly, nonexistent.

One channel could be whether foreign investment is associated with higher levels of total investment. Figure 4.7 suggests that there may be a positive relationship between foreign direct investment (FDI) and the investment rate, but this relationship may be weak. (Data in the figure are from ninety-two developing countries in 2012–2014, but the trend is similar to the pattern in the 1970s.) If higher FDI is associated with more domestic inequality, a negative relationship would suggest that more IIA protections stimulate investment but do not necessarily increase domestic inequality.

Do BITs reduce the cost of political insurance for foreign investors? Once again, the existing evidence indicates that the cost of political insurance is independent of the existence of BITs (Skovgaard Poulsen 2010). Replacing BITs with political insurance would require a global abrogation of the existing system of BITs.

The enormous compensation awards granted by tribunals could serve as a direct channel between BITs and domestic inequality. However,

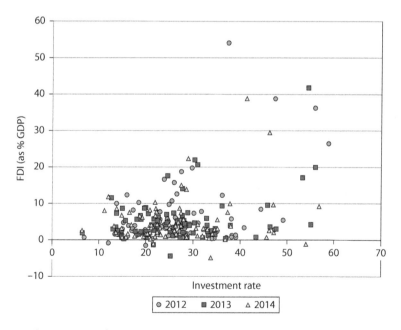

Figure 4.7   Foreign direct investment versus investment rate (in percent of GDP).

investigating this requires first overcoming the secrecy surrounding these awards. Awards will exacerbate domestic inequality, even though most are one-time bonanzas for already wealthy investors. For developing countries, their own citizens and residents may have benefited as awardees as foreign investors, entering as owners in incoming investment from treaty country partners. The overwhelming majority of BITs awardees are enterprises resident in developed countries. These awards would exacerbate domestic inequality in *developed* countries. These enterprises have a more diffuse ownership structure, including pension funds, in which arbitral awards could benefit labor. For large U.S. corporations, however, a big proportion of these awards are captured by management based on the nature of compensation practices that have become standard for these corporations (Lazonick 2014).

IMPACT OF BITS THROUGH PUBLIC POLICY AND RESOURCES

One important channel is the impact of BITs on domestic inequality through the public sector. BITs affect public policy, and the practice of BITs also has an effect on fiscal resources (through the cost of arbitral awards). It must be recognized that this impact is mediated by the stance of public policy. If public policy is indifferent or tolerant of increasing inequality as the price of greater investment and faster growth, the costs of investor protection cannot be easily implicated in increasing domestic inequality.

The case studies presented in section 4 illustrate the expanding influence BITs may have on domestic inequality, particularly the dimensions of inequality that go beyond income and wages. Ownership requirements, environmental and health protections, and access to land have been adversely affected by the domestic policy straitjackets introduced through investor protection obligations. The integrity of the domestic judicial system, exemplified by awarding 2G licenses in India in the late 2000s, speaks to the unequal access to redress for damages introduced by the BITs network. Although the United States has carved out many policies that allow states to avoid BITs disciplines (including minimum wage requirements and local content), most developing country national governments are liable for the adverse impact on investors of the policies of their subnational governments.

The other channel of impact by BITs is through public resources and the claims on public revenues due to the cost of arbitral litigation and awards, constraints on reductions in investment incentives, and tax policy in general. The Philippine Fraport case throws light on the substantial costs of investor-state arbitration in poor countries, which depletes resources for teacher salaries and immunization programs, among others. These countries often settle to avoid additional costs, but there is no guarantee that such fiscal savings will be directed to social programs that reduce inequality.

7. FINAL COMMENTS

This paper does not present direct evidence that the BITs international governance mechanism has a strong effect on domestic inequality. The case examples in section 4 suggest that BITs obligations obstruct public interventions oriented toward reducing inequality and can impose severe fiscal costs, draining resources that could be applied to combat domestic inequality. However, there are a host of intervening variables, not the least of which is the policy stance of host governments subject to BITs disciplines.

As discussed in section 2, under the prevailing regime of investor protection, obligations are set only for host states, not for investors. These obligations have tended to be stated in ambiguous terms and interpreted expansively in arbitral proceedings. With very few exceptions, corresponding responsibilities on the part of investors are not defined in the regime. The feasibility of a global, multilateral path toward reforming the system is extremely limited; a multilateral approach cannot overturn the obligations codified in the 3,304 treaties in place today. Nonetheless, developing countries are introducing initiatives to sidestep this problematic system.

New efforts on the part of both developed and developing countries to reform the "classic" form of investor protections suggest that this is a remnant of the high tide of the globalization era from the 1980s. Inequality is the most prominent motive force behind the burgeoning rethinking of the current form of globalization. In a piece provocatively entitled "Neoliberalism: Oversold?," Ostry and colleagues at the IMF suggest that a policy considered part of an ideal standard set—"removing restrictions on the movement of capital across a country's borders (so-called capital account liberalization)"—cannot be associated with increased growth and is associated with increased inequality, which "in turn hurts the level and sustainability of growth" (2016, 38–39).

Developing country authorities "practice" this neoliberal standard not only in structural adjustment programs but in accepting investor-protection obligations in treaties that have an expansive definition of the investments covered, such as this list from the final TPP text: "shares, stock and other forms of participation in an enterprise," "futures, options and other derivatives," and "bonds, debentures, other debt instruments and loans" (U.S. Trade Representative 2016, 3). The text goes on to "permit all transfers relating to a covered investment to be made freely and without delay into and out of its its territory" (9). An IMF legal counsel opinion on the U.S.-Singapore Free Trade Agreement in 2003 stated that in complying with the blanket prohibitions against capital restrictions of the free trade agreement, a member could become ineligible to access IMF resources in the event of a balance-of-payments crisis because the Articles of Agreement authorize the staff to request the imposition of capital controls[14] in such situations (Montes 2012).

The new investment treaty models from Brazil and India exclude portfolio flows from investor protection. However, these proposals have not been tested in agreements that include G7 countries, whose financial centers are a key element of their international competitiveness. In the United States, in particular, it is difficult to find an instance when the investment coverage and "freely and without delay" provisions have strayed from the U.S. model in investment treaties.

Reflecting on CETA, it appears that Canada and the EU are prepared to move toward a clearer definition of fair and equitable treatment and to restore the state's regulatory power for public purposes. A related development is the pattern in the developing countries' new model BITs, which introduce responsibilities of investors. These proposals have not been tested in treaties with developed countries.

Still another trend in the international sphere is the growing effort to include human rights responsibilities in business activities. In 2011, the United Nations Human Rights Council endorsed the Guiding Principles for Business and Human Rights, which extends voluntary human rights standards to the activities of private companies. On June 26, 2014, the Human Rights Council adopted Resolution A/HRC/26/9: "Elaboration of an International Legally Binding Instrument on Transnational Corporations and other Business Enterprises with respect to Human Rights." The resolution provides for the establishment of an open-ended intergovernmental working group with the mandate to develop a legally binding international instrument to regulate, in international human rights law, the activities of transnational corporations and other business enterprises. Should this line of work prosper over the resistance of developed countries in the council, it will create a set of obligations and responsibilities on the part of investors and international business.

These developments point to a retreat from the guarantees over an uninhibited space for private profit-making, which had been considered a fundamental ingredient of globalization and which the provisions of classic investment treaties have upheld. The Brazilian and Indian innovations and the drastic actions by Bolivia, Ecuador, and South Africa to revoke existing treaties are more in line with pressing for thoroughgoing and more rapid reform. The real test is whether this divide will leave behind countries that are not as prominent in the foreign investment game. Evidence suggests that the classic treaties have had an insignificant impact on investment flows, but smaller countries may feel compelled to accede to investment treaties to achieve a minimum qualification to be considered as investment destinations. Will they take the leap and accept the alternative approaches being experimented with in the developing world?

NOTES

1. For convenience and given that their provisions are highly comparable, in this chapter the term "BITs" is used to refer to both bilateral investment treaties and investment chapters in free trade agreements. The important difference between BITs and investment chapters is that a BIT can be terminated as a stand-alone treaty, whereas abrogating the obligations in an investment chapter in a free trade agreement requires withdrawal from the whole agreement, including, for example, any mutual trade concessions in other parts of the treaty.

2. The problems of expansive interpretations of vague treaty provisions by arbitral panels are well known. For an example of the kind of "highly malleable" constraints put on governments by these vague provisions see van Harten (2011a).

3. In 2004, one of the fifteen privileged arbitrators, Gabrielle Kaufmann-Kohler of Switzerland, "was appointed as arbitrator by water company Vivendi and energy and gas supplier EDF in two different claims against Argentina. Two years later, in 2006, Kaufmann-Kohler was appointed to the Board of the Swiss bank UBS, which was the single largest shareholder in Vivendi and which has stakes in EDF. Kauffman-Kohler claimed she was unaware of the connections. Argentina challenged her impartiality on the case. A committee deciding on the challenge denied Argentina's claim, but lambasted her for failing to disclose her role as a corporate board member" (CEO/TNI 2012, 40).

4. In fact, investment lawyers Wiśniewski and Górskaon (2015) suggest that the threat of sparking a dispute is a legitimate company tactic to prevent any changes in the regulatory regime in which they operate.

5. The EU Parliament and national parliaments of EU member states must approve CETA before it can take full effect.

6. Even though the first dispute against a state was lodged in 1987, the North American Free Trade Agreement (NAFTA) of 1994 is the true grandfather of the system in which an investor can seek damages against a state (see chapter 11 of the agreement). NAFTA happens to include two developed countries—the United States and

Canada—and one developing country, Mexico. At this writing, only Canada, arguably the less developed of the two, has made payments for damage claims brought by U.S. investors. Canadian investors have not won a single case against the U.S. government.

7. CETA must still be ratified by each EU member state, and the EU is currently seeking an opinion on the compatibility of ICS to European treaties resulting from a last minute concession to the objections to CETA by the Wallonian region of Belgium.

8. ICSID's dominance is partly due to the ICSID requirement to report the existence of cases it accepts. The number of actual cases is unknown.

9. The costs of the process include the cost of the services and travel for members of the arbitral panel, the cost of services for counsel of the opposing sides, and other costs with respect to information-gathering, travel of witnesses, and so on.

10. There are also differences in the kinds of investors tumbling out of the United States and other countries whose incentive structures are based on maximizing managerial incomes and shareholder values. See Lazonick (2011) for a window into this literature, which also argues that in the long-term the United States could be at a competitive disadvantage because these "financialized" management approaches privilege short-term returns and penalizes innovations that create new products and markets. Coming from underdeveloped financial markets, it can be argued that investors from developing countries experience relatively less pressure toward maximizing financial returns than do those from the United States.

11. Schreuer expresses this worldview in a paper about the ICSID Convention thus: "The role of FDI for development is practically uncontested today and has been recognized by nearly all developing countries. Therefore, the Convention's original idea, the promotion of economic development through FDI, has turned out to be a clear success" (2002, 5).

12. The Tribunal issued Procedural Order No. 4 concerning production of documents on December 21, 2015. https://icsid.worldbank.org/apps/icsidweb/cases/Pages/casedetail.aspx?CaseNo=ARB/12/15.

13. Treaty negotiations with Mozambique, Angola, and Mexico have been concluded. A treaty with Chile is being negotiated.

14. China, being party to BITs, continues to maintain capital controls. It is not known if it has been hauled into arbitral disputes over such controls, for which nonnationals willing to risk a permanent souring of relations with the host government would likely be the aggrieved parties. Known cases of disputes over capital controls stem from balance-of-payments crises, which China has not experienced recently.

REFERENCES

Anderson, Sarah, and Manuel Perez-Rocha. 2013. "Mining for Profits in International Tribunals: Lessons for the Trans-Pacific Partnership." Washington, DC: Institute for Policy Studies. https://justice-project.org/wp-content/uploads/2017/07/mining-for-profits-2013-english.pdf.
Bastin, Luke. 2013. "Amici Curiae in Investor—State Arbitrations: Two Recent Decisions." *Australian International Law Journal*: 96–104. http://www.austlii.edu.au/au/journals/AUIntLawJl/2013/7.pdf.

Basu, Parantap, and Alessandra Guariglia. 2007. "Foreign Direct Investment, Inequality, and Growth." *Journal of Macroeconomics* 29 (4): 824–39.

Bechtel v. Bolivia. 2002. ICSID Case No. ARB/02/3, Award (25 February 2002). http://icsidfiles.worldbank.org/icsid/ICSIDBLOBS/OnlineAwards/C210/DC629_En.pdf.

Bernasconi-Osterwalder, Nathalie, Aaron Cosbey, Lise Johnson, and Damon Vis-Dunbar. 2011. "Investment Treaties and Why They Matter to Sustainable Development." Winnipeg, Canada: International Institute for Sustainable Development. https://www.iisd.org/publications/investment-treaties-and-why-they-matter-sustainable-development-questions-and-answers.

Bernhard von Pezold v. Zimbabwe. 2015. ICSID Case No. ARB/10/15, Award (28 July 2015). https://www.italaw.com/sites/default/files/case-documents/italaw7095_0.pdf.

Bilcon of Delaware et al. v. Canada. 2015. PCA Case No. 2009–04, Award (March 17, 2015). https://pcacases.com/web/view/50.

Border Timbers Limited and others v. Zimbabwe. 2010. ICSID Case No. ARB/10/25, (20 December 2010). https://www.italaw.com/sites/default/files/case-documents/ital043.pdf.

CEO/TNI. 2012. *Profiting from Injustice: How Law Firms, Arbitrators and Financiers Are Fuelling an Investment Arbitration Boom.* Brussels: Corporate Europe Observatory and the Transnational Institute.

Dar, Biswajit. 2015. "India's Experience with BITs: Highlights from Recent ISDS Cases." South Centre Investment Policy Brief No. 3. Geneva.

Foresti v. South Africa. 2010. ICSID Case No. ARB(AF)/07/1, Award (4 Aug. 2010). http://investmentpolicyhub.unctad.org/ISDS/Details/262.

ICSID. 2016. "About ICSID." https://icsid.worldbank.org/en/Pages/about/default.aspx.

Khor, M. 2014. "A Note on the Investor-State Dispute Settlement System (ISDS) in the Context of BITs." Geneva: South Centre.

Koeth, Wolfgang. 2016. "Can the Investment Court System (ICS) Save TTIP and CETA?" European Institute of Public Administration Working Paper 2016/W/01.

Lakner, Christoph, and Bramko Milanovic. 2016. "Global Income Distribution: From the Fall of the Berlin Wall to the Great Recession." *World Bank Economic Review* 30 (2): 203–32.

Lazonick, William. 2011. "The Innovative Enterprise and the Developmental State: Toward an Economics of "Organizational Success." Paper prepared for the Institute for New Economic Thinking annual conference: "Crisis and Renewal: International Political Economy at the Crossroads." Mount Washington Hotel Bretton Woods, NH, April 8–11.

——. 2014. "Profits Without Prosperity." *Harvard Business Review.* https://hbr.org/2014/09/profits-without-prosperity.

Memiş, Emel. 2013. "Deriving Macro Policy from Income Inequality Decompositions by Subgroups: A Cautionary Discussion." *Ekonomik Yaklasim* 24 (87): 69–84. https://www.researchgate.net/publication/312164063_Deriving Macro Policy from Income Inequality Decompositions by Subgroups A Cautionary Discussion.

Metalclad v. Mexico.2000. ICSID Case No. ARB(AF)/97/1, Award (30 August 2000). http://www.italaw.com/sites/default/files/case-documents/ita0510.pdf.

Mohamadieh, Kinda, and Manuel F. Montes. 2014. "Investment Agreements: Expansive Interpretation of Provisions and Constraints on Development Policy Space." Paper submitted to ESCAP. Geneva : South Centre.

Mohamadieh, Kinda, and Daniel Uribe. 2016. "The Rise of the Investor-State Dispute Settlement in the Extractive Sectors: Challenges and Considerations for African Countries." Research Paper 65. Geneva: South Centre.

Montes, Manuel F. 2012. "Capital Controls, Investment Chapters and Asian Development Objectives." Policy Brief 15. Geneva: South Centre.

——. 2015. "Démocratie, bonne gouvernance et état de droit s'appliquent-ils dans le système économique international?" In *Tous responsables: Chroniques de la gouvernance 2015*, 33–40. Institut de recherche et débat sur la gouvernance. Éditions Charles Léopold Mayer.

Ostry, Jonathan D., Prakash Loungani, and Davide Furceri. 2016. "Neoliberalism: Oversold?" *Finance & Development* 53 (2): 38–41.

Peterson, Luke E. (2012) "French Company, Veolia, Launches Claim Against Egypt over Terminated Waste Contract and Labor Wage Stabilization Promises." *Investment Arbitration Reporter*. https://www.iareporter.com/articles/french -company-veolia-launches-claim-against-egypt-over-terminated-waste-contract -and-labor-wage-stabilization-promises/.

Roberts, Anthea. 2014. "Recalibrating Interpretive Authority." New York: Vale Columbia Center. http://ccsi.columbia.edu/files/2014/01/FDI_No113.pdf.

Sauvant, Karl, and Lisa E. Sachs. 2009. *The Effect of Treaties on Foreign Direct Investment: Bilateral Investment Treaties, Double Taxation Treaties and Investment Flows*. Oxford: Oxford University Press.

Schreuer, Christoph. 2002. "The World Bank/ICSID Dispute Settlement Procedures." In *Settlement of Disputes in Tax Treaty Law*, ed. Michael Lang and Mario Zuger, 501–31. Vienna: Linde Verlag Wien. http://www.oecd.org/dataoecd/47/25/2758044 .pdf.

Skovgaard Poulsen, Lauge N. 2010. "The Importance of BITs for Foreign Direct Investment and Political Risk Insurance: Revisiting the Evidence." In *Yearbook on International Investment Law and Policy 2009/2010*, 539–74. New York: Oxford University Press.

——. 2011. "Sacrificing Sovereignty by Chance: Investment Treaties, Developing Countries, and Bounded Rationality." (PhD diss., Department of International Relations of the London School of Economics and Political Science, London.)

Steptoe. 2016. "Matthew Coleman, Partner." http://www.steptoe.com/professionals -Matthew_Coleman.html.

UN Conference on Trade and Development (UNCTAD). 2014. *World Investment Report 2014*. Geneva: UNCTAD.

——. 2015. *World Investment Report 2015: Reforming International Investment Governance*. Geneva: UNCTAD.

——. 2016. *World Investment Report 2016: Investor Nationality: Policy Challenges*. Geneva: UNCTAD.

Uribe, Daniel, and Manuel F. Montes (2017) "Taxation Carve-Out Clauses: Do they Work?" (manuscript). Geneva: South Centre.

U.S. State Department. 2012. "2012 U.S. Model Bilateral Investment Treaty." https://www.state.gov/documents/organization/188371.pdf.

U.S. Trade Representative. 2016. "Investment." In TPP Final Text, https://ustr.gov /sites/default/files/TPP-Final-Text-Investment.pdf.

Van Harten, Gus. 2011a. "Thinking Twice About a Gold Rush: PacRim Cayman LLC v. El Salvador." In *FDI Perspectives: Issues in International Investment*, ed. Karl Sauvant, Lisa Sachs, Ken Davies, and Ruben Zandvliet, 94–96. New York: Vale Columbia Center on Sustainable International Investment.

——. 2011b. "Foresti v South Africa (Italy—South Africa BIT)." http://www.iiapp .org/media/cases_pdfs/Foresti_v_South_Africa.rev.pdf.

Veolia v. Egypt. 2015. ICSID Case No. ARB/12/15, (13 April 2015). http:// investmentpolicyhub.unctad.org/ISDS/Details/458.

Whitehouse.gov. 2017. "Presidential Memorandum Regarding Withdrawal of the United States from the Trans-Pacific Partnership Negotiations and Agreement." https:// www.whitehouse.gov/the-press-office/2017/01/23/presidential-memorandum -regarding-withdrawal-united-states-trans-pacific.

Wiśniewski, Cezary, and Olga Górskaon. 2015. "A Need for Preventive Investment Protection?" Kluwer Arbitration (blog). http://kluwerarbitrationblog .com/blog/2015/09/30/a-need-for-preventive-investment-protection/?utm _source=feedburner&utm_medium=email&utm_campaign=Feed%3A+Kluwer ArbitrationBlogFull+%28Kluwer+Arbitration+Blog+-+Latest+Entries%29.

Yackee, Jason W. 2010. "Do Bilateral Investment Treaties Promote Foreign Direct Investment? Some Hints from Alternative Evidence." *Virginia Journal of International Law* 51 (2): 397–442.

CHAPTER 5

Investment Treaties, Investor-State Dispute Settlement, and Inequality

HOW INTERNATIONAL RULES AND INSTITUTIONS CAN EXACERBATE DOMESTIC DISPARITIES

Lise Johnson and Lisa Sachs

INTRODUCTION

Government officials from around the world have been erecting a framework of economic governance with major, but underappreciated, implications for intranational inequality for four decades. The components of this framework are thousands of bilateral and multilateral treaties designed to protect international investment. In many jurisdictions, the treaties have been concluded without public awareness or scrutiny—or even much discussion or analysis by government officials, including those responsible for negotiating the agreements (Poulsen 2015)—and without an adequate understanding of how these agreements could affect intranational inequality. Long imperceptible, the size and power of this framework for economic governance has become increasingly apparent. Governments have continued to expand and entrench this framework through negotiation of several new bilateral and multilateral agreements, including the Trans-Atlantic Trade and Investment Partnership Agreement between the European Union and the United States, the agreements China is negotiating with the United States and the European Union, and the Regional Comprehensive Economic Partnership (RCEP) agreement being negotiated by sixteen countries throughout Asia and the Pacific.

International investment treaties protect multinational corporations from suffering losses due to government actions, or even government failures to act. Wholly or partly foreign-owned corporations can use investment treaties to sue their "host" governments for laws, regulations, court decisions, or other actions the governments take or do not take. Companies covered by investment treaties include the internationally dispersed corporate families of oil companies exploring for, extracting, or selling fossil fuels; pharmaceutical companies conducting research, manufacturing drugs, holding patents, and marketing or selling products; companies invested in providing water services; banks making investments and providing services; media companies; and a variety of manufacturing and services firms that have established overseas affiliates.

These international investment treaties (often referred to as "international investment agreements" or IIAs) can affect inequality in various ways. In principle, they could potentially reduce inequality. A key stated objective of the treaties is to promote cross-border investment by covered firms. Those cross-border investment activities could establish operations and inject capital into areas where they are badly needed, spurring economic growth, job creation, and wage increases. To the extent that these treaties catalyze cross-border investment activity, increasing the pay of low-income workers or increasing the tax revenue that can be used to redistribute wealth, they could help combat intranational inequality.

Additionally, IIAs could combat intranational inequality due to a common rule shared by most of those 3,000 agreements that bar governments from discriminating against foreigners. That rule could be used by foreign-owned companies to challenge the nepotism and cronyism that elites within a country use to concentrate market power and wealth within their networks (Justino and Moore 2015). IIAs, which give foreign investors and the companies they own powerful rights to enforce the treaties' rules, could be used to unlock opportunities and make market participation more equal.

But IIAs also exacerbate intranational disparities between haves and have-nots in legal, political, and economic terms. Other chapters in this book have examined how the investment-liberalization rules in IIAs can lead to inequality. IIAs can increase intranational inequality in social, economic, legal, and political terms in other ways as well. In this chapter, we focus on two of them: the potential for IIAs to increase inequality by (i) providing unequal procedural rights for protection of wholly or partially foreign-owned firms, giving them greater power than other stakeholders both with respect to relations with the host state government and with disputes with other private parties; and (ii) providing foreign firms with greater substantive standards of protection that strengthen the legal force of their economic rights and "expectations," which may have a negative impact on competing rights and interests held by others. This chapter provides a sketch of each of these two channels, with particular reference to circumstances in the United States.

BRIEF OVERVIEW OF IIAS: FEATURES AND RATIONALE

The substantive protections promised to covered companies in IIAs are broadly consistent across the more than 3,000 treaties that have been negotiated. The agreements typically include these obligations:

1. Prohibit host states from discriminating against partially or wholly foreign-owned companies (which we refer to simply as multinational enterprises or MNEs).
2. Require host states to provide "fair and equitable" treatment to MNEs.
3. Require governments to pay prompt, adequate, and effective compensation for MNEs or MNEs' assets that states expropriate.
4. Prevent host states from restricting the ability of MNEs to transfer capital in and out of the country.

IIAs also give MNEs powerful rights to sue their host states for alleged violations of treaty obligations and to seek compensation for the breach. MNEs are able to pursue these claims through arbitration before a panel of three private, party-appointed arbitrators. This method of dispute settlement, typically referred to as "investor-state dispute settlement" (ISDS), is a defining feature of the international investment-protection framework discussed in this chapter, and it strengthens the force of investment-protection treaties' substantive legal provisions.[1]

One key justification for IIAs is that they are needed to protect MNEs from disadvantages suffered in host countries due to the MNEs' foreignness. MNEs doing business abroad lack voting power in those jurisdictions, and foreign-owned businesses may be discriminated against in favor of locally owned firms. IIAs, it is argued, compensate for those vulnerabilities by giving MNEs special protections, which in turn may make MNEs more willing to invest their capital abroad. In this sense, IIAs can be seen as instruments that level the otherwise unequal playing field between foreign and domestic economic actors within a given country, minimizing MNEs' concerns about discrimination and political risk, and facilitating the cross-border capital flows and technology transfers that can be crucial for advancing broad-based sustainable development.

We challenge the depiction of IIAs as equalizers. As an initial matter, as arbitral tribunals have interpreted IIAs, actual "foreignness" is not a prerequisite to protection. Tribunals have extended IIA protections to firms in the host state that are beneficially owned by individuals or enterprises of that host state. In other words, tribunals have permitted individuals and firms from Country A to route their investments through holdings overseas in Country B and then send them back into Country A as "foreign"-owned firms. Country A's individuals and enterprises with the means and knowledge to do so can adopt this "round-tripping" strategy to benefit from protections offered under IIAs that are more favorable than protections otherwise offered to citizens and firms under Country A's domestic laws.[2] Indeed, the "approach to corporate nationality illustrated by [some ISDS decisions] encourages the use of round-tripping structures in developing and emerging markets." This is "at cross purposes with global initiatives in favor of transparency and against corruption, money laundering and tax avoidance" (Nougayrède 2015, 340). Those initiatives, which can help combat intranational inequality, may therefore be undermined by IIA rules that provide special treatment for investments made through round-tripping.

Even when an MNE is truly foreign owned, there are a number of reasons to question the premise that these companies are disadvantaged in the host country and need special protections. First, an MNE may have the same power to influence policy making as does a domestically owned company, if not more. Although neither entity could cast a vote in elections, both have equal indirect influence on policy issues that affect them through, for example, their own lobbying efforts and the positions taken and votes exercised by employees, consumers, suppliers, neighbors, and others with a stake in the firm's operations and how those operations are governed (Henisz 2016; Freeman et al. 2010).

Second, foreign-owned MNEs are more likely than domestic firms to move their operations out of the country, so they can use their relative mobility to gain bargaining power over their host governments (Aisbett and Poulsen 2016). Third, foreign-owned MNEs may be able to leverage their home governments or international financial institutions to encourage or pressure host countries to provide favorable treatment. Fourth, foreign-owned MNEs may be even more closely connected to the political elite in the host country than are domestic firms. And fifth, foreign-owned MNEs may be more experienced than domestic firms in using "highly skilled negotiators and lobbyists to ensure favorable government treatment in host states" (Aisbett and Poulsen 2016, 5).

Even if discrimination against foreign MNEs was common when the "global economy could much more easily be divided along national lines" and the nationality of different companies was clear, the modern era of globalization and liberalized capital flows has changed that picture (Lester 2015, 214; UN Conference on Trade and Development [UNCTAD] 2016, 182). Domestic companies traditionally considered as "national champions" linked closely with domestic identity and prosperity are now often wholly or partially foreign-owned. Moreover, a firm that is popularly considered to be of or tied to its "home" country may conduct major segments of its activities and book large parts of its profits overseas. These new patterns have highlighted questions about the need and basis for distinguishing between foreign and domestic firms (UNCTAD 2016).

To the extent that governments are drawing distinctions between domestic and foreign firms, the trend among governments is to compete for foreign capital, not to discriminate against it. Governments, for example, often offer incentives and establish investment-promotion agencies to attract foreign-owned companies, and they provide those firms with dedicated "after-care" services designed to help keep them in the country. Indeed, some studies have shown that governments treat foreign-owned firms better than they treat domestically owned companies (Aisbett and Poulsen 2016; Huang 2003). Others have found that governments treat multinational corporations—whether domestic- or foreign-owned—better than domestic firms with no international affiliates (Aisbett 2010). Discrimination against foreign-owned firms today, therefore, may be more myth than reality.

Furthermore, with the ability to structure firms across national lines and to access specialist advice from lawyers and consultants, MNEs (which may include those domestic firms involved in round-tripping) can identify and take advantage of benefits that domestic firms cannot. These include benefits derived from using corporate affiliates to book profits in low-tax jurisdictions, engage in trade mispricing and regulatory arbitrage, and take advantage of international tax treaties (Nougayrède 2015). Based on these practices, MNEs may pay less in taxes than their domestic counterparts. MNEs are also able to strategically locate assets outside a host state's borders in an effort to shield those assets from creditors seeking to secure payment for tax, environmental, or other liabilities. Given these modern realities and benefits enjoyed by MNEs, the case for extra special treatment is far from self-evident.

Even if there were discrimination against MNEs, justifying enhanced supranational protection, the solution could be much more limited than that currently provided for in IIAs. For foreign-owned MNEs to have equal protection under the law and before courts would simply require domestic and international rules preventing discriminatory treatment.[3]

But IIAs typically do much more than merely require host states to grant MNEs the same rights and access to judicial remedies available to domestic individuals and enterprises. IIAs require host states to provide MNEs certain standards of treatment that are often more favorable than treatment to which domestic individuals and entities are entitled, and it is this differential treatment that can undermine intranational equality. The next section looks at how IIAs provide uniquely powerful *procedural* rights for MNEs as compared to (a) other private individuals and entities under international law, (b) governments under domestic law, and (c) other private individuals and entities under domestic law. We also highlight how IIAs provide privileged substantive property rights and economic power to MNEs relative to those of other private stakeholders, creating and exacerbating inequality.

IIAS AND UNEQUAL PROCEDURAL RIGHTS FOR MNES

In their IIAs, host states give MNEs the extraordinary power to bring ISDS claims against them in order to challenge, and seek compensation for, government conduct that breaches the IIA provisions. This power to challenge government conduct through ISDS is uniquely strong compared to the powers of other private actors under both international law and domestic law. These asymmetries in power to initiate legal action and claim relief, standing alone, are examples of inequality before the law. And, even more important, ISDS tribunals can then shape the substantive contours of the law in a way that generates increased inequality.

EXTRAORDINARY POWER UNDER INTERNATIONAL LAW

ISDS is a fundamental departure from traditional practice under international law. Traditionally, only states have had the power to enforce other states' international law obligations. Only member states of the World Trade Organization (WTO), for example, are entitled to use the WTO's dispute-resolution system to allege other WTO treaty parties have violated their commitments and to seek remedies for breach of WTO law. Most other treaties follow this model. The terms of the treaties might benefit private individuals and corporations, but they do not provide those actors with direct rights of actions to enforce the treaties' provisions.

Some international human rights treaties adopt a different approach. Under these human rights instruments, individuals and, in some cases, corporations[4] are able to initiate claims against governments for violating their human rights. Nevertheless, there are limits on the abilities of those private actors to challenge government conduct. One key limit is the requirement that those seeking to challenge government conduct first exhaustively pursue relief through the domestic legal system. Accordingly, allegedly wrongful legislation, administrative actions, or judicial decisions of lower courts would typically need to be challenged through the judicial system before those measures or decisions could be challenged at the international level as violations of international law. Only once domestic remedies are exhausted can private actors ask international human rights tribunals to adjudicate their claims and provide relief. This exhaustion requirement provides opportunities for governments to correct wrongs and narrows the scope of measures that may give rise to international claims.

IIAs' provisions on ISDS depart from both of those approaches and give MNEs extraordinary privileges under international law. In contrast to the general norm in international law that only states may enforce other states' treaty obligations, MNEs are able to initiate ISDS proceedings to challenge a host state's breach of IIA standards. This, in turn, creates hundreds of thousands of potential claimants with the power to police compliance and seek remedies.[5] Moreover, unlike under international human rights law, arbitral tribunals have relatively consistently ruled that MNEs bringing ISDS claims are not required to first exhaust their domestic remedies. This means that MNEs are able to challenge a broad set of administrative, judicial, and legislative measures before international arbitral tribunals. If they prevail in their claims, MNEs are also able to use other treaties for the enforcement of international arbitral awards to ensure governments comply with the decisions issued against them.[6] Thus, in international law, MNEs are uniquely positioned to be able to sue governments in supranational forums for the governments' breach of their treaty commitments and to enforce decisions issued in their favor.

Substantive protections given to MNEs are therefore more easily enforceable than other rights and interests, including human rights, that are protected under international law. One potential consequence of that disparity in enforcement regimes is that it will prompt governments to devote more resources to ensuring compliance with obligations regarding treatment of MNEs than to ensuring compliance with obligations owed under human rights or other treaty instruments. Moreover, if there are tensions or arguable conflicts between observance of different treaty obligations (such as conflicts between protection of human rights and adherence to MNE protection standards), host states may favor adherence to the MNE protection obligations on the basis that breach of those obligations would be more likely to trigger litigation and financial liability.

Thus the exceptional nature of ISDS threatens to result in disproportionate host government attention being paid to the rights and interests of MNEs when compared to the rights and interests of other stakeholders under international law.

EXTRAORDINARY POWER TO CHALLENGE GOVERNMENT ACTION

The ability of MNEs to initiate ISDS proceedings is similarly exceptional when compared to the ability of private individuals and entities to challenge government conduct under many domestic legal systems. Domestic jurisdictions typically employ various doctrines that both permit and restrict government exposure to litigation and liability for different types of conduct. Comprehensive immunity of governments to lawsuits is critiqued on the ground that it prevents accountability and facilitates—and even encourages—negligent or knowingly wrongful conduct. When a government erects a legal framework enabling it to act with impunity, people are right to be concerned. But this is not to say that any person or entity aggrieved by any type of government conduct should have a right to challenge that conduct and to seek compensation or other relief as a remedy. Broadly allowing individuals and entities to contest any government action or omission that has a negative impact on their rights or interests, or the rights or interests of others, could unduly tie the hands of governments seeking to adopt and enforce important measures taken in the public interest. Ultimately, excessive exposure to claims and liability could grind governments to a halt.

Decisions on whether and in what circumstances (i) to impose liability on governments and (ii) to compensate individuals or entities for harm can have important behavioral impacts, incentivizing certain types of conduct and discouraging others. When shaping liability and compensation regimes, it is crucial to assess and understand those effects and ensure that claims and remedies are designed to send the right signals and to advance desired outcomes. It is also important to assess how the availability of claims or remedies (or absence thereof) may be unequal in design or effect. Erecting systems that in law or in practice grant certain actors heightened powers to challenge governments can chill important regulatory policy or grant remedies for harms that only injure those actors' interests but protect important public interests.

Based on these and other factors, domestic jurisdictions often have myriad rules on claims against the government. These rules relate to policy questions such as which entity of government is best suited to make the appropriate determination of whether conduct is or is not lawful or appropriate. For example, should courts, administrative officials with technical expertise, legislators, or executive officials make the ultimate decision on wrongfulness? Should courts or administrative tribunals be able to revisit other government entities' decisions and, if so, through which procedures? What impact will allowing claims or allowing certain types of remedies have on future government performance and for redress to victims? Who can bring claims: those who have been directly harmed, or anyone with an interest in the outcome of an issue? What types of harms should be actionable through a legal challenge: economic losses, losses to property, infringements of personal liberties, or government abdication of duties? And what types of remedies should be available: monetary compensation, punitive damages, or changes in the relevant law or policy?

All domestic individuals and firms are bound by the rules of the domestic jurisdiction. Firms covered by IIAs, however, can either bring their claims to domestic forums subject to these rules or bypass the domestic judicial system and go directly to the ISDS system, in which domestic procedural restrictions do not apply. Under some IIAs, MNEs can pursue relief through domestic channels *and* ISDS simultaneously.[7]

The ability to sidestep domestic restraints on litigation gives MNEs greater power than non-MNEs to challenge government action and inaction. Even before an ISDS claim is filed or a decision reached, the mere fact that MNEs alone have recourse to ISDS may cause the government to devote greater attention and accord greater deference to the preferences and interests of MNEs. This heightened attention may be to the detriment of competing preferences and interests (Van Harten and Scott 2017).

If, for instance, a government decision to issue a permit would be opposed by environmentalists, and a decision to deny the permit would be opposed by an MNE, the agency responsible for deciding which option to pursue may be influenced by knowledge that the environmentalists could not mount a lawsuit challenging the government's decision but that the MNE could sue the government for vast sums through ISDS. Similarly, when administrative and judicial enforcement of consumer-protection laws are opposed by industry but supported by consumer advocates, governments may be influenced by the fact that the decision to prosecute a violator could trigger an ISDS claim by the firm but that a decision to let the violation go unpunished could not be challenged by the citizens the law was designed to protect. An ISDS suit by an MNE may, therefore, have a negative impact on the rights and interests of the MNE's competitors, consumers, employees, and creditors. More diffuse interests, such as those who benefit from or ideologically support the environmental, labor, tax, antitrust, or other government policy, may also affected by an MNE's use of ISDS to challenge relevant government conduct.

As one commentator has explained when discussing the ability of different stakeholders to sue administrative bodies and challenge regulations, the type of inequality in procedural powers that is inherent in ISDS has

> fundamental and insidious impacts on the law-generating process as well. Government agencies do not want to spend time and resources defending regulations in court. If one side of the regulatory equation generally has standing to sue, and the other side does not, agencies are likely to favor the side that can sue them in their rulemaking decisions to avoid the expenditure of resources necessary to defend regulations in court, the negative publicity, and disappointment inherent in having regulations struck down. (Coplan 2009, 408)

Giving MNEs such broad and privileged access to "judicial" review through ISDS is especially problematic in an era in which political legislative and executive branches of government are already disproportionately attentive to (or captured by) wealthy individuals and corporate interests (Andrias 2015; Drutman 2015, 71; Gilens and Page 2014; Stiglitz 2012). Gilens's (2012) analysis of federal legislative activity in the United States found that the "political system is tilted very strongly in favor of those at the top of the income distribution" (70) and that legislative responsiveness to the policy preferences of the middle class and poor in the United States is "virtually nonexistent," except when those preferences happen to align with the preferences of the top 10 percent in terms of income (83). Political scientists have highlighted how political decisions are creating and entrenching economic inequality through the issues they prioritize, and those they do not (Hacker and Pierson 2010; Andrias 2015). To combat the trends of wealth influencing politics and politics further generating wealth inequality, judicial review of government action can play a key role.

Indeed, the judicial branch of government has come to be seen as the branch most insulated from the influence of powerful, wealthy stakeholders (Schlozman and Tierney 1986). It is therefore best-placed to address and remedy the weighty influence wealthy individuals and firms can have over legislative, executive, and administrative decisions (Andrias 2015; Schiller 2000; Peterson 2014). Because MNEs (and their investors) are able to challenge government conduct outside of domestic courts using the ISDS process, they are able to avoid the checks on undue power that courts can provide. Consequently, the influence of wealthy individuals and industry over government decision making is strengthened, exacerbating domestic inequality.

Several additional characteristics of IIAs and ISDS make MNEs' unique access to arbitral tribunals extraordinarily powerful and intensify concerns that ISDS will worsen, not ameliorate, wealth's influence over lawmaking. In contrast to most advanced systems of corporate law, IIAs have been interpreted to allow direct shareholders—including even minority, noncontrolling shareholders—to bring ISDS claims seeking compensation for harms to the company in which they hold shares (Gaukrodger 2014). In addition, many IIAs have been interpreted to permit claims by MNE shareholders up the ownership chain, such as claims by intermediate holding companies and ultimate beneficial owners. Thus, when a measure affects a single MNE within its borders, a government may face a number of ISDS claims from that firm's various direct and indirect shareholders.[8]

When a government measure affects a whole industry, the number of potential claims and claimants multiplies. Each separate claim will likely require the state to incur additional defense and arbitration costs,[9] estimated at US$ 5 million per case per side, which are significant (Hodgson 2014).[10] MNEs who lose their ISDS claims are only infrequently (38 percent of the time) ordered to compensate states for their legal expenses, whereas losing states are required to compensate successful MNEs for their legal expenses in 53 percent of cases (Hodgson 2014, 756).

As well as increasing states' defense costs, multiple claims give MNEs multiple chances to win their claims. MNEs can advance different arguments or appoint different arbitrators with the hope that their arguments will prevail in at least one of the cases. There is no system of precedent in ISDS arbitration that binds one tribunal to decisions previously issued by another, so losing before one arbitral tribunal does not prevent other shareholders from bringing a case against the same government challenging the same measure and subsequently prevailing.[11] When a government seeks to shift policies in an industry in which multiple firms have at least some foreign shareholders, that government may face a veritable barrage of ISDS litigation and potential liability, a risk that further increases the leverage of

MNEs in their negotiations and disputes with host governments. Given these issues, it is foreseeable, if not expected, that firms will increasingly organize themselves, and shareholders will increasingly structure their holdings, to ensure that when governments act or fail to act in their interests firms can mount ISDS claims to contest or secure damages for that conduct.

EXTRAORDINARY POWER TO CHALLENGE THE RIGHTS
AND INTERESTS OF NON-MNES

ISDS also gives MNEs greater power than non-MNEs in legal disputes directly between those two groups. For example, if a domestic citizen successfully sues an MNE in the courts of the host country for harms caused by the MNE and is awarded monetary compensation for injuries suffered, the MNE may then be able to turn to ISDS to undo or otherwise eliminate the effects of its court loss. If the reverse were true and the MNE prevailed in domestic court proceedings, the domestic citizen would not be able to seek a different outcome through ISDS. With access to ISDS, MNEs thus have greater opportunities to get their desired results than their non-MNE opponents do.

One case that followed this pattern is *Chevron v. Ecuador*.[12] Ecuadorian citizens sued Chevron for pollution caused by oil operations in the Ecuadorian Amazon. An Ecuadorian court sided with the Ecuadorian plaintiffs, commonly referred to as the "Lago Agrio Plaintiffs" due to the location of the oil operations, and ordered Chevron to pay them roughly $18 billion in damages (which was reduced by an Ecuadorian appellate court decision to $9 billion). To avoid paying the Lago Agrio Plaintiffs that compensation, Chevron initiated an ISDS case against Ecuador.

In the ISDS proceedings, Chevron argued that the Ecuadorian legal processes that produced the award were marred by government corruption and collusion between the Lago Agrio Plaintiffs and judicial officials. Even if there were no fraud or corruption, Chevron also argued that "the Lago Agrio Judgment's factual findings, legal holdings, and assessment of damages are so unjust" that they constitute a denial of justice in breach of the IIA.[13] As part of that position, Chevron disputed a number of findings made by the Ecuadorian courts on issues such as the extent of environmental damage in the Amazonian region, the cause of contamination, and the crucial question of who is legally responsible to pay for harms done.

Through its ISDS case, Chevron asked for a number of remedies that would directly impact the Lago Agrio Plaintiffs and their ability to obtain compensation for environmental harms. Chevron, for example, asked the arbitral tribunal to declare that "Chevron is not liable for any judgment rendered in the Lago Agrio Litigation,"[14] and that the Lago Agrio judgment itself is a "nullity as a matter of international law," is "unlawful and consequently devoid of any legal effect,"[15] and is "not final, conclusive or enforceable." Chevron also requested that the tribunal "order Ecuador to use all measures necessary" to prevent the Lago Agrio Plaintiffs from collecting their award of compensation.[16]

In response, the tribunal ordered Ecuador to take immediate steps to render the Lago Plaintiffs' award undenforceable and to preclude the plaintiffs from recovering any of the sums awarded in their favor.[17]

Although Chevron's case was principally against Ecuador, it also sought to and succeeded in affecting the outcome of the underlying Ecuadorian court litigation between Chevron and the Lago Agrio Plaintiffs. The case is relevant for the important question of who pays for environmental harms caused by oil operations: those affected by the pollution, taxpayers, or oil companies? Under the tribunal's order, the costs of those harms will continue to be borne by affected individuals and communities, not by Chevron nor by the government of Ecuador.

Although affected by the tribunal's award, the Lago Agrio Plaintiffs have had no right or ability to participate in the ISDS proceedings nor to dispute Chevron's claims and protect the judgment they had fought for years to secure. ISDS is limited to claims by MNEs (or their investors) against their host states; treaties concluded to date do not permit third parties to intervene and join these arbitrations even if the subject of the arbitration or the arbitration itself, as in the *Chevron v. Ecuador* dispute, affects those third-parties' rights or interests. By allowing investors to access ISDS and excluding full participation by affected third parties, IIAs give rise to inequalities in procedural rights. These procedural inequalities can exacerbate substantive inequalities such as who suffers from, who benefits from, and who pays for environmental damage.

Another dispute in which the loser in domestic court proceedings turned to ISDS for relief is *Eli Lilly v. Canada*.[18] That case arose out of litigation between a generic drug company and Eli Lilly regarding the validity of two pharmaceutical patents held by Eli Lilly. When the generics company sought to manufacture and sell generic versions of Eli Lilly's patented drugs, Eli Lilly sued it for patent infringement. The generics company prevailed in court, permitting it and other generic drug manu-facturers to sell their versions of the drugs in Canada.

Having lost in Canada, Eli Lilly turned to ISDS under the North American Free Trade Agreement (NAFTA) and alleged that Canada's courts had developed new patent law doctrines that improperly imposed new, heightened, and arbitrary requirements for patentability on firms, and that the change in requirements—and the requirements themselves—violated NAFTA. According to Eli Lilly, the decisions by Canadian courts invalidating Eli Lilly's patents entitled Eli Lilly to at least CAD$ 500 million as compensation for what it claims was a wrongful interfer-ence with its intellectual property rights.

As in *Chevron v. Ecuador*, Eli Lilly attempted to use ISDS to secure an outcome different from the private litigation in the host country. It asked the arbitral tribunal to declare that the substantive contours of Canadian patent law violated NAFTA. Similar to the Ecuadorian case, the generic drug company in the underlying Canadian litigation could not be party to the ISDS arbitration despite the fact that the case centered on the validity of the decisions on Canadian patent law that the generics firm had successfully fought for and secured.

Eli Lilly further illustrates how ISDS can provide one party in domes-tic litigation with extra procedural avenues to prevail over its opponent. Although Eli Lilly did not directly ask the arbitral tribunal to undo or prevent enforcement of the Canadian court judgments, the relief Eli Lilly sought—an order requiring Canada to compensate Eli Lilly for loss of its monopoly rights and other companies' use of "its" patents—could have made it cost-prohibitive for Canada to uphold those court decisions.

Ultimately, Eli Lilly lost its NAFTA case. The tribunal decided that Eli Lilly had failed to prove that the shift in Canada's intellectual property laws was sufficiently dramatic or arbitrary to violate NAFTA. Nevertheless, the arbitrators declared that it was entirely proper for ISDS tribunals to reevaluate the outcomes of domestic court cases between pri-vate litigants even in the absence of any denial of justice or evidence of corruption in those proceedings.

Cases like *Eli Lilly* have weighty public policy implications regarding incentives for and the abilities of individuals and firms to innovate, the extent of openness and competition in a given market, and the pricing of medicines and other products. Strong patent protections, such as those sought by drug developers, convey monopolistic power on patent holders, which can influence the relative strength and success of other firms who develop or manufacture products (for example, favoring innovative drug companies holding patents over generics firms seeking to produce the patented technologies). Disproportionately strong patent protections also exacerbate inequality among individuals in terms of their ability to access health care and other goods and services derived from patented innovations (Liu 2014; Chang 2012). Consequently, by giving MNEs disproportionate powers to argue for and protect monopoly rights, ISDS may reshape the substantive contours of the law in a manner that generates more inequality among both producers and consumers.

Chevron and *Eli Lilly* underscore how ISDS grants MNEs a formidable and privileged procedural mechanism, and how investors' use of that procedural mechanism to get one more "bite at the apple" may create or exacerbate substantive inequalities between, on one hand, MNEs and their shareholders and, on the other hand, all other stakeholders. Other ISDS cases illustrate the breadth of the problem. Investors have used ISDS to contest decisions regarding the relative rights of creditors and debtors in bankruptcy proceedings,[19] contests over land ownership,[20] citizen suits challenging permitting decisions for extractive industry operations,[21] and other unfavorable litigation proceedings and outcomes between the MNEs and other private individuals and entities before domestic courts.

Treaties could be drafted to preclude investors from using ISDS to alter the effect of domestic litigation with other private parties. They could, for example, contain language stating that a case must be dismissed if individuals and entities whose interests would be affected by the ISDS proceedings are not able to join them. Treaties could also contain language giving those whose interests may be affected by the proceedings the right to join the arbitration as full parties. However, this would potentially require them to incur the costs of investment arbitration (on average estimated to be US$5 million per party per case) and might not be feasible for all to pay (Hodgson 2014). Such provisions can be found in procedural rules of domestic courts to prevent court decisions from overriding the rights and interests of those who are not party to the case.[22]

Even absent such express language, tribunals could arguably invoke existing principles of international law to decline to hear cases or order relief that would affect the rights of nonparties. To date, however, tribunals have not been receptive to these issues or arguments. In *Chevron v. Ecuador*, for example, pursuant to principles of international law, Ecuador argued that the tribunal should not take jurisdiction over Chevron's claims or grant its requested relief because doing so would affect the rights of the Lago Agrio Plaintiffs.[23] The tribunal rejected that argument, declaring with little analysis that its hearing of the case would not affect the rights of the Lago Agrio Plaintiffs; then it issued awards preventing the Lago Agrio Plaintiffs from collecting their award of compensation.[24]

IIAS AND UNEQUAL SUBSTANTIVE PROPERTY RIGHTS

Property rights are a zero-sum game in which "protecting the resource claims of some parties requires preventing others from using those same resources" (Lawson-Remer 2012, 151), so decisions on their definition and scope are a product of a rich history and ongoing contestation (Kennedy 2011, 10). Distributions of economic, social, and political power shape property rights; and, in turn, property rights can shape those distributions of power (12).

Traditionally, international law has left domestic jurisdictions and the social forces, political processes, and legal institutions within them significant latitude to define the scope of property rights and to allocate them among members of society (Sasson 2010). To the extent that international law has been relevant to protection of property, it has largely been confined to assessing whether states have violated extant or vested property rights in breach of customary international law or treaties protecting human rights (Sasson 2010).[25] International law has generally not defined or created property rights; rather, it has limited state interference with them.

IIAs have changed that. Rather than merely protecting property rights as defined and redefined through domestic processes, IIAs—and, in particular, their "fair and equitable treatment" obligations[26]—have effectively become a tool for creating new property rights to be enjoyed only by MNEs. These IIA provisions, as interpreted, limit the ability of governments to take actions that interfere with those IIA-created rights and can diminish the property rights of other stakeholders, undermining efforts to reduce inequality.

CREATING NEW SUBSTANTIVE RIGHTS THROUGH THE FAIR AND EQUITABLE TREATMENT STANDARD

IIAs require host states to provide MNEs with "fair and equitable treatment" (FET). However, protecting MNEs' conceptions of what is fair and equitable may have unfair or inequitable impacts on others. For example, environmental laws imposing new and costly emissions standards on manufacturing plants may be viewed as unfair or inequitable from a firm's perspective unless those laws exempt existing plants that had long operated under more lax regimes and for which compliance costs would be high. Exempting older, existing facilities is unfair and inequitable from the perspective of those individuals living near the polluting plants, however, as they are left to disproportionately suffer the harms of air pollution from unregulated facilities (Gorovitz Robertson 1995). Additionally, measures that provide special exceptions or flexibilities to environmental laggards are likely unfair and inequitable from the perspective of manufacturing firms that voluntarily incurred costs to upgrade their facilities in anticipation of future regulation. Similar questions about the equities and inequities of law arise with respect to taxation, labor law and employee benefits, social services, tort law, and myriad other areas.

IIAs and ISDS expressly seek to ensure fair and equitable treatment only for MNEs and their owners, with no meaningful opportunity for those who may be unfairly or inequitably affected by MNEs or MNEs' ISDS claims to present their views to tribunals. Of course, the FET obligation could be interpreted to take into account fairness to others, but there are no guarantees arbitral tribunals will adopt such a holistic vision of fairness. Indeed, cases decided to date suggest otherwise.

In fact, tribunals have been effectively creating new property rights through their pronouncements that the FET obligation in IIAs protects the "legitimate expectations" of MNEs. Specifically, arbitral tribunals have created a legal doctrine through which certain expectations held by foreign investors regarding future government treatment are protected, and tribunals will order host states to pay compensation if actual government conduct deviates from those expectations. Arbitral tribunals thereby effectively convert mere expectations regarding treatment of foreign-owned firms into legally recognized rights enforceable against the state.

The expectations that have been effectively turned into legally enforceable property rights are extremely diverse, including the right to continue to enjoy government subsidies,[27] the right to be free from having to pay higher taxes,[28] the right to be awarded permits for activities such as developing hazardous waste sites,[29] the right to enjoy certain rates of return in public infrastructure projects,[30] and the right to have tariffs for public services (such as water or energy) determined in accordance with particular investor-approved formulas or at levels "expected" by the investors.[31] In none of these cases was the "expectation" held by the MNE clearly recognized as a "right" under the host country's domestic legal framework.

Rather, the existence and nature of those rights were contested due to questions regarding the scope of the state's power to adjust economic benefits and burdens or the effects on those holding competing interests or rights claims.

For example, in *Micula v. Romania*,[32] a dispute regarding foreign-owned firms' alleged right to receive government subsidies, Romania contended that the MNEs had no vested right to continue to receive subsidies in future years and that the government had the power to terminate those supports. Romania further argued that recognizing a right to continued receipt of subsidies would be inconsistent with applicable law and policy restricting government grants of subsidies due to concerns that such subsidies could result in welfare-reducing effects on competition, constituted a waste of government resources, and were an inappropriate transfer of wealth from taxpayers to select private interests.

The arbitral tribunal in the *Micula* case determined that it need not decide whether Romanian law had created and conferred property rights on the MNEs to continue to receive government subsidies. Nor did the tribunal engage with the concerns underlying the government's efforts to terminate subsidies deemed to be inconsistent with policy aims, or the question of whether, based on those concerns and policies, the MNEs might have expected their government benefits would end. Instead, the tribunal decided that the MNEs had "legitimate expectations" that they would be able to continue to benefit from those subsidies and that the government's decision to terminate the subsidies violated those expectations. The tribunal then ordered the government to pay the value of those future subsidies as compensation.

The arbitral tribunal effectively created and conferred on the MNEs and their investors the right to continue to receive government subsidies at the expense of other Romanian taxpayers and business competitors. The tribunal also undermined the power of Romania's legal and political institutions to determine whether MNEs had such a right to receive government subsidies and, if so, on what terms. Arbitral tribunals in ISDS proceedings have assumed the role of identifying which economic interests are recognized and protected by the law and have assigned themselves the power to erect a property rights framework that can depart from norms established in domestic legal systems through constitutions, legislation, court decisions, or other channels. By converting "legitimate expectations" of investors and MNEs regarding their economic activities to enforceable property rights, and requiring the state (taxpayers) to compensate investors for loss of those rights, tribunals have effected a transfer of wealth from the public to investors and MNEs.

According to tribunals, legitimate expectations can arise from the general legal and regulatory framework in place at the time an investor makes its investment, especially when those expectations are based on government officials' representations or assurances to investors. Those with the strongest claims to favorable legitimate expectations, therefore, are those who have had direct communications with presidents, ministers, or other high-level government representatives and have received promises or other encouragements regarding prospects for the investments and advantages offered by the host state's legal and businesses environment. These MNEs are frequently companies developing or operating major infrastructure projects for water, energy, and transportation services; firms engaged in exploration for and extraction of oil, gas, or minerals; and businesses constructing or operating major real estate or tourism projects. In short, companies that have the best claims to legitimate expectations are often firms that have benefited from a closeness with government that most individuals and entities will never enjoy. This widens the gap between the power of those with the ear of the government and those without.

ISDS decisions have held that investors' legitimate expectations based on government representations or assurances must be upheld even if those representations or assurances were nonbinding or illegal under domestic law.[33] If, for instance, a government official were to represent to a foreign-owned firm that the contract terms the MNE sought for an infrastructure project were acceptable, but a court later deemed the relevant contract invalid under the constitution or other domestic law, the firm may be able to prevail on an ISDS claim that the court decision violated its legitimate expectations of benefiting from the contract. The ISDS decision would effectively allow the government official's representation to prevail over broader domestic legal norms.

Binding the government to (or requiring compensation for) unlawful, nonbinding, and often nontransparent representations or commitments can upset the normal separation of powers by effectively giving government officials the ability to knowingly or negligently override or bypass limits set by the legislature. Moreover, enforcing such unlawful or unauthorized promises can encourage improper collusion between the project proponent and those in the government who support the proposed investment. Assume, for instance, that government officials want to give a project proponent a broad guarantee of fiscal stability to encourage the project's development. However, to preserve tax policy flexibility over time and to ensure that tax policy is set by the legislature, those officials do not have authority under domestic law to provide any commitment that fiscal policies will remain unchanged. The doctrine of legitimate expectations means that the officials could nevertheless agree to a contractual stabilization clause, knowing that the contractual promise might become too costly to break.

In some domestic legal systems, courts protect against such collusive conduct by imposing strict rules against enforcement of unauthorized or illegal promises. Affirming the U.S. rule that legal force will not be given to illegitimate representations by agency officials, the U.S. Supreme Court stated:

> If agents of the Executive were able, by their unauthorized oral or written statements to citizens, to obligate the Treasury for the payment of funds, the control over public funds that the [Constitution] reposes in Congress [governing appropriation of funds] in effect could be transferred to the Executive. If, for example, the President or Executive Branch officials were displeased with a new restriction on benefits imposed by Congress . . . and sought to evade them, agency officials could advise citizens that the restrictions were inapplicable. [A legal doctrine binding the government to the officials' advice] would give this advice the practical force of law, in violation of the Constitution.[34]

Not only does the doctrine of legitimate expectations in ISDS reject that approach, favoring protection of investors' reliance interests over protection of the rule of law in the domestic legal system, but it could result in an IIA breach if domestic courts, such as those in the United States, were to refuse to enforce illegal promises. If a domestic court ruled that the fiscal stabilization provision was invalid, the MNE could bring an ISDS suit challenging that court decision as a violation of its expectations.

Recourse to ISDS also gives rise to another opportunity for improper collusion between investors and certain government officials and provides a mechanism to disrupt the balance of government powers.

The executive branch, which has control over decisions regarding litigation and settlement of ISDS claims in many countries, could simply agree as part of a settlement to abide by an unauthorized or illegal stabilization commitment to dispose of the case and entrench its policy preferences regarding fiscal stabilization. That settlement agreement can then be enshrined as an "award" by the ISDS tribunal, making it binding on the host country even if the terms of the agreement were illegal under that country's domestic law.

Apart from intentional corrupt conduct outside normal lawmaking processes, serious questions remain regarding whether and under what circumstances negotiated settlements adequately reflect the interests of all those with a stake in the litigation. Because governments serve diverse constituents with different and potentially competing interests, it may be difficult if not impossible for the government to equally and fully represent all views when litigating and settling cases.[35] The perspectives of some constituents—particularly those who are politically weak—may not be taken into account in government positions when the government is seeking to dispose of a case.

In light of those risks and realities, some jurisdictions have developed rules and mechanisms under domestic law to ensure that government settlements represent broader public interests and are consistent with the law, and that they enable stakeholders to directly protect their interests in court. These include allowing interested individuals and entities to intervene in disputes between the government and other private parties and to challenge terms of settlement agreements; additional rules may require the judicial branch to assess whether settlement agreements are in the public interest before approving them. The ISDS process provides no mechanisms for third-party intervention or public interest oversight. Consequently, given the often "numerous complex and conflicting interests" at the local, regional, or national level that a state sued in an ISDS case may be responsible for defending, there is a real risk that the interests of the most marginalized "may become lost in the thicket of" or sacrificed in "sometimes inconsistent governmental policies."[36]

Assume the following fact pattern: an MNE seeking to develop a coastal tourism project secures a concession from national-level officials for that project and is told that the land is government-owned and not inhabited by others. Local residents, however, claim ownership of the land and argue that, under domestic law of eminent domain, the land cannot be expropriated from them and given to another private party.

The local residents file and succeed on a claim before domestic courts that the concession was in fact improperly granted, and the court orders termination of the concession. After the court award, the MNE brings an ISDS claim challenging the decision and seeking (i) an order from the tribunal mandating the government to take all steps necessary to prevent enforcement of that domestic court judgment; or (ii) an award of hundreds of millions of dollars in damages from alleged lost future profits. Indeed, there are many actual examples of tribunals similarly ordering governments to interfere in judicial proceedings or outcomes,[37] as well as ordering governments to pay hundreds of millions of dollars in future lost profits for frustrated projects.[38]

The government entity responsible for defending the case may opt to settle the case and allow the development to proceed notwithstanding the competing rights and interests of the local citizens, whether because it wants the tourism project to go ahead, does not want to risk an adverse judgment and potential liability for hundreds of millions of dollars, or does not want to face the reputational costs and potential lost future investment that an ISDS claim can bring (Alee and Peinhardt 2011). If the settlement agreement is then reflected in an arbitral award, the government could argue that its international law obligations trump domestic law decisions, and that therefore the domestic court decision is invalid or preempted, undermining the rights of the affected communities.

In summary, because the doctrine of legitimate expectations provides disproportionate protection to those with unique access to government officials and can bind governments to promises irrespective of whether those promises are authorized or legal, MNEs can distort the law in their favor without having to secure the support necessary for legislative or constitutional change.

USING LEGITIMATE EXPECTATIONS TO PROTECT THE STATUS QUO

Protecting the legitimate expectations of MNEs is particularly favored by existing asset holders and powerful interests because they can be compensated for changes to the status quo. The general rule adopted by tribunals is that the doctrine of legitimate expectations protects expectations held at the time the investment is made, including that the legal framework governing or affecting an MNE will not change over time (or will not change much)[39] through court decisions, administrative actions, shifts in policies or practices, changes in legislation, or other means of legal evolution.

If subsequent government conduct exceeds the MNE's legitimate expectations, granting more favorable treatment than the MNE had anticipated at the time of the investment, the MNE keeps those gains; but if the government frustrates the investor's expectations, the government may be ordered to compensate firms for any difference between their hoped-for and actual economic position.

One likely effect over time is that the legal and policy framework will become increasingly favorable to MNEs. Because IIAs typically only permit investors to initiate claims against states (neither states nor other individuals or entities may initiate IIA claims against MNEs), the outcomes of ISDS decisions will only ever be (i) to *uphold* the property rights framework that existed under the host state's domestic law, or (ii) to *expand* the property rights protections enjoyed by covered investors under that law. ISDS proceedings never narrow the property rights enjoyed by MNEs under host state law. Thus, beyond the specific effects protection of legitimate expectations has in a particular case, the structure of the ISDS system will inevitably lead to a general expansion of the legal protections for MNEs' economic interests and corresponding expansion of state (taxpayer) liability for conduct interfering with those interests.

Protecting the status quo against change can also entrench or increase inequality among firms by safeguarding the power of market incumbents when compared to new players. If, for example, a government decides to remove or decrease subsidies given to existing businesses (such as coal-fired power plants), or to increase subsidies given to potential new competitors (such as generators of renewable energy), that may trigger an ISDS claim for breach of the FET obligation by the incumbents. Similarly, if the government passes new environmental or other obligations that would impose new costs on firms, it may agree to exempt incumbents from having to comply to avoid triggering an ISDS dispute, thereby favoring incumbents relative to newcomers.

In addition to disadvantaging those competitors without access to ISDS, the ability of MNEs to entrench favorable aspects of the status quo harms other interests that would benefit from adjustments to law and policy. As one scholar studying the powerful impact of money in slowing U.S. lawmaking has concluded, "wealth interests affect inaction disproportionately and benefit from it uniquely" (Andrias 2015, 425–26). Indeed, FET provisions are not the only forces working against change. Scholars studying legal trends have found a general status quo bias limiting legal reform in democratic states (Gilens and Page 2014, 74; Hacker,

Pierson, and Thelen 2015, 183), and political scientists have identified the phenomenon of drift through which vested, nonmajoritarian interests can work behind the scenes to prevent voters and other public interests from updating the legal framework to take into account changing circumstances (Hacker et al. 2015, 184). Thus, inequality-entrenching policy stagnation appears to be a reality even in the absence of IIAs and ISDS; but IIAs and ISDS provide new and powerful channels for counteracting legal and policy adjustments.

Notably, MNEs have relied on FET protections to prevent legal systems from evolving to combat three of the most inequality-inducing effects that can arise from property rights systems: negative externalities, abusive practices of monopoly rights holders, and undue appropriation of gains. The first, negative externalities, result from property rights holders seeking to maximize gains from their uses of property by pushing costs onto others (Merrill 2012). A typical example is a company that generates harmful pollutants when producing a product for sale and is able to dispose of those pollutants in the air, water, or on land owned by the general public, who will then suffer the harms and bear the costs of such pollution. The second negative effect occurs when the holder of a monopoly right is allowed to extract onerous payments from those seeking to use or benefit from that right. For example, a pharmaceutical company holding a patent over a life-saving drug for which there are no substitutes can therefore charge sick patients an exorbitant price. Another example is when a company has a monopoly over the right to distribute and sell water and can set high prices for that essential resource without fear of losing consumers to competitors. A third negative consequence that systems of property rights protections can produce is a direct increase in inequality that can arise when systems allow the rights holder to appropriate all of the gains in value attributable to the right it holds (Merrill 2012). This aspect of property rights systems, through which "property beget[s] more property" can be positive in that it can "create an incentive for the owner to work hard to make the resource" it holds "productive and valuable" (Merrill 2012, 2093). Yet allowing property rights holders to uniquely capture all of the gains from the property they hold can also lead to growing inequality. As Merrill has described:

> Not all gains in the value of resources are attributable to the skill and industry of the owner. Some will be due to rising market demand for resources generally; others will be due to sheer luck. . . . The portion that

can be attributed to luck or general conditions of scarcity represents a
kind of built-in multiplier, whereby those that have property get more
property without regard to their individual effort or desert. (2093)

Problematically, government efforts to address each of these negative,
inequality-exacerbating effects of property rights systems have been successfully challenged under IIAs. Investors have used ISDS to secure compensation for environmental laws and decisions that seek to minimize or
avoid environmental externalities;[40] regulate tariffs, tackle anticompetitive
pricing in provision of public services[41], and limit intellectual property
rights; and assess "windfall profits taxes" seeking to capture a greater share
of gains derived from the rising price of natural resources (that is, gains
not derived from the investor's increased efficiency or skill).[42] These types
of decisions focus on MNEs' expectations and do not take into account
the broader implications that such protections have for inequality.

Some scholars have argued that property law can increase equity and
inclusiveness if the notion of what is protected "property" is expanded
and a greater set of interests are folded within the definition of "property"
rights (Super 2013). Although that may be possible, the FET standard
(coupled with the ISDS system) is a particularly noninclusive approach,
permitting only MNEs and their shareholders to expand and enforce their
property rights (Van Harten and Malysheuski 2016). Compounding the
problem, IIAs correspondingly reduce the power of those excluded from
or marginalized by status quo systems of property rights protections to
improve their situation by "destabilizing" existing norms (Rosser 2015,
465; Peñalver and Katyal 2010, 1). When changing property rights systems
would require government action that interferes with MNEs' expectations,
governments may lack the will and resources to risk IIA-based retribution.

CONCLUDING REMARKS

IIAs provide MNEs with privileged access to procedural remedies and
strong substantive protections that favor MNEs' property rights and
expectations, creating and exacerbating inequality among a diverse
group of other stakeholders. Furthermore, they allow MNEs to entrench
the status quo, favoring incumbents and MNEs' interests more generally. More analysis could usefully demonstrate how these two particular channels operate in theory and practice. To what extent do claims or
threats of claims result in governments devoting their time, resources,

and policies to the interests and needs of MNEs within their borders? To what extent do MNEs engage in round-tripping to exploit these procedural and substantive benefits? To what extent do MNEs use the extra legal route provided by ISDS to insulate themselves from the effects of generally applicable domestic law; to prevent, stall, or reshape redistributive policies; or to modify outcomes in litigation between domestic parties? A number of known ISDS cases illustrate each of these practices and effects, but the extent of the trends has not been well-researched, in part because of the confidentiality of MNE-government interactions and in part because of the challenge of isolating government motivations.

Additional research investigating other channels through which IIAs might affect intranational (and international) inequality include research on the amount, destination, distribution, and effects of monetary compensation awarded under the treaties;[43] the impact of IIA rules limiting use of performance requirements or subsidies aimed at developing economic opportunities for socioeconomically disadvantaged individuals or communities; the ways in which IIA policies are developed at the domestic level and the influence such policy input has on policy outputs and impacts; and the effects of IIA rules requiring that host governments accept and respond to MNE input on proposed or actual laws and regulations. Finally, further research could explore whether and how IIAs could be enlisted as a tool to combat intranational inequality. As the system of international economic governance is expanding, and as intranational inequality is increasing, it is crucial to understand the links between the two phenomena and how the law can be used to advance rather than undermine equality.

NOTES

1. Under the traditional ISDS mechanism, modeled on international commercial arbitration, arbitrators are appointed by the parties and paid by one or both of the disputing parties. This leads, inter alia, to concerns that the arbitrators will be loyal to those who appoint them as opposed to being neutral decision makers; it also leads to concerns that the arbitrators have a personal interest in seeing a high number of cases as this will generate business income for them. Exacerbating these concerns is the fact that arbitrators typically operate free from the rules on independence and impartiality that typically govern judicial officials. The European Commission has recently been pushing for arbitration by a more permanent tribunal that would address some of the concerns raised by party-appointed and party-paid arbitrators, but that would still provide investors with a private right of action to sue host states to enforce treaty violations.(Coleman et al. 2017).

2. See, for example, *Tokios Tokelés v. Ukraine*, International Centre for Settlement of Investment Disputes (ICSID) Case No. ARB/02/18, Decision on Jurisdiction (April 29, 2004); but see also the Dissenting Opinion of Chairman Prosper Weil, April 29, 2004.

3. There may be certain valid grounds for distinguishing between firms based on ownership. A number of countries have special rules and restrictions on foreign ownership for national security reasons. The presence of those rules, however, does not necessarily imply an absence of rights or remedies for improper discrimination. When, for example, U.S. President Barack Obama ordered a U.S. firm owned by Chinese nationals to sell certain assets in the United States following an evaluation of the firm's investment by the Committee on Foreign Investment in the United States (CFIUS), U.S. courts were open to the firm to challenge the CFIUS process and the president's decision. The Appeals Court for the District of Columbia declared that the process and resulting decision were unconstitutional violations of the Chinese-owned company's due process rights. *Ralls Corp. v. Committee on Foreign Investment in the United States, et al.*, No. 1:12-cv-01513 (D.C. Ct. App. July 15, 2014).

4. Legal entities such as corporations are recognized as having rights under the European Convention on Human Rights. Other international human rights bodies, such as the Inter-American Court of Human Rights and the African Court on Human and People's Rights, however, only permit claims by natural persons.

5. These claimants are the hundreds of thousands firms that have been established around the world, and even the various shareholders in those firms (UNCTAD 2016; Gaukrodger 2014).

6. These treaties are the 1958 Convention on the Recognition and Enforcement of Foreign Arbitral Awards and the 1965 Convention on the Settlement of Investment Disputes between States and Nationals of other States.

7. To the extent that foreign or domestic stakeholders dislike these rules limiting litigation in a given legal system, those stakeholders can, in at least some systems, seek to change them through legislative, administrative, or judicial action. See the discussion on the *Ralls* case in note 3.

8. Some treaties attempt to address these issues by requiring consolidation of certain claims or by allowing only controlling shareholders to bring claims seeking relief for harms to the company, but those treaties are few in number and do not offer complete solutions to the problems they seek to address.

9. States may be able to consolidate claims brought by different investors, which can minimize defense costs. Nevertheless, even if the effort to consolidate is successful, that effort itself will likely result in additional arbitration-related expenses.

10. Hodgson found the defense costs for respondent states to average USD 4.5 million, plus the state's portion of the tribunal's costs, which averaged USD 750,000.

11. For examples of cases involving the same investment and the same government conduct, but brought by different investors and coming to different conclusions, see (1) *CME v. Czech Republic*, UNCITRAL, Award, September 13, 2001, and *Lauder v. Czech Republic*, UNCITRAL, Award, September 3, 2001; also (2) *Teco v. Guatemala*, ICSID Case No. ARB/10/23, Award, December 19, 2013, and *Iberdola Energía v. Guatemala*, ICSID Case No. ARB/09/5, Award, August 17, 2012.

12. *Chevron Corp. v. Ecuador*, Permanent Court of Arbitration (PCA) Case No. 2009–23.

13. *Chevron Corp. v. Ecuador*, PCA Case No. 2009–23, Claimants' Supplemental Memorial on Track 2, para. 104 (May 9, 2014).

14. *Chevron Corp. v. Ecuador*, PCA Case No. 2009–23, Claimants' Memorial on the Merits, para. 547 (September 6, 2010).

15. *Chevron Corp. v. Ecuador*, PCA Case No. 2009–23, Claimants' Supplemental Memorial on Track 2, para. 199 (May 9, 2014).

16. *Chevron Corp. v. Ecuador*, PCA Case No. 2009–23, Claimants' Memorial on the Merits, para. 547 (September 6, 2010).

17. *Chevron Corp. v. Ecuador*, PCA Case No. 2009–23, Second Partial Award on Track II, Part X, para. 10.13 (August 30, 2018).

18. ICSID Case No. ARB/14/2.

19. See *Dan Cake v. Hungary*, ICSID Case No. ARB/12/9, Decision on Jurisdiction and Liability, August 24, 2015.

20. See *Awdi v. Romania*, ICSID Case No. ARB/10/13, Award, March 2, 2015.

21. See *Infinito Gold v. Costa Rica*, ICSID Case No. ARB/14/5, Request for Arbitration, February 6, 2014, and Petition for Amicus Curiae Status, September 15, 2014.

22. See US Federal Rules of Civil Procedure, R.19.

23. See *Chevron v. Ecuador*, Third Interim Award on Jurisdiction and Admissibility, paras. 3.83–3.85, 3.139 (February 27, 2012); *Chevron v. Ecuador*, Respondent Track 2 Counter-Memorial on Merits, paras. 516–525 (February 18, 2013).

24. *Chevron v. Ecuador*, Third Interim Award on Jurisdiction and Admissibility, paras. 4.59–4.71 (February 27, 2012); *Chevron v. Ecuador*, Second Awards on Interim Measures, para. 3 (February 16, 2012); *Chevron Corp. v. Ecuador*, PCA Case No. 2009–23, Second Partial Award on Track II, Part X, para. 10.13 (August 30, 2018).

25. But see Nigel Bankes (2010); also see Sasson (2010) discussing Anglo-Italian Conciliation Commission, *Raibl* Claim, June 19, 1964, 40 ILR 260–288 (1970).

26. Also relevant are tribunals' interpretation of the indirect expropriation standard. This paper, however, focuses on the fair and equitable treatment obligation and its role as a tool for creating new property rights.

27. *Micula v. Romania*, ICSID Case No. ARB/05/20, Award, December 11, 2013.

28. *Perenco v. Ecuador*, ICSID Case No. ARB/08/6, Decision on Remaining Issues of Jurisdiction and Liability, September 12, 2014.

29. *Tecmed v Mexico*, ICSID Case No. ARB(AF)/00/2, Award, May 29, 2003.

30. *Walter Bau v. Thailand*, UNCITRAL, Award, July 1, 2009.

31. *Teco v. Guatemala*, ICSID Case No. ARB/10/23, Award, December 19, 2013.

32. ICSID Case No. ARB/05/20, Award, December 11, 2013.

33. *Fraport AG Frankfurt Airport Services Worldwide v. Republic of the Philippines* [II], ICSID Case No. ARB/11/12, Award, December 10, 2014, paras. 482–519; *Railroad Development Corporation v. Republic of Guatemala*, ICSID Case No. ARB/07/23, Second Decision on Objections to Jurisdiction, May 18, 2010, para. 146; *Desert Line Projects LLC v. Republic of Yemen*, ICSID Case No. ARB/05/17, Award, February 6, 2008, para. 120; *Fraport AG Frankfurt Airport Services Worldwide v. Republic of the Philippines* [I], ICSID Case No. ARB/03/25, Award, August 16, 2007, para. 346 (subsequently annulled on other grounds); *MTD Equity Sdn. Bhd. v. Chile*, ICSID Case No. ARB/01/7, Award, May 25, 2004.

34. *Richmond v. Office of Personnel Management*, 496 U.S. 414, 428 (1990).

35. U.S. cases in support of this principle include *Utah Association of Counties v. Clinton*, 255 F.3d 1246, 1255 (10th Cir. 2001); *Kleissler v. United States Forest Service*, 157 F.3d 964, 973–974 (3rd Cir. Ct. App. 1998); *Am. Farm Bureau Fedn v. United States EPA*, 278 F.R.D. 98 (M.D. Pa. 2011). For a discussion of some of these issues, see Morley (2014), 637.

36. *Kleissler v. United States Forest Service*, 157 F.3d 964, 973–974 (3rd Cir. Ct. App. 1998).

37. See notes 12–17 and 23–24 discussing *Chevron v. Ecuador*.

38. See *Gold Reserve v. Venezuela*, ICSID Case No. ARB(AF)/09/1, Award, September 22, 2014.

39. See *Tecnicas Medioambientales Tecmed S.A. v. Mexico*, ICSID Case No. ARB(AF)/00/2, Award, para. 154, May 29, 2003.

40. See *Bilcon v. Canada*, PCA Case No. 2009–04, Award on Jurisdiction and Liability, March 17, 2015entre for Settlement of Investment Disputes (Inew property rights. however, focuses on the FET obligation and its role as a pro.

41. See *EDF v. Hungary*, UNCITRAL, Award, December 4, 2014; *Teco v. Guatemala*, ICSID Case No. ARB/10/23, Award, December 19, 2013.

42. See *Murphy Exploration and Production Co. v. Ecuador*, Permanent Court of Arbitration, Award, February 10, 2017; *Perenco v. Ecuador*, ICSID Case No. ARB/08/6, Decision on Remaining Issues of Jurisdiction and Liability, June 30, 2011.

43. Such research could build, for example, upon Van Harten and Malysheuski (2016). Additional research could trace the ultimate destination of compensation: to the firm itself, owners in the host country, owners in the home country, or owners in a tax haven.

REFERENCES

Aisbett, Emma. 2010. "Foreign Firms: Powerful or Persecuted?" Proceedings of the German Development Economics Conference. Hannover, No. 39. https://www.econstor.eu/handle/10419/39969.

Aisbett, Emma, and Lauge Poulsen. 2016. "Relative Treatment of Aliens: Evidence from Developing Countries." Global Economics Governance Working Paper 122. https://www.geg.ox.ac.uk/publication/geg-wp-2016122-relative-treatment-aliens-firm-level-evidence-developing-countries.

Allee, Todd, and Clint Peinhardt. 2011. "Contingent Credibility: The Impact of Investment Treaty Violations on Foreign Direct Investment." *International Organization* 65 (3): 401–32.

Andrias, Kate. 2015. "Separations of Wealth: Inequality and the Erosion of Checks and Balances." *University of Pennsylvania Journal of Constitutional Law* 18 (2): 419–504.

Bankes, Nigel. 2011. "Protection of the Rights of Indigenous Peoples to Territory Through the Property Rights Provisions of International Regional Human Rights Instruments." *Yearbook of Polar Law* 3 (1): 57–112.

Chang, Thomas K. 2012. "A Developmental Approach to the Patent-Antitrust Interface." *Northwestern Journal of International Law & Business* 33 (1): 1–79.

Coleman, Jesse, Lise Johnson, Lisa Sachs, and Kanika Gupta. 2017. "International Investment Agreements, 2015–2016: A Review of Trends and New Approaches." In *Yearbook on International Investment Law and Policy 2015–2016*, ed. Lisa Sachs and Lise Johnson, 42–115. Oxford: Oxford University Press.

Coplan, Karl S. 2009. "Ideological Plaintiffs, Administrative Lawmaking, Standing, and the Petition Clause." *Maine Law Review* 61: 377–466.

Drutman, Lee. 2015. *The Business of America Is Lobbying: How Corporations Became Politicized and Politics Became More Corporate*. Oxford: Oxford University Press.

Freeman, R. Edward, Jeffrey S. Harrison, Andrew C. Wicks, Bidhan L. Parmar, and Simone de Colle. 2010. *Stakeholder Theory: The State of the Art*. Cambridge, UK: Cambridge University Press.

Gaukrodger, David. 2014. "Investment Treaties and Shareholder Claims for Reflective Loss: Insights from Advanced Systems of Corporate Law." OECD Working Papers on International Investment 2014/02. http://www.oecd.org/daf/inv/investment -policy/WP-2014_02.pdf.

Gilens, Martin. 2012. *Affluence and Influence: Economic Inequality and Political Power in America*. Princeton, NJ: Princeton University Press.

Gilens, Martin, and Benjamin I. Page. 2014. "Testing Theories of American Politics: Elites, Interest Groups, and Average Citizens." *Perspectives on Politics* 12 (3): 564–81.

Gorovitz Robertson, Heidi. 1995. "If Your Grandfather Could Pollute, So Can You: Environmental 'Grandfather Clauses' and Their Role in Environmental Inequity." *Catholic University Law Review* 45 (1): 131–79.

Hacker, Jacob S., and Paul Pierson. 2010. *Winner-Take-All Politics: How Washington Made the Rich Richer—and Turned Its Back on the Middle Class*. New York: Simon & Schuster.

Hacker, Jacob S., Paul Pierson, and Kathleen Thelen. 2015. "Drift and Conversion: Hidden Faces of Institutional Change." In *Advances in Comparative-Historical Analysis*, ed. James Mahoney and Kathleen Thelen, 180–208. Cambridge: Cambridge University Press.

Henisz, Witold J. 2016. "The Dynamic Capability of Corporate Diplomacy." *Global Strategy Journal* 6 (3): 183–96.

Hodgson, Mathew. 2014. "Costs in Investment Treaty Arbitration: The Case for Reform." In *Reshaping the Investor-State Dispute Settlement System: Journeys for the 21st Century*, ed. Jean E. Kalicki and Anna Joubin-Bret, 748–59. Leiden, Netherlands: Martinus Nijhoff.

Huang, Yasheng. 2003. *Selling China: Foreign Direct Investment During the Reform Era*. New York: Cambridge University Press.

Justino, Patricia, and Mick Moore. 2015. "Inequality: Trends, Harms and New Agendas." IDS Evidence Report 144. Brighton, UK: Institute of Development Studies.

Kennedy, David. 2011. "Some Caution About Property Rights as a Recipe for Economic Development." *Accounting, Economics, and Law* 1 (1): 1–62.

Lawson-Remer, Terra. 2012. "Property Insecurity." *Brooklyn Journal of International Law* 38 (1): 145–91.

Lester, Simon. 2015. "Rethinking the International Investment Law System." *Journal of World Trade* 49: 211–22.

Liu, Deming. 2014. "Patent, But Where Is Home and Where Is Global Justice? A Rawlsian and Senian Inquiry." *Chicago-Kent Journal of Intellectual Property* 14 (1): 173–215.

Merrill, Thomas W. 2012. "The Property Strategy." *University of Pennsylvania Law Review* 160: 2061–95.

Morley, Michael T. 2014. "Consent of the Governed or Consent of the Government? The Problems with Consent Decrees in Government-Defendant Cases." *University of Pennsylvania Journal of Constitutional Law* 16 (3): 637–96.

Nougayrède, Delphine. 2015. "Yukos, Investment Round-Tripping, and the Evolving Public/Private Paradigms." *American Review of International Arbitration* 26 (3): 337–64.

Peñalver, Eduardo M., and Sonia K. Katyal. 2010. *Property Outlaws: How Squatters, Pirates and Protestors Improve the Law of Ownership*. New Haven, CT: Yale University Press.

Peterson, Niels. 2014. "The German Constitutional Court and Legislative Capture." *International Journal of Constitutional Law* 12 (3): 650–69.

Poulsen, Lauge. 2015. *Bounded Rationality and Economic Diplomacy*. Cambridge, UK: Cambridge University Press.

Rosser, Ezra. 2015. "Destabilizing Property." *Connecticut Law Review* 48 (2): 397–472.

Sasson, Monique. 2010. *Substantive Law in Investment Treaty Arbitration: The Unsettled Relationship Between International Law and Municipal Law*. Alphen aan den Rijn, Netherlands: Kluwer Law International.

Schiller, Reuel E. 2000. "Enlarging the Administrative Polity: Administrative Law and the Changing Definition of Pluralism, 1945–1970." *Vanderbilt Law Review* 53: 1389–1453.

Schlozman, Kay L., and John T. Tierney. 1986. *Organized Interests in American Democracy*. New York: HarperCollins.

Stiglitz, Joseph. 2012. *The Price of Inequality*. New York: Norton.

Super, David A. 2013. "A New New Property." *Columbia Law Review* 113: 1773–1896.

United Nations Conference on Trade and Development (UNCTAD). 2016. *World Investment Report 2016: Investor Nationality: Policy Changes*. Geneva, Switzerland: UNCTAD.

Van Harten, Gus, and Pavel Malysheuski. 2016. "Who Has Benefited Financially from Investment Treaty Arbitration? An Evaluation of the Size and Wealth of Claimants." Osgoode Legal Studies Research Paper Series, No. 14, vol. 12, no. 3: 1–18.

Van Harten, Gus, and Dayna N. Scott. 2017. "Investment Treaties and the Internal Vetting of Regulatory Proposals: A Case Study from Canada (Part 2)." In *Yearbook on International Investment Law and Policy 2015–2016*, ed. Lisa Sachs and Lise Johnson, 412–44. Oxford: Oxford University Press.

CHAPTER 6

Capital Openness and Income Inequality

SMOOTH SAILING OR TROUBLED WATERS?

Kevin P. Gallagher, Guillermo Lagarda, and Jennifer Linares

1. INTRODUCTION

Capital openness has long been associated with financial and banking crises. Most recently, the financial crisis raised concerns among policy makers about the effects of capital openness and the growing income inequality within countries. This reaction is not baseless: over the past three decades, increases in financial liberalization and economic downturns have coincided with income inequality aggravation. In response, there has been an increase in capital controls and the re-regulation of the financial account.[1] This return to orthodoxy could be a setback for supporters of global coordination.

The troubling decision of choosing sides between closing rather than opening has not been exclusive to policy makers. Capital controls are making an intellectual comeback too: "The general presumption was that capital account liberalization was always good, and capital controls were nearly always bad. I've seen the thinking change, partly because it was already wrong then, and because it was particularly wrong in the crisis," said Olivier Blanchard, former professor of the Massachusetts Institute of Technology (MIT) and former Chief Economist of the International Monetary Fund (IMF) (cited in Bird 2016). As Blanchard said, openness has traditionally been seen as Pareto-improving because it expands possibility frontiers. In contrast, closing or restricting the capital account is considered by many to be detrimental to countries' economies. It can, for instance, discourage inward investment because investors may fear they will not be able to easily withdraw their money during an economic downturn.

But is capital account liberalization the way to go? Claimants of openness have long argued that it increases risk-sharing and domestic-consumption smoothing. However, when financial institutions are weak and access to credit is not inclusive, liberalization may bias financial access in favor of those better-off and therefore increase income inequality. It could go the other way as well: on the likelihood of financial crises, income inequality could fall because bankruptcies and falling asset prices may have a greater impact on those with access to financial markets. On the other hand, long-lasting recessions may disproportionately hurt the poor because they have limited access to banking services to hedge against risks. Finally, capital account openness may affect the distribution of income through its effect on the labor share of income. The best way to think of this is in the context of a bargaining game between labor and capital. If capital account liberalization represents a credible threat to reallocate production abroad, it may lead to an increase in the profit-wage ratio and to a decrease in the labor share of income (Harrison 2002).

Should we shift gears and revert capital openness? A surge of discussions addressing this question suggests that this issue is far from being a closed, or even a cold, case. Most of the available literature focuses on within-country experience (Larrain 2014, 88) or on a limited set of countries (Das and Mohapatra 2003, 217–48), leaving key issues unaddressed. Important questions remain, including under what circumstances is capital openness negatively related to income inequality, and is there evidence that capital account openness only exacerbates income inequality during downturns and improves it during economic expansion? Ultimately, we would like to know if there is a right moment to restrict the capital account during contractions, and if these measures should be coordinated worldwide.

This paper contributes to the empirical literature on the effects of capital openness on income inequality by examining the distributional consequences of capital account liberalization for a large (unbalanced) panel of 141 countries from 1990 to 2013. We specifically focus on answering three questions: (i) Is there (on average) a positive or negative relation between income inequality and capital account openness? (ii) Are the negative effects of income distribution larger during booms, busts, or regular periods? and (iii) Have ex ante and ex post capitalopenness policies contributed to reduced income inequality? To the best of our knowledge, no research covers these issues. Therefore, our research contributes to existing literature and brings into consideration whether capital account liberalization occurs too rapidly relative to the implementation of other policies.

The level of financial development and the occurrence of crises play key roles in shaping the response financial globalization reforms have on income inequality. In particular, we present evidence that capital account liberalization reforms are associated with a statistically significant and persistent increase in income inequality ex post a crisis. However, results also suggest that restrictive measures aimed at limiting distributional negative effects during economic downturns have ambiguous outcomes and are conditional on the duration of the bust. Closing the accounts ex post, for instance, reduces the Gini by 0.02 but only when the downturn lasts more than a year. Otherwise, when the bust is gone after a year, the policy changes are ineffective because the pace at which they affect the economy is slower. The increase of income inequality is, however, conditional on the structural policies that accompanied liberalization reforms.

The paper is organized as follows. Section 2 presents a summary of the related literature. Section 3 focuses on describing data and showing some descriptive statistics regarding the evolution of inequality and capital account openness. Section 4 specifies the methodology and is followed by a discussion of results in section 5. Finally, in section 6 we present our conclusions.

2. RELATED LITERATURE

In the last twenty-five years, more than a dozen countries in the developing world have eased restrictions on cross-border capital flows, resulting in a more financially integrated world. Theory suggests that these policies are Pareto-optimal because they allow resources to flow from capitalabundant countries in the developed world, where return to capital is low, to capitalscarce nations in the developing world, where return to capital is higher (Henry 2006). This influx of capital to the developing world reduces the countries' cost of capital and consequently encourages investment, ceteris paribus. Investment triggers economic growth and therefore raises the standard of living of these countries. However, as explained by Hellmann, Murdock, and Stiglitz (2000), financial market liberalization could increase the moral hazard problem: liberalization is associated with an increase in bank competition, which in turn erodes profits. A decrease in profits is associated with lower franchise values, which lowers the incentive for making good loans, thus increasing moral hazard. A similar case of information asymmetries is presented in McKinnon and Pill (1996). Even Gourinchas and Jeanne (2006) show limited benefits of transitioning from an autarkic state to an open economy with regard to improvements in domestic productivity. Thus theory does not conclude whether capital account liberalization is ultimately beneficial or not. This ambiguity is also found in empirical studies. Jeanne, Subramanian, and Williamson (2012) provided a full review of this literature and found that capital account liberalization is not correlated with economic growth but rather is correlated with banking crises—especially in developing countries.

3. MEASURES AND CORRELATIONS

INCOME INEQUALITY

The Gini coefficient is the most widely used measure of income inequality. The Standardized World Income Inequality Database (SWIID) created by Solt (2016) contains post-tax income estimates represented in one hundred separate imputations per country. For simplification purposes, we averaged the one hundred imputations for each country, per year. Figure 6.1a shows time series data for eight world regions. Income inequality has increased in most regions, especially in the developed economies. Interestingly, in Latin America, the most unequal region of the world, income distribution was improving, even after the late 1990s when the large countries in the region experienced economic slowdowns. Figure 6.1b shows all countries divided by income groups. Once again, high-income countries have the worst trend. This may be associated with the 2008–09 crisis because these countries are very open to the global economy. Low-income countries were the least affected, possibly because of the countries' fewer linkages with the global economy.

CAPITAL ACCOUNT LIBERALIZATION

Capital account liberalization de jure measures are typically constructed from the IMF's Annual Report on Exchange Arrangements and Exchange Restrictions (AREAER), which measures more than sixty different types of controls. Measures typically result in binary variables in which one equals the presence of financial controls, and zero otherwise. One such de jure measure is the Chinn-Ito index, which has been fine-tuned for the extent of openness in capital account transactions (Chinn and Ito 2008). It does not, however, measure the intensity of capital controls as Quinn (1997) and Quinn (2003) do. Chinn-Ito's correlation with Quinn is 0.84, however, suggesting that it captures capital control intensity to a reasonable extent.

Fernandez et al. (2015) recently developed a de jure dataset (KA-Uribe hereafter) using AREAER and the methodology in Schindler (2009).

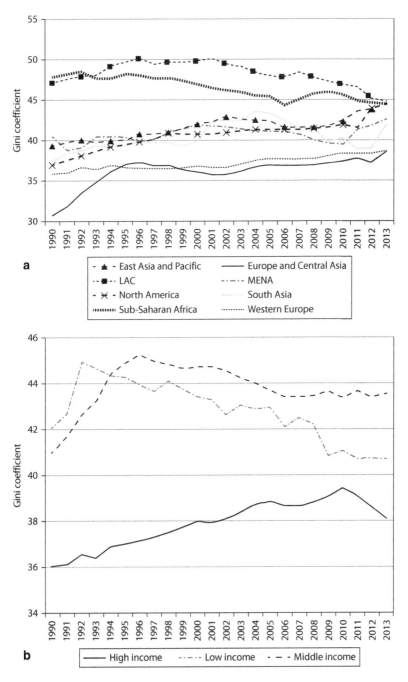

Figure 6.1 (*a*) Gini coefficient in eight world regions. *Source*: Solt (2016).
(*b*) Gini Coefficient by Income Group. *Source*: Solt (2016).

The dataset offers information on capital controls disaggregated by both type—whether the controls are on inflows or outflows—and ten categories of assets, including money market instruments, derivatives, collective investment securities, guarantees, sureties, financial backup facilities, and direct investment accounts. KA-Uribe constructed an index from these data that ranges from zero to one, where zero is equivalent to a capital account lacking restriction and one is equivalent to a fully "closed" account. The correlation between KA-Uribe and the Chinn-Ito index is strong at –0.87. It is important to recall that it is normal for the Chinn-Ito index and KA-Uribe to move in opposite directions: in the former the maximum value is equivalent to a fully liberalized account, whereas in the latter the maximum value is equivalent to a fully restricted account.

Several de facto measures have also been generated in response to de jure measures' shortcomings. Lane and Milesi-Ferretti (2007) proposed a stock-based de facto database that captures a country's exposure to international financial markets. It includes countries' aggregate assets and liabilities in the following categories: portfolio equity, foreign direct investment, debt, and financial derivatives. For this paper, we summed all portfolio investment and debt assets and liabilities[2] as a percentage of gross domestic product (GDP). The resulting "index" was used as a de facto measure. It should be noted that gross capital flows are more volatile than equity-based measures (Quinn, Schindler, and Toyoda 2011).[3]

For our empirical analysis, we considered both de jure and de facto measures because many countries allow capital account transactions but do not receive flows.[4] Only a handful of countries with liberalized capital accounts receive a high percentage of capital flows. Therefore, utilizing only de jure measures could bias results. Similarly, omitting variables that explain the difference between the degree of de jure and de facto liberalization could cause heterogeneity issues if we only use de facto measures. To reduce the possibility of omitting these variables, we used additional controls, including depth of financial system (credit to private sector as a percentage of GDP) and institution strength.

It should be noted that having a closed capital account does not guarantee a lack of investment flows into a country. For instance, direct investment and funds recorded as "other investment" in the balance of payments can enter a country through the banking system or any other means offered by the central bank. However, this research focuses on portfolio investment flows. It would be unlikely for portfolio investment flows to enter a country without a de jure framework that allows for it.

RELATIONSHIP BETWEEN FINANCIAL LIBERALIZATION
AND INCOME INEQUALITY

A quick glance at our panel (for a list of all countries included in the panel, please refer to table A.1 in the chapter appendix) shows that the Chinn-Ito and the Gini coefficient are negatively correlated. In other words, the opening of the capital account is associated with a reduction in income inequality. However, this correlation is rather weak (–0.15). The effect of openness is also beneficial (but weaker) when comparing the Fernandez-Uribe index to the Gini coefficient. Considering that limiting oneself to using de jure measures can provide an inaccurate picture of reality, we also evaluated the relationship between capital flows (as a percentage of GDP) from the Lane and Milesi-Ferretti database and the Gini index. The result (–0.07), although very weak, also suggests that a greater amount of capital flows is associated with a fall in income inequality.

These correlations contrast with the econometric findings in the literature—a proof that the effects of financial openness on inequality are not uniform across countries. There is clearly more to explore than a simple correlation. Some of the reasons for these contrasting effects discussed in the literature include political, institutional, and market efficiency differences. Although the reasons are many, researchers seem to agree on the role of institutions because countries with solid institutions usually have a higher penetration of financial services. To control for institutions, we assume that the degree of institutional strength is correlated with GDP per capita, and we classified countries into three income groups—high income, middle income, and low income—based on the following rule:[5]

$$Income\ Group = \begin{cases} Low & if & GDPpc < 4,999 \\ Middle & if & 5000 \le GDPpc \le 19,999 \\ High & if & GDPpc > 20,000 \end{cases}$$

Correlations by income group, although generally weak, vary significantly. For instance, the correlation between the Chinn-Ito index and Gini is negative for the entire panel, but it is positive (although weak) for the low- and middle-income groups, implying that only high-income groups have benefited (in terms of inequality reduction) from liberalizing their capital account.

In addition to income groups, we further disaggregated the panel into three periods that we consider to be fundamentally different from each other: 1990–1999, 2000–2007, and 2008–2013. Between 1990 and 1999, more than eighty countries opened their capital accounts. However, beginning in 2000 de facto openness accelerated. Finally, 2008 marks the beginning of the Great Recession.[6] This additional disaggregation allowed us to visualize whether there were characteristics between income groups and over time that contrast the aforementioned correlations.

Correlations by period also show inconsistent results. For the high-income group, the relationship between capital account liberalization (using Chinn-Ito) and income inequality is unfavorable during most periods;[7] that is, capital account liberalization is associated with an increase in income inequality. The correlations are even stronger when using the Fernandez-Uribe index. We ran a final check by exploring the relationship between Gini and the lags of each of the de jure measures, given that the Gini coefficient usually reports the previous year's inequality. However, correlations remain virtually identical to those found with their contemporary values.

We also explored the relationship between our de facto measure and income inequality by income groups. For these correlations, we used the lag of the de facto measure for the reasons mentioned above. The results are ambiguous: liberalization is usually unfavorable for low- and middle-income countries[8] but is beneficial for high-income countries. This correlation, along with the correlations mentioned above, are consistent with the arguments of Klein and Olivei (2008) and Prasad and Rajan (2008) on the importance of the strength of institutions for a beneficial reception of capital flows.

RELEVANT SHOCKS

The academic literature has identified several shocks that may have an effect on the reduction of income inequality. For our purposes, we focused on impacts that are transmitted through portfolio investment. Monetary policy, in particular (Coibion et al. 2012), can have global effects that are reflected in the cost of capital. An exogenous shock that suddenly increases liquidity and persistently maintains low rates can generate changes in investment patterns. In this case, income inequality could improve or worsen, depending on the sector of the economy that absorbs the benefits. The reasoning behind this is that most households primarily rely on labor earnings instead of business and financial income: if expansionary monetary policy shocks raise profits more than wages, then those with claims to ownership of firms will tend to benefit disproportionately. These people also tend to be wealthier, so this channel should lead to higher income inequality in response to monetary policy shocks. Also, if some agents frequently trade in financial markets and are affected by changes in the money supply prior to other agents, then an increase in the money supply will redistribute wealth toward those agents most connected to financial markets.

Another variety of shocks could be related to internal conditions that suddenly change from optimistic to pessimistic, such as the difference between growth expectations and the actual GDP growth rate. Although there is usually a strong correlation between this variable and other factors, and this variable is not the best representation of a domestic shock, it allows for the estimation of an orthogonal component to external factors. In addition, this difference between expectations and reality may be interacting with the capital account liberalization policy or with de facto capital flows. Finally, including this variable in our analysis enabled us to see the effect that an underperforming economy[9] has on income distribution during periods of capital account liberalization.

We controlled for these two types of shocks by including the following variables in our analysis:

- Romer and Romer (2004) (hereafter RR) shocks, which reflect changes in U.S. monetary policy (agreed at each Federal Open Market Committee meeting) orthogonal to the set of information from the Fed, obtained from the GREENBOOK forecasts. This variable can be used to identify monetary policy innovations purged from anticipated effects related to economic conditions.
- To characterize unusual economic episodes, we generated a proxy variable that is only weakly correlated with world economic performance. To do so, we used the real GDP growth rate of each country and projected it to current and lagged GDP growth of the United States, Japan, Germany, and China,[10] both lagged and contemporaneous. The estimation results were then used to find the forecast error of the proxy we seek.
- We also used a simple categorization of GDP growth performance: regular episode whenever GDP growth is within a 1.5 (historical) standard deviation, boom when it is above, and bust when it is below.

$$Unusual\ Event = \begin{cases} Bust & if & GDPg < \mu_i - 1.5\sigma_i \\ Regular & if & \mu_i - 1.5\sigma_i \leq GDPg \leq \mu_i + 1.5\sigma_i \\ Boom & if & GDPg > \mu_i + 1.5\sigma_i \end{cases}$$

4. METHODOLOGY

We first performed a baseline estimation that inherits some elements from Bumann and Lensink (2016) and Furceri and Loungani (2015). We improved the baseline estimations by adding variables we believe are useful in the identification of unusual economic episodes. Doing so allowed for a better understanding of correlations and helped to identify the direction of causality between capital account openness and income inequality over different time periods. We focused on answering three questions: (i) On average, is there a positive or negative relation between income inequality and capital account openness? (ii) Are the negative effects of income distribution larger during booms or busts? and (iii) Have ex ante and ex post capital openness policies contributed to reduced income inequality?

To answer the first question, we began by describing the general econometric model:

$$g_{i,t} = c + \varphi_i + \rho g_{i,t-1} + \alpha KAOP_{i,t} + \varepsilon_{i,t}. \tag{1}$$

In this equation, $i = 1, \ldots, N$ and $t = 1, \ldots, T$ are indices for country and time, respectively. Our measure for income inequality $g_{i,t}$ is expressed in natural logarithms,[11] and φ_i are country fixed effects. We include the lag of the Gini coefficient as an explanatory variable to account for the persistence of inequality that was observed in the data. Capital account openness (or KAOP) corresponds to the capital openness indicator, and $\varepsilon_{i,t}$ is the error term.

Our hypothesis here is that on average, for the entire sample, $\alpha \leq 0$ with some good level of significance. We believe this should be the case because capital openness has been widespread, suggesting that policy makers at least perceive that open policies are contributing to less inequality. However, given that the literature indicates that institutions play a key role on the distribution of benefits, we expanded the basic regression to quantify whether there is a significantly different level effect between countries with strong, medium, and weaker institutions. To do so, we included a full set of dummies to identify whether a country is in a high-, medium-, or low-income group. Furthermore, we added other controls to better identify the correlation between capital openness and inequality.

$$g_{i,t} = c + \varphi_i + \rho g_{i,t-1} + \alpha KAOP_{i,t} + \sum_j \beta D_{i,j} + \sum_j \gamma x_{i,j,t} + \varepsilon_{i,t}, \quad (2)$$

where $D_{i,j}$ are *j-dummies* variables income groups per each *i* countries. $x_{i,j,t}$ is a set of *j-variables* usually associated with inequality changes including inflation, financial depth, trade openness, age dependency ratio, and secondary education enrollment as control variables. Academic research has identified these variables as key correlates of income equality. Some of the arguments follow:[12]

1. Low-income households normally keep a large percentage of their income in cash to buy goods, so they are more likely to be affected by a generalized increase of prices (Albanesi 2007). However, the effect of price-level changes on income inequality might be conditional on the capacity of households to shield against them (through the banking system, for instance). Therefore, we added credit to the private sector as a percent of GDP as a measure of financial depth.

2. Trade openness also might be a channel inducing income inequality because trade flows could cause sudden changes in the relative demand of high-skilled workers. In the absence of migration policies or an adequate education system, these trade flows could cause a rise of relative wages, thus increasing income inequality (Anderson 2005).

3. Education deficiencies may induce income inequality because education levels could create wage differentials (Goldin and Katz 2007).

4. A country's age structure may have an effect on income inequality. For instance, inequality could be lower among retirees, but so is their average income (Alesina and Perotti 1996).

Unlike Bumann and Lensink (2016, 62), we do not include GDP per capita as a proxy for the development of institutions. Instead, we group countries by income level. This allows us to indirectly control for institutions without having to regress one additional variable.

To address the second question, we followed two approaches. The first one is based on the link between higher RR values and an unusual episode that surprises the world economy as a whole. To briefly recapitulate, RR is large when the increase of interest rates is higher than expected. Recall that RR constructs this variable in such a way that it is strongly exogenous to other macroeconomic variables. Therefore, RR acts as a shock that may help determine a causal relation between a boom or bust episode and the changes in inequality. We use this event to contrast the coefficients for KAOP. Given a more than expected decrease of the interest rate (worse economic conditions than expected), we hypothesized that $\alpha^s < \alpha$. When countries are caught in an unexpectedly worse economic condition than anticipated, low-income households are unable to adjust their spending fast enough and lack the financial instruments to mitigate the downturn, reducing the beneficial multiplier of KAOP. A second estimation to account for economic conditions considers a simple categorization of GDP growth performance based on the categories of unusual events previously defined. We do not have a prior or a particular position here. However, we sought to discover whether, on average, KAOP has led to increased inequality during busts compared to booms.

Finally, to investigate whether ex ante and ex post capitalopenness policies have contributed to reduce income inequality, we categorized the magnitude of changes in our capital openness variable. First, we defined that a liberalization policy occurred whenever there was a positive change on KAOP between $t-1$ and t. Otherwise, the policy remained unchanged ("none") or had a negative change ("close"):

$$Policy = \begin{cases} Close & if & \Delta KAOP_{i,t} < 0 \\ None & if & \Delta KAOP_{i,t} = 0 \\ Open & if & \Delta KAOP_{i,t} > 0 \end{cases}$$

We then use these variables to discover whether income distribution improved. A key element here is that policies on capital account openness are typically nonlinear. For instance, a decision to add capital controls is more likely to occur during a bust or when economic conditions might induce capital flights. Therefore, we modified equation (1) to add these features:

$$g_{i,t} = c + \varphi_i + \rho g_{i,t-1} + \sum_j \mu Policy_{i,j,t} * Z_{i,t-1} + \sum_j \gamma x_{i,j,t} + \varepsilon_{i,t}, \quad (3)$$

where $Policy_{i,j}$ are j-dummies variables for Policy groups per each i country. $x_{i,j,t}$ is a set of j-variables usually associated with inequality changes and $Z_{i,j,t}$ includes a 1 and those variables that denote a macroeconomic shock. It is worth noting that KAOP is omitted from equation (3) given that the objective is to assess restrictive policies.

5. RESULTS AND DISCUSSION

CAPITAL ACCOUNT LIBERALIZATION AND INCOME INEQUALITY

The initial hypothesis—that capital openness is correlated with less inequality—largely holds in the full sample regression. On average, we find that for every unit of capital liberalization the Gini coefficient falls about 2.3 percent, with 99 percent confidence. This result broadly confirms the trends we have seen in the data: since the 1990s, countries across the globe have liberalized their capital account to some degree, perhaps after observing success stories elsewhere. The sign of this estimation also seems consistent with other recent studies, such as Furceri and Loungani (2015).

Surely, this is not the whole story. Figure 6.1 shows that some income groups had improved in terms of reducing inequality, but high-income countries had seen a steady increase in inequality that has only recently receded. How is this possible? Gini estimates are usually sensitive to the measure of income or wealth that is taken into consideration. However, an increase of the mass of people in the lowest income percentiles will affect the Gini calculation, for instance, because of low-skill migration. Nonetheless, we hypothesized that strong institutions should, or at least could, explain the positive correlation between financial liberalization and the inequality reduction.

Under this hypothesis, stronger institutions suppose a better governance environment that could lead to more inclusive policies. Therefore we tested for a negative correlation between inequality and capital openness (KAOP) differentiating income groups. In other words, the direct effect of KAOP on the Gini should be stronger as countries gain stronger institutions. Columns (2)–(4) in table 6.1 show different estimations to test the hypothesis. The income group effect is divided into two sets: weak institutions (low- and middle-income countries) and strong institutions (high-income countries). In all these estimations, KAOP continues to be negatively correlated with the Gini although with slightly less impact. Nonetheless, a simple t-test provides evidence of nonsignificant difference of the KAOP coefficient between the dummy regression and the baseline estimation. These same estimations (column (2)) show us that conditional on being part of the group of weak institutions the level impact is positive; that is, on average, these countries have more inequality—an expected result.

The estimations in column (3) provide us with an interesting result. Here we do not use single dummies but their interaction with KAOP. The previous dummy estimation offered no additional information regarding the KAOP coefficient, and here we are looking for a likely slope effect. It is clear that there is a different level of inequality between each group, but our intuition behind this option is that the way capital account openness has affected inequality could vary according to the degree of openness countries decide to keep. According to the estimations, conditional on whether a country has strong or weak institutions, the total accounting of direct and indirect effects seems to balance in favor of our hypothesis. In fact, we first note that the direct effect—the coefficient of KAOP—reduces the impact level from approximately 2 percent to 1.6 percent. But the story does not end here. What will determine the final overall effect is whether a country has weak or strong institutions. This second component is measured by the interaction term. The estimation outcomes suggest that there is certain evidence of differential effects between countries with different degrees of institutional strength. Having weak institutions for a certain level of capital openness will more likely drive inequality up, although this is only significant at 10 percent. Contrastingly, under stronger institutions, the coefficient is negative (that is, inequality reducing) with larger significance. To complete this analysis, the final column in table 6.1 combines the dummy analysis with the interaction terms. The results are consistent with what we have discussed here. The dummies track the same sign as before and the interaction terms follow suit. The direct effect of KAOP on Gini growth remains below 2 percent, the strong institution coefficients remain basically unchanged, the weak institution dummy reduced almost half its magnitude, and the weak institution interaction term doubled its detrimental effect on inequality growth.

It seems reasonable to associate income inequality with institutional strength. The estimations in table 6.1, a snapshot, correspond to the common belief that stronger institutions will identify and take advantage of the benefits of capital account openness, whereas weaker institutions might not seize the benefits, resulting in more inequality. However, a better interpretation is linked to discovering whether transitioning from weak to strong institutions is associated with a significant improvement in equality. With the dummy regressions, plus interaction terms, we can answer this question. Because the dummy estimation uses a discrete set of binary variables, the only way to evaluate how inequality growth changes as a country moves from weak to strong institutions is a simple difference. We now pay attention to the estimation in column (4). To learn whether

Table 6.1   Baseline Regression

	(1)	(2)	(3)	(4)
Gini ($t-1$)	0.837**	0.829**	0.839**	0.729**
	(40.81)	(39.13)	(38.37)	(58.77)
KAOP	−0.0230**	−0.0209**	−0.0162*	−0.0178**
	(−3.00)	(−2.72)	(−2.11)	(−6.07)
Dummies				
Weak		0.0275**		0.0103+
		(2.77)		(1.72)
Strong		−0.0195*		−0.0134+
		(−2.11)		(−1.89)
KAOP*Weak			0.0244+	0.0401**
			(1.66)	(5.99)
KAOP*Strong			−0.0227+	−0.0278**
			(−1.69)	(−6.43)
Constant	0.620**	N/A	0.614**	N/A
	(8.06)		(7.52)	
Observations				

t statistics in parentheses

$^+p < 0.10$, $^*p < 0.05$, $^{**}p < 0.01$

Source: Arellano-Bover.

transitioning to a better income group induces a significantly different effect on Gini growth, we calculate the following:

$$E\left[g_{i,t} \mid \text{Institutions} = \text{Strong}\right] - E\left[g_{i,t} \mid \text{Institutions} = \text{Weak}\right]$$
$$= [\beta^{(s)} - \beta^{(w)}] + [\delta^{(s)} - \delta^{(w)}]KAOP_{i,t} \tag{5}$$

The above equations divide the total effect of improving institutions into two parts. The first component, $\beta^{(s)} - \beta^{(w)}$, quantifies a direct effect of improving institutions. However, the global effect is conditional on the degree of capital openness, which supposes an indirect effect $\delta^{(s)} - \delta^{(w)}$. Column (4) demonstrates that there is a reduction in income inequality when a country strengthens its institutions. However, the effect is stronger when this is coupled with a liberalized capital account.

Another way to think about these correlations is to quantify how the marginal contribution of capital openness changes given the strength of institutions. This analysis derives straightforwardly from the previous estimations. That is, we are interested in determining the magnitude and size for:

$$\frac{dg_{i,t}}{dKAOP_{i,t}} = \alpha + \sum_{j}\delta^{(j)}D_{i,j}. \tag{6}$$

We once again examine the results shown in column (4) of table 6.1. In this case, we see that the marginal contribution to the elasticity has different patterns. For instance, having weaker institutions will lead to a positive overall value, thus implying that capital openness could lead to increased inequality. In contrast, the effect of strong institutions is completely the opposite; the total effect would reduce inequality by 10 percent.[13] Both calculations seem to go in the same direction: capital openness seems to be inequality-reducing as institutions are strengthened.

The analysis based on level effect differences by income groups—our proxy for institutional strength—gives us some initial thoughts about inequality patterns. Although institutions are key when handling distributional policies, multiple factors are usually correlated strongly with inequality growth. Endogeneity may arise when a public policy, say, in education, gradually has a feedback effect on institutional strength. As human capital increases, institutions may gain strength, and this in turn may lead to better policies in education. It remains unclear whether initial implementation of the educational policy would have happened without any previous changes in institutions. This sort of ambiguity is a source of endogeneity that requires further study. So far we can only attest to the correlation between changes in inequality and the degree of openness unconditional on other latent factors. We have discussed the variables usually linked with inequality. These variables speak to structural features of the economy that form part of the way income is distributed within a country. To isolate as much as we can the direct effect of capital openness on inequality, we must control for the usual variables that correlate with inequality.

Because countries with weak institutions have important differences from those with strong institutions, we test our hypotheses in a slightly different way. We divide the sample into two groups, those with weak or strong institutions. In this way, we proxy per capita income and quality of institutions. By doing so, we implicitly constrain the distribution of the other factors so[14] most of the observations with a private credit ratio below 25 percent come from low-income and middle-income countries; the high school enrollment rate is usually below 44 percent in low-income countries; and so on. For each sample, we perform a set of estimations incrementally adding the structural variables. We then proceed by asking how relevant these variables are for countries with weaker institutions.

The estimations for the weak institutions sample is reported in table 6.2. We find that the sign of the correlation between inequality and KAOP holds with strong significance in the baseline case. Sign and

Table 6.2 Weak Institutions: Controlled Fixed-Effects

	(1)	(2)	(3)	(4)	(5)	(6)
Gini ($t - 1$)	0.849**	0.885**	0.845**	0.743**	0.703**	0.737**
	(66.39)	(68.70)	(62.79)	(47.10)	(48.59)	(47.77)
KAOP	-0.0279**	-0.0243**	-0.00170+	-0.0119	-0.01285+	-0.0147*
	(-6.19)	(-4.80)	(-1.32)	(-1.02)	(-1.22)	(-2.20)
Structural Controls						
Inflation		0.00140+	0.00124+	0.00221	0.00308+	0.00260+
		(1.46)	(1.30)	(1.28)	(1.81)	(1.52)
TradeOP			-0.0771**	-0.0551**	-0.0514**	-0.0538**
			(-13.50)	(-9.96)	(-9.38)	(-9.71)
Schooling				-0.000271**	-0.000360**	-0.000329**
				(-3.06)	(-3.94)	(-3.58)
Financial Controls						
Fin. Depth					-0.00679+	-0.00128
					(-1.45)	(-1.05)
KAOP*Fin.Depth						0.0171**
						(2.70)
Constant	0.582**	0.442**	0.643**	1.027**	1.006**	1.053**
	(12.06)	(9.14)	(12.46)	(16.68)	(16.90)	(16.98)
Observations	1704	1548	1518	1087	1065	1065

t statistics in parentheses

$^+p < 0.10$, $^*p < 0.05$, $^{**}p < 0.01$

Source: Arellano-Bover.

magnitude are similar in the whole sample baseline. Significance, though, falls for some of the subsequent regressions. Table 6.2 incrementally shows how the main structural variables affect the KAOP correlation with inequality. Inflation, although significant at 10 percent, has the expected detrimental effect on equality. The KAOP coefficient slightly shifts down compared to the baseline. A larger change occurred when we added trade openness. The KAOP coefficient drops in absolute value from 0.0243 to 0.0170, about 42 percent, albeit with much less statistical significance. Also important is the fact that the trade coefficient has a negative correlation with inequality. As reported in the literature review, the extent to which trade has contributed to a reduction in inequality is still being debated. Here we find that in this time span and with this combination of controls, trade seems to be mostly beneficial in this subsample. Education also pulls down the magnitude of the KAOP's coefficient. According to the estimation, schooling is an important element for inequality. Schooling has an interesting interpretation. Because increasing the average years of schooling is a long-term process, the sample beginning with

1990 can only capture a few generations of young individuals. In spite of this, we can see the positive effects that schooling has through possible salary channels in the non-high-income countries.[15]

So far, all correlates, including inflation, trade openness, and school enrollment, preserve the expected sign: inflation associated with inequality growth, trade openness with a decrease of inequality, and high school enrollment with less inequality. According to these outputs, capital openness—when controlling for inflation, age structure, trade openness, and secondary enrollment—is associated with a 1.2 percent to 2.4 percent decrease in income inequality. We validate these differences again through a means test between each marginal contributor and the baseline estimation. The differences are all statistically significant.

Findings for the strong institutions set of countries differ from those for countries with weak institutions in several ways. First, the baseline estimation for this sample shows a positive coefficient for KAOP. This is true for most of the subsequent estimations, although most of them have very low significance. This seems to contradict the results obtained from the whole sample, but it does not. In our sample, high-income countries reached their highest levels of capital account openness in the 1990s. Since then they have experienced increases in inequality only when new countries join this income group. At the same time, inequality has been increasing, passing from an average Gini coefficient of 36 in the 1990s to nearly 40 in the 2000s. Despite this, our incremental estimations seem to move KAOP from a positive coefficient to a negative and significant one.

Table 6.4 shows the estimations for countries with strong institutions. Once again, our structural correlates keep their signs consistent with most of the literature. But this should not surprise us at all. Schooling differentials, increases in price level, or trade openness are usually at desired levels throughout the time span of this sample. Inflation is positively correlated, as expected, although never significant. For these countries, inflation has been relatively steady during most of the sample, inducing a low covariance between these two and a resulting low t-statistic. Just as with the weak institutions sample, we observe a larger change in the KAOP coefficient when we control for trade openness. The KAOP coefficient drops from 0.01 to 0.001, albeit with low statistical significance. The trade coefficient has a negative and significant correlation with inequality too. This is also the case for the weak institutions sample, but the magnitude is much lower here (in absolute terms). Recall that the point estimate in the weak institution case was –0.07, much higher (in absolute terms) than the –0.002 of the high-income countries.[16]

Education seems to be a key factor in high-income countries. When we added the high school enrollment rate to the estimation, the KAOP coefficient became negative. Although the significance of the KAOP coefficient is very low, this movement might be telling us that capital openness can have a beneficial effect on equality once we account for education. Two important things should be kept in mind. Increasing the average years of schooling is a long-term process, and these countries usually already have high schooling indexes. The main beneficiaries of schooling affect people who migrated from areas with lower schooling, or in the case of the European Union, new countries with lower schooling that joined the EU may have been experiencing a faster catch up. Thus we can think about the intergenerational positive effects schooling has through possible salary channels for these population groups.

It is worth pointing out that KAOP in countries with strong institutions shows a persistent lower significance. Given that these countries are usually either completely or highly open to capital flows (both de jure and de facto) throughout the entire period of study, variation is very limited, thus resulting in a weaker relationship between capital account openness and income inequality. It is likely that other factors, such as financial depth, have a stronger effect on inequality in these countries.

Estimations (5) and (6) in table 6.2 add our proxy for financial development to the incremental estimations for weak institutions. The first change to note is the increase (in absolute terms) of the KAOP estimate. When controlling for financial development, the correlation between capital openness and income inequality becomes stronger in magnitude and significance. The level moves from −0.0119 to −0.01285, with a 15 percent significance. The final estimation includes the interaction between financial development and KAOP and is quite promising. First, it induces a more negative coefficient for KAOP and improves the statistical significance of the direct effect of financial development. The KAOP point estimate moves from −0.0128 to −0.0147, with 95 percent confidence. Also, the interaction term has a negative sign, which means there is an indirect spillover effect from deepening the financial system when the capital account is open. The interpretation of the interaction term is straightforward: financial liberalization, when accompanied by financial depth, benefits equality because more people have access to ways to ensure their stream of income and consumption via credit or savings.

It is worthwhile to expand the discussion of the differences among low-income and middle-income countries. Capital openness is again associated with slow inequality growth after splitting the group into low- and middle-income groups. Yet our findings suggest that lower-income countries are associated with lower statistically significant correlations.[17] Financial development remains a relevant variable to consider in the analysis, and in every case there is some kind of beneficial effect as depth increases. Auxiliary regressions for the low-income group are shown in table 6.3. Incremental regressions show evidence of KAOP losing significance in low-income countries. However, this fact is not surprising. As shown in table 6.2, low-income countries, regardless of their de jure openness, have very small portfolio flows as a percentage of GDP, which also explains the implicitly high p-values in the same table. In middle-income countries, capital openness improved its significance once we added financial depth and the interaction term. The middle-income countries' parameters pool the weak institution ones. For instance, in the low-income group financial depth is not significant, but in the middle-income group it is strongly significant, thus leading to a significant outcome in the weak institution estimation.

Table 6.3   Low-Income Countries: Fixed-Effects Estimation

	(1)	(2)	(3)	(4)	(5)	(6)
Gini $(t-1)$	0.951**	1.041**	1.011**	0.973**	0.987**	0.989**
	(55.16)	(55.95)	(51.27)	(38.32)	(36.66)	(36.15)
KAOP	−0.0312**	−0.0572**	−0.0179*	−0.0331	−0.0182	0.0115
	(−4.06)	(−6.58)	(−1.95)	(−1.49)	(−1.37)	(0.37)
Structural Controls						
Inflation		−0.000209*	−0.000109	−0.000209	−0.000289*	−0.000282*
		(−2.43)	(−1.04)	(−1.42)	(−2.06)	(−2.00)
TradeOP			−0.00105**	−0.000719**	−0.000597**	−0.000565**
			(−13.68)	(−8.84)	(−7.22)	(−6.45)
Schooling				0.000281*	0.000269*	0.000218+
				(2.14)	(1.97)	(1.54)
Financial Controls						
Fin.Depth					−0.00366	0.000337
					(−1.31)	(0.07)
KAOP*Fin. Depth						−0.0119
						(−1.07)
Constant	0.195**	−0.134+	0.0386	0.152+	0.0947	0.0786
	(2.99)	(−1.91)	(0.51)	(1.56)	(0.91)	(0.73)
Observations	790	705	682	422	403	403

t statistics in parentheses

$^+ p < 0.15$, $^* p < 0.05$, $^{**} p < 0.01$

The high-income economies are typically the most financially integrated and normally are more financially open. In high-income countries, financial development has served as a buffer for inequality increases (table 6.4). Here the estimations also confirm the beneficial effects of a developed financial system. The role of financial depth, measured by crediting the private sector as a percentage of GDP, is significant for both the linear and the nonlinear components. The key here is the two-piece decomposition of the total effect on income inequality of opening the capital account. On one side, the marginal effect of opening the capital account reduces inequality by 0.0105 (KAOP coefficient). On the other, financial depth further alleviates the detrimental effects as indicated by the significant coefficient on the interaction term. More precisely, the negative sign implies that the greater the financial depth the smaller (less detrimental) will be the effect of capital account liberalization on income inequality. In fact, both, the single effect and the interaction term render a negative coefficient. The power of the estimates also increase, with significance of 1 percent and 5 percent.

The estimations of the financial controls also show key differences between groups of weak and strong institutions. Recall that for lower- and middle-income countries (weak institutions) the magnitude of the financial correlates are near −0.0170 for the interaction term and about −0.001 for the single effect. Table 6.4 shows that the corresponding estimates are both near −0.0170. The fact that the magnitude is similar for the interaction term is simply a sign that the role of a deeper financial system in an openness environment is equally beneficial. In contrast, the larger difference in the single effect denotes a weaker correlation between variations of inequality and large changes in financial depth. The higher significance of financial depth in table 6.4 compared to table 6.2 might not be totally unreasonable. Although there are no meaningful differences in terms of financial development (they all have similar depth indicators), high-income countries have more access to banking services for households at all income levels, which would explain the correlations with higher significance.

This is a very optimistic result, and we could question whether this holds only for those countries in which households and firms are able to acquire insurance or hedge their savings portfolios during downturns. Table 6.5 shows these same estimations for both strong and weak institution groups. The results confirm that financial depth is usually beneficial, although some evidence suggests that these direct effects are not as strong in weaker institution countries in which bankarization is lower. A second way to address this is by using a variable that better describes access to households.

Table 6.4 Strong Institutions: Controlled Fixed-Effects

	(1)	(2)	(3)	(4)	(5)	(6)
Gini ($t-1$)	0.852**	0.849**	0.843**	0.811**	0.780**	0.777**
	(39.90)	(36.58)	(27.77)	(24.13)	(22.33)	(22.26)
KAOP	0.0113	0.0101	0.0010	−0.0084	−0.00999	−0.0105*
	(1.26)	(1.02)	(0.82)	(−1.06)	(1.09)	(−1.63)
Structural Controls						
Inflation		0.000326	0.000334	0.000161	0.000106	0.000196
		(0.92)	(0.94)	(0.38)	(0.25)	(0.46)
TradeOP			−0.00213+	−0.00807*	−0.0131+	−0.0149+
			(−1.26)	(−1.90)	(−1.31)	(−1.48)
Schooling				−0.00202+	−0.00064+	−0.000968*
				(−1.27)	(−1.37)	(−1.55)
Financial Controls						
Fin. Depth					−0.00304	−0.0163*
					(−1.02)	(−1.62)
KAOP*Fin. Dept						−0.0169*
						(−1.78)
Constant	0.533**	0.547**	0.565**	0.709**	0.799**	0.756**
	(6.96)	(6.53)	(5.38)	(5.99)	(6.55)	(6.01)
Observations	734	709	707	635	599	599

t statistics in parentheses

+$p < 0.10$, * $p < 0.05$, ** $p < 0.01$

Source: Arellano-Bover.

Financial depth aggregates all credit available to the private sector, but different countries may have different rates of access among different income groups within the country. We use lending interest rates as a proxy. The underlying assumption is that a country with high credit interest rates is typically either subject to low credit screening or low credit availability, and both factors are linked to the perceived risk by the financial institutions. In this case, lower-income households are usually the most affected.

Table 6.5 show these estimations for weak and strong institution groups. Weak institutions have magnitude levels less than half that of strong institutions. For instance, level impact of or proxy for access is −0.0015 in the weak institutions subset, below a −0.0386 of strong institutions. Significance differs too. The single effect of our proxy for access preserves the negative sign but is not significant. In contrast, the point estimate for strong institutions is quite high (1 percent p-value). Similar reasoning applies to the interaction term. Our findings confirm the previous argument: in high-income countries, financial development seems to be a factor in better income distribution, whereas the correlation is significantly weaker in the opposite group.

Table 6.5   Access: Fixed-Effects Estimation, Arellano-Bond

	Weak (1)	Weak (2)	Strong (1)	Strong (2)
Gini $(t-1)$	0.716**	0.716**	0.715**	0.658**
	(43.93)	(43.92)	(17.92)	(15.53)
KAOP	−0.0155*	−0.0204*	−0.0163	−0.0184**
	(−2.10)	(−2.54)	(−1.42)	(−4.15)
Structural Controls				
Inflation	0.000221	0.000232	0.000231	0.000105
	(1.11)	(1.16)	(0.48)	(−0.21)
TradeOP	−0.0612**	−0.0614**	−0.0145+	−0.0204+
	(−11.19)	(−11.22)	(−1.264)	(−1.72)
Schooling	−0.000260**	−0.000259**	−0.000110**	−0.000153**
	(−2.82)	(−2.80)	(−2.54)	(−2.75)
Financial Controls				
LendRate	−0.00142	−0.00149	−0.000314+	−0.00386**
	(−0.42)	(−0.36)	(−1.56)	(−3.29)
KAOP*LendRate		−0.000216+		−0.00653**
		(−1.47)		(−4.06)
Constant	1.131**	1.131**	1.053**	1.217**
	(17.92)	(17.90)	(7.50)	(8.31)
Observations	921	921	492	492

t statistics in parentheses

$^+p < 0.15$, $^*p < 0.05$, $^{**}p < 0.01$

TIMING MATTERS

Capital account liberalization policies are aimed at allowing a free flow of financial resources in and out of a country. Countries running current-account deficits need to find financing for all the goods and services they purchase abroad. Whenever direct investment is not enough to cover the deficit, capital inflows may find their way in, of course assuming that the return on investment compensates for the risk. We have shown that the benefits of opening the capital account become more apparent as a country strengthens its institutions. Structural conditions such as schooling, trade openness, or financial depth also play important roles in the potential to seize these benefits. If macroeconomic conditions are considered relevant, a natural question to ask is whether capital openness is beneficial (or detrimental) exclusively during episodes of economic expansion (or contraction). This seems to be a critical question because policy makers may be tempted to restrict openness if they believe it may harm the distribution of wealth. Taking our previous findings as a starting point, the main hypothesis here is that a deep financial system will allow households of all income levels to maintain their consumption and income streams even during sudden busts. However, this is contingent on the persistence of the poor economic conditions.

To test our hypothesis, we estimate a parsimonious version of equation (3) that includes the Gini lag, the usual controls, capitalopenness policy changes, and a variable representing the cyclical behavior of GDP growth. The estimations consider the whole sample and identify booms and busts via dummy episodes. Table 6.6 shows a sequence of incremental regressions focused on booms and busts. Taking the controlled regression as the baseline, the indicator variable for booms agrees with our hypothesis. The coefficient is negative and has a 10 percent significance. On average, during booms the inequality indicators fall at a rate of 1.93 percent, which is coincidental with a larger point estimate for KAOP, which increased (in absolute terms) two times more than the baseline. Structural variables see a beneficial effect only in trade openness, and there is no significance on either inflation or schooling. Financial depth continues to be important in explaining the reduction in income inequality. In turn, busts seem to lead to important increases in inequality. The point estimate for the busts dummy is large: 0.0476. The estimate is only significant at the 15 percent level. Although this is low compared to booms, it is worth taking into consideration. Consider a scenario in which the economy slumps into a recession, say, for four years. On average, expected inequality will rise about 5 percent. To compensate for this would require an enormous increase on KAOP or financial access or any of the other structural variables, which is highly unlikely.

Policy reactions are fundamental to avoid worsening income distributions. Deciding whether a policy is going to be effective requires consideration of its timing and strength. This reminds us of the steps taken by Iceland to control the volatility of flows and massive outflows. Economists use theory to choose the best policy in terms of time and instrument, but it is only ex post that we can test whether these policies had the intended effect. In this sense, a policy change in response to a bust that only persists for a year will not be as effective as a policy change for a bust that persists for a longer period. Implementing a policy takes time, and the adaptability of agents is not immediate. Table 6.6 includes an interaction term for a change in the capitalopenness policy in estimation (3). The change of policy is a restriction on openness measured by a negative change in KAOP compared to the previous year as defined in the methodology section. As a reminder, KAOP is not needed as a control because the objective in this group of regressions is to assess restrictive policies.

Table 6.6 Booms and Busts: Fixed-Effects Estimations

	(1)	(2)	(3)	(4)
Gini ($t-1$)	0.768**	0.769**	0.768**	0.733**
	(24.03)	(24.00)	(23.98)	(24.06)
KAOP	-0.0135*	-0.0298*		
	(-1.72)	(-1.75)		
Structural Controls				
Inflation	0.00306	0.00306	0.00161	0.00310
	(0.74)	(0.74)	(0.39)	(0.75)
TradeOP	-0.0255**	-0.0246**	-0.0257**	-0.0255**
	(-2.76)	(-2.61)	(-2.72)	(-2.71)
Schooling	-0.000338+	-0.000370	-0.000740+	-0.000583+
	(-1.59)	(-1.21)	(-1.42)	(-1.33)
Financial Controls				
Fin. Depth	-0.00288+	-0.00326+	-0.00224	-0.00283
	(-1.38)	(-1.42)	(-1.15)	(-1.17)
KAOP*Fin.Depth	-0.0148*	-0.0182+	-0.0145+	-0.0183+
	(-1.74)	(-1.37)	(-1.38)	(-1.40)
Dummies				
Boom		-0.0193+		
		(-1.39)		
Bust		0.0476		
		(1.26)		
ΔKAOP*Bust ($t = -1$)				-0.0176*
				(-1.72)
ΔKAOP*Bust (t = 0)			0.0109+	0.0089*
			(1.56)	(1.76)
ΔKAOP*Bust (t = 0; $t \geq 1$)				-0.0202*
				(-1.96)
Constant	0.907**	0.903**	0.886**	0.711**
	(7.62)	(7.58)	(7.62)	(7.66)
Observations	1664	1664	1664	1664

t statistics in parentheses

$^+p < 0.10$, $^*p < 0.05$, $^{**}p < 0.01$

Note: ΔKAOP*Bust (t = -1) means that ΔKAOP happened at (t = -1) where (t = 0) is the year when the bust begins. ΔKAOP*Bust (t = 0) means that ΔKAOP happened at (t = 0) where (t = 0) is the year when the bust begins. ΔKAOP*Bust (t = 0; t ≥ 1) means that ΔKAOP happened at (t = 0) where (t = 0) is the year when the bust begins and is multiplied for all the periods the bust lasted.

Source: Arellano-Bover.

The estimation suggests that restricting the capital account during the first year of a bust has no beneficial effect on income inequality; in fact, it shows an average increase of about 1 percent, with 90 percent confidence. This reinforces the previous discussion about timing and the adaptability of agents to policy changes. By the time the first year had passed, income distribution had already been affected (on average). Anticipating the bust and applying a restrictive policy the year before the bust ($t=-1$) does have a beneficial effect, reducing inequality by about 2 percent (see estimation (4)). The estimation is significant at the 5 percent level, but it is only evidence that countries that were already processing changes to restrict openness weathered the bust better than those that did not. It does not test whether countries that reduced their openness obtain benefits during earlier booms.

Estimation (4) also give us some insight into why timing matters. Once again, a policy change in $t=0$ registers a correlation with the increase of inequality, albeit at a lower magnitude but with higher significance. The more interesting result is from the interaction between the change of policy at $t=0$ and the period over which the bust lasted. In this case, on average, the point estimate suggests a 2 percent beneficial effect with 95 percent confidence, which is in agreement with our hypothesis. A plausible story backing these findings is that a policy restricting capital openness enacted early during the bust will meet some of its goals. However, it is unlikely that it will avoid distributional effects within a year. Thus, if the same level of restriction is held in place throughout the duration of the bust, we should expect to observe an average reduction in inequality.

Could unexpected shocks be magnified through the capital account? It is common to find arguments supporting this view. We previously tested for policy reactions to an already unfavorable environment, but we have not talked about sudden shocks. The sudden crash in 2008–09 affected the most financially integrated economies first. This occurred in part because the crash started at the core of the world's largest financial system. However, contagion entered through the financial and monetary channel before affecting the rest of the real economy. Our previous estimations gave us a taste for the advantages of deepening the financial system, but the Great Recession suggests otherwise. Where's the catch? Financial depth variables are usually negatively correlated with the Gini, but the years after the crisis led to larger inequality in high-income economies. Larger economies are typically the most open, but the financial sector could not avoid hurting households because the core of the crash was the financial system. Faced with an ill financial system, the real economy contraction had few mechanisms to smooth income and consumption. Households, especially lower-income ones, could not react to protect their income streams. We hypothesize that this unexpected component is behind the steep increases in inequality since this crisis.

Table 6.7 assembles a set of estimations to study the correlation between capital openness and inequality after an unexpected shock. A monetary

Table 6.7   Unexpected Shocks (proxies): Fixed-Effects Estimations

	(1)	(2)	(3)
Gini (t-1)	0.768**	0.754**	0.768**
	(24.03)	(23.57)	(23.71)
KAOP	–0.0135*	–0.0101*	–0.0117*
	(–1.72)	(–1.84)	(–1.69)
Structural Controls			
Inflation	–0.00306	–0.00277	–0.00321
	(–0.74)	(–0.68)	(–0.77)
TradeOP	–0.0255**	–0.0237**	–0.0252**
	(–2.76)	(–2.58)	(–2.72)
Schooling	–0.000338+	–0.000262+	–0.000352
	(–1.59)	(–1.55)	(–1.20)
Financial Controls			
Fin. Depth	–0.00288+	–0.00289	–0.00376
	(–1.38)	(–0.38)	(–0.48)
KAOP*Fin.Depth	–0.0148*	0.00416	0.00408
	(–1.74)	(0.41)	(0.39)
Shocks			
R&R		0.0123	
		(1.20)	
KAOP*R&R		0.00521*	
		(1.91)	
Growth.Forecast			0.00140+
			(1.62)
KAOP*Growth.Forecast			0.0402*
			(1.89)
Constant	0.907**	0.958**	0.910**
	(7.62)	(8.04)	(7.52)
Observations	1664	1664	1664

t statistics in parentheses

+p < 0.10, * p < 0.05, ** p < 0.01

Note: ΔKAOP*Bust (t = –1) means that ΔKAOP happened at (t = –1) where (t = 0) is the year when the bust begins. ΔKAOP*Bust (t = 0) means that ΔKAOP happened at (t = 0) where (t = 0) is the year when the bust begins. ΔKAOP*Bust (t = 0; t ≥ 1) means that ΔKAOP happened at (t = 0) where (t = 0) is the year when the bust begins and is multiplied for all the periods the bust lasted.

Source: Arellano-Bond.

shock, as the one represented by RR, has been used to proxy markets performance or economic expectations. It also carries an important feature: it is based on U.S. monetary policy, which is linked directly to the financial system and is a key factor for distributional effects. We keep the direct effect KAOP may have on the Gini in the regression, but we also introduce the RR to track the marginal effect of changes in KAOP; that is,

$$\frac{dg_{i,t}}{dz_{i,t}} = \gamma_1 + \gamma_2 KAOP_{i,t} \tag{7}$$

When controlling for unexpected shocks, the correlation between KAOP and Gini weakens the magnitude of the impact. In the baseline regression (shown in table 6.6, column (1)), the point estimate was –0.0135. When controlling by our proxies for exogenous shocks, the point estimates increased their correlation with inequality growth. In particular, the RR estimation resulted in a coefficient of –0.0101, substantially below the baseline. This seems to be on the expected track: shocks are detrimental to equality. Only changes in policies that negatively shifts the Chinn-Ito index could change the direction of equation (7). Even if the KAOP change is null, the total effect will be an increase of 0.0123, but only 85 percent of the time. A similar conclusion results from estimation (3) in the same table. The interaction effects track about the same significance as (2), but the single effect is now both detrimental and significant at 10 percent. In summary, unanticipated deviations from growth forecasts may induce increases in inequality by nullifying any positive spillover of opening the capital account further. In both cases, we did find weak statistical evidence to argue a possible conditional effect γ_2, but only with p-values between 10 percent and 5 percent.

Overall the estimations broadly support our hypothesis. First, global exogenous shocks, such as the RR monetary shocks, increase the level of inequality in income distribution. Moreover, the size of the shock plays an important role by increasing income inequality through a direct effect and as a magnifier through KAOP. The RR shock is linked to the development level of the financial system. We would expect its effect on inequality to be larger in lower- and middle-income countries than in high-income countries. Nonetheless, there was no strong evidence to support this assumption. Under these circumstances, the financial system is the channel that acts as a magnifier or shock. Therefore, opening the capital account further will not provide the positive returns it did previously. Second, whenever an unusual economic performance is correlated with global economic cycles, the negative effects on income distribution will magnify. This is consistent with the boom-bust discussion: capital openness is unambiguously worse for income equality during a bust. As atypical economic performances depart from global cycles, capital account openness correlates negatively with inequality, suggesting the existence of a magnifying effect whenever the global economies are the main cause of an atypical event.

What lessons can we extract? The rationale behind policies that restrict capital openness have been discussed. Controls on capital account transactions represent a country's attempt to shield itself from risks associated with fluctuations in international capital flows. Capital controls take on special circumstances in the context of a fixed exchange-rate regime. In a country with a fragile banking system, allowing households to invest abroad freely could precipitate an exodus of domestic savings and jeopardize the banking system's viability. Likewise, short-term capital inflows can be quickly reversed when a country is hit with an adverse macroeconomic shock, thereby amplifying its macroeconomic effect. In theory, capital account liberalization should allow for more efficient global allocation of capital from capitalrich industrial countries to capitalpoor developing economies. This should have widespread benefits by providing a higher rate of return on people's savings in industrial countries and by increasing growth, employment opportunities, and living standards in developing countries. Access to capital markets should allow countries to "insure" themselves to some extent against fluctuations in their national incomes so national consumption levels are relatively less volatile. Since good and bad times often are not synchronized across countries, capital flows can, to some extent, offset volatility between countries.

As we have seen, the evidence is not quite as compelling as the theory. Middle-income countries that have liberalized their capital accounts typically have had questionable improvements in inequality. Our findings indicate that this is associated with swings in the domestic and world economy, which magnify the negative effects. Is there any evidence of the value of closing the external accounts? We tested whether restrictive measures on the capital account were significantly followed by periods of lower inequality (table 6.7). The coefficients broadly kept the same patterns as the baseline regression. However, to support a "closing policy" requires more thought. The key element is when the policy is enacted and the period of time that it will affect the markets. Evidence suggest that policies restraining openness in the year of a bust that lasts about a year are ineffective in mitigating distributional effects. However, these policies might turn the balance favorably if the bust persists.

The only way to avoid distributional negative effects in busts is to anticipate them, which is not easy to do. If no policy changes occur, unexpected shocks will be detrimental, especially when the financial system is affected. So should a country close, open, or settle on a mixture of the two? It seems that the right direction is to respond with an active mechanism. Certainly, timing matters because restricting the capital account to face a shock reduces the negative effects on income distribution when the event lasts more than a year. However, evidence that policies should be focused on the financial account are inconclusive. Governments usually can expand their social spending during recovery periods (assuming there is a certain level of public spending efficiency). Our analysis opens the door to explore the role of safety nets as co-policy instruments to mitigate the negative effects during downturns.

6. CONCLUSIONS

The idea that capital account liberalization may have negative effects on growth through financial instability in emerging markets is widely accepted. Moreover, the links between economic and financial distress and income inequality have frequently been revisited, especially in the last decade. In this paper, we attempt to build upon these two ideas and examine the extent to which capital account liberalization is associated with income inequality. We conclude that capital openness is associated with a decrease in inequality when a country transitions into a higher income group, in which stronger institutions are in place. Our findings offer supportive evidence that financial development is key to extending the benefits of the capital account liberalization to all income levels. Financial development that enables households to access smooth consumption and income streams is important. However, unexpected shocks, especially those affecting the financial channels, require active policy responses to reduce their detrimental impact on income distribution.

We have demonstrated the differential impacts of capital account liberalization on inequality during periods of economic expansion and contraction. The impact of financial liberalization on income inequality is positive during normal economic times, whereas during contractions, capital account liberalization appears to significantly increase income inequality. Strong institutions and financial depth are key factors in limited the extent of the negative impacts. One possible reason behind this is that financial services may provide households with better risk-sharing and the possibility of shielding themselves against economic swings. Furthermore, our findings suggest that when a country decides to implement regulations to slow and steer financial flows during atypical economic events, the detrimental effects on income distributions diminish. These findings offer support for countercyclical, temporary, and flexible "speed bumps" during sudden stops or similar atypical events. However, combining capital account measures with other social redistributive policies may provide more favorable results than using a narrower focus.

Finally, in developing countries with weak institutions, the absence of ex ante policies means that capital account liberalization will probably increase income inequality during periods of economic contraction. To ensure dignifying living conditions, developing countries must implement additional protective measures for disadvantaged groups such as what is being tried in Latin America and the Caribbean. Further work is needed to determine whether safety nets (especially conditioned cash transfers) are behind these observed differences and whether liberalization should be synchronized with social safety net coverage.

We have considered two kinds of policies. One type of policy is geared toward seizing the positive spillovers of openness during economic expansion, albeit these policies must also act as safety nets during contractions. Second, our findings support resorting capital restrictions during busts, especially if social safety nets have low coverage or are nonexistent. For developing countries with weak institutions, capital account liberalization will likely increase income inequality in the absence of safety net policies. To ensure dignified living conditions for all, additional protective measures are necessary for these disadvantaged groups.

APPENDIX: COUNTRIES IN THE SAMPLE

Table A1 shows all countries by income group. Some countries (such as Chile) appear in two groups because the income criteria we used (section 3) allow countries to transition between income groups.

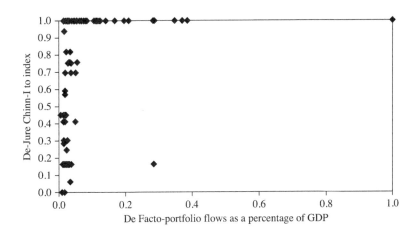

Figure A1   De facto and de jure measures of portfolio flows.

Table A1 Income Groups

High Income	Middle Income		Low Income	
Australia	Albania	Mongolia	Afghanistan	Nepal
Austria	Algeria	Morocco	Albania	Nicaragua
Belgium	Armenia	Namibia	Armenia	Niger
Canada	Azerbaijan	Nigeria	Azerbaijan	Nigeria
Chile	Barbados	Panama	Bangladesh	Pakistan
Croatia	Belarus	Paraguay	Benin	Papua New
Cyprus	Belize	Peru	Bhutan	Guinea
Czech	Bhutan	Philippines	Bolivia	Philippines
Republic	Bolivia	Poland	Bosnia and	Rwanda
Denmark	Bosnia and	Russia	Herzegovina	Senegal
Estonia	Herzegovina	Seychelles	Burkina Faso	Sierra Leone
Finland	Botswana	Slovakia	Burundi	Sri Lanka
France	Brazil	Slovenia	Cambodia	Tajikistan
Germany	Bulgaria	South Africa	Cameroon	Tanzania
Greece	Chile	Sri Lanka	Central African	Togo
Hong Kong	China	St. Lucia	Republic	Turkmenistan
Hungary	Colombia	Suriname	Chad	Uganda
Iceland	Costa Rica	Swaziland	China	Ukraine
Ireland	Croatia	Thailand	Comoros	Uzbekistan
Israel	Czech Republic	Trinidad and	Cote d'Ivoire	Vietnam
Italy	Dominican	Tobago	Djibouti	Zambia
Japan	Republic	Tunisia	El Salvador	Zimbabwe
Kazakhstan	Ecuador	Turkey	Ethiopia	
Latvia	El Salvador	Turkmenistan	Gambia	
Lithuania	Estonia	Ukraine	Georgia	
Malaysia	Fiji	Uruguay	Ghana	
Malta	Georgia	Venezuela	Guinea	
Netherlands	Guatemala		Guinea-Bissau	
New Zealand	Hungary		Guyana	
Norway	Indonesia		Haiti	
Poland	Iran		Honduras	
Portugal	Israel		India	
Russia	Jamaica		Indonesia	
Seychelles	Jordan		Kenya	
Singapore	Kazakhstan		Kyrgyz Republic	
Slovak	Latvia		Lesotho	
Republic	Lebanon		Madagascar	
Slovenia	Lithuania		Malawi	
Spain	Macedonia		Mali	
Sweden	Malaysia		Mauritania	
Switzerland	Maldives		Moldova	
Trinidad and	Mauritius		Mongolia	
Tobago	Mexico		Morocco	
United	Moldova		Mozambique	
Kingdom				
United States				

Table A2   Summary Statistics for Entire Sample

Variable	Mean	Std. Dev.	Observations
KA-Uribe	0.354	0.346	1469
KAOP	0.538	0.369	2556
Gini	42.099	7.511	2676
RR Shocks	0.028	0.205	2676
Inflation	28.466	244.945	2418
De Facto	0.042	0.448	2533
Private Credit to GDP	49.480	47.170	2523
School Enrollment	76.862	31.275	2045
Trade	83.051	52.101	2623
Age dependency	63.834	18.446	2676
Real GDP growth	3.836	6.622	4460

Table A3   Summary Statistics for Low Income Countries

Variable	Mean	Std. Dev.	Observations
KA-Uribe	0.556	0.349	329
KAOP	0.318	0.290	840
Gini	43.314	7.109	885
RR Shocks	0.036	0.210	885
Inflation	19.911	143.501	761
De Facto	−0.020	0.254	828
Private Credit to GDP	19.703	18.232	816
School Enrollment	43.646	27.621	553
Trade	70.071	36.890	860
Age dependency	81.689	16.100	885
Real GDP growth	4.155	5.828	859

Table A4   Summary Statistics for Middle Income Countries

Variable	Mean	Std. Dev.	Observations
KA-Uribe	0.436	0.346	562
KAOP	0.488	0.334	951
Gini	43.713	8.406	1003
RR Shocks	0.027	0.205	1003
Inflation	47.104	347.036	903
De Facto	0.024	0.311	954
Private Credit to GDP	41.440	30.618	974
School Enrollment	76.972	17.653	788
Trade	84.387	37.991	994
Age dependency	58.370	12.414	1003
Real GDP growth	4.098	4.824	979

Table A5   Summary Statistics for High Income Countries

Variable	Mean	Std. Dev.	Observations
KA-Uribe	0.160	0.224	578
KAOP	0.841	0.276	765
Gini	38.681	5.326	788
RR Shocks	0.020	0.198	788
Inflation	14.778	163.882	754
De Facto	0.132	0.686	751
Private Credit to GDP	93.313	55.238	733
School Enrollment	102.832	18.781	704
Trade	95.839	74.326	769
Age dependency	50.736	10.043	788
Real GDP growth	2.712	3.678	776

NOTES

1. The concept of capital flow liberalization is used in this paper interchangeably with capital account liberalization and financial account liberalization.

2. The data were available in flows.

3. These measures usually suffer from endogeneity and may not reflect changes induced by policies.

4. A scatterplot of Chinn-Ito versus a de facto measure (see figure A1 in the chapter appendix) provides evidence for this argument.

5. We used GDP per capita, PPP, and constant 2011 international dollars from the World Bank.

6. According to the U.S. NBER, the great recession started in December 2007. Given that the panel contains annual data, we marked 2008 as the start of the recession.

7. This is true except for the low- and middle-income groups during 1990–1999, when the relationship was practically nonexistent.

8. This hold true except for middle-income countries from 2008 to 2013.

9. That is, an economy performing slower than was expected.

10. China's GDP and lagged GDP are only included from 2004 on.

11. We follow Furceri (2015), using the logarithm of the Gini index as it behaves more like a normally distributed variable and thus is more amenable for an ordinary least squares estimation.

12. Bumman and Lensink (2016) include a complete discussion on the selection of these variables.

13. We did not find statistical support for the correlations in low-income countries.

14. Tables A2 through A5 in the chapter appendix have summary statistic tables per income group

15. Although not the core of the discussion here, it is important to keep in mind that as countries open to trade schooling improves. This would be compatible with the increasing job opportunities due to trade.

16. Once again, this could be related to the fact that these countries usually are more capital intensive and from the perspective of the sources of jobs it generates

might have a more limited penetration in the lower percentiles. This is just a possibility because trade of labor-intensive goods should reduce or keep certain prices relatively stable, potentially helping low-income households.

17. It is important to note that low-income countries tend to be less unequal and receive smaller capital flows relative to other income groups.

REFERENCES

Albanesi, Stefania. 2007. "Inflation and Inequality." *Journal of Monetary Economics* 54 (4): 1088–1114.

Alesina, Alberto, and Roberto Perotti. 1996. "Income Distribution, Political Instability, and Investment." *European Economic Review* 40 (6): 1203–28.

Anderson, Jonathan. 2005. "Capital Account Controls and Liberalization: Lessons for India and China." In *India's and China's Recent Experience with Reform and Growth*, ed. Wanda Tseng and David Cowen, 264–74. New York: Palgrave Macmillan.

Bird, Mike. 2016. "The Hottest Idea in Finance: Capital Controls are Good." *Wall Street Journal*, February 4. https://www.wsj.com/articles/the-hottest-idea-in-finance-capitalcontrols-are-good-1454581800.

Bumann, Silke, and Robert Lensink. 2016. "Capital Account Liberalization and Income Inequality." *Journal of International Money and Finance* 61: 143–62.

Chinn, Menzie D., and Hiro Ito. 2008. "A New Measure of Financial Openness." *Journal of Comparative Policy Analysis* 10 (3): 309–22.

Coibion, Olivier, Yuriy Gorodnichenko, Lorenz Kueng, and John Silvia. 2012. "Innocent Bystanders? Monetary Policy and Inequality in the U.S." IMF Working Paper WP/12/199.

Das, Mitali, and Sanket Mohapatra. 2003. "Income Inequality: the Aftermath of Stock Market Liberalization in Emerging Markets." *Journal of Empirical Finance* 10 (1): 217–48.

Fernández, Andrés, Michael W. Klein, Alessandro Rebucci, Martin Schindler, and Martin Uribe. 2015. "Capital Control Measures: A New Dataset." IMF Working Paper WP/15/80.

Furceri, Davide, and Prakash Loungani. 2015. "Capital Account Liberalization and Inequality." IMF Working Paper WP/15/243.

Goldin, Claudia, and Lawrence F. Katz. 2007. "Long-Run Changes in the U.S. Wage Structure: Narrowing, Widening, Polarizing." *Brookings Papers on Economic Activity* 38 (2): 135–68.

Gourinchas, Pierre-Olivier, and Olivier Jeanne. 2006. "The Elusive Gains from International Financial Integration." *Review of Economic Studies* 73 (3): 715–41.

Harrison, Ann E. 2002. "Has Globalization Eroded Labor's Share? Some Cross-Country Evidence." Unpublished manuscript. http://www.econ.fea.usp.br/gilberto/eae0504/Harrison_Glob_Labor_Share_2002.pdf/.

Hellmann, Thomas F., Kevin C. Murdock, and Joseph E. Stiglitz. 2000. "Liberalization, Moral Hazard in Banking, and Prudential Regulation: Are Capital Requirements Enough?" *American Economic Review* 90: 147–65.

Henry, Peter B. 2006. "Capital Account Liberalization: Theory, Evidence, and Speculation." National Bureau of Economic Research Working Paper No. 12698.

Jeanne, Olivier, Arvind Subramanian, and John Williamson 2012. *Who Needs an Open Capital Account?* Washington, DC: Peterson Institute for International Economics.

Klein, Michael W., and Giovanni P. Olivei. 2008. "Capital Account Liberalization, Financial Depth, and Economic Growth." *Journal of International Money and Finance* 27 (6): 861–75.

Lane, Philip R., and Gian M. Milesi-Ferretti. 2007. "The External Wealth of Nations Mark II: Revised and Extended Estimates of Foreign Assets and Liabilities, 1970–2004." *Journal of International Economics* 73 (2): 223–50.

Larrain, Mauricio. 2014. "Capital Account Opening and Wage Inequality." *The Review of Financial Studies* 28 (6): 1555–87.

McKinnon, Ronald I., and Huw Pill. 1996. "Credible Liberalizations and International Capital Flows: The Overborrowing Syndrome." In *Financial Deregulation and Integration in East Asia, NBER-EASE*, vol. 5, ed. Takatoshi Ito and Anne O. Krueger, 7–50. Chicago, IL: University of Chicago Press.

Prasad, Eswar S., and Raghuram Rajan. 2008. "A Pragmatic Approach to Capital Account Liberalization." *Journal of Economic Perspectives* 22 (3): 149–72.

Quinn, Dennis. 1997. "The Correlates of Change in International Financial Regulation." *American Political Science Review* 91 (3): 531–51.

Quinn, Dennis, Martin Schindler, and A. Maria Toyoda. 2011. "Assessing Measures of Financial Openness and Integration." *IMF Economic Review* 59 (3): 488–522.

Quinn, Dennis P. 2003. "Capital Account Liberalization and Financial Globalization, 1890–1999: A Synoptic View." *International Journal of Finance & Economics* 8 (3): 189–204.

Romer, Christina D., and David H. Romer. 2004. "A New Measure of Monetary Shocks: Derivation and Implications." *American Economic Review* 94 (4): 1055–84.

Schindler, Martin. 2009. "Measuring Financial Integration: A New Data Set." IMF Staff Papers, Palgrave Macmillan 56 (1): 222–38.

Solt, Frederick. 2016. "The Standardized World Income Inequality Database." *Social Science Quarterly* 97 (5): 1267–81.

CHAPTER 7

Intellectual Property

A REGULATORY CONSTRAINT TO REDRESS INEQUALITIES

Carlos M. Correa

1. INTRODUCTION

In the last two decades, a steady increase in the protection of intellectual property (IP) has taken place in both developed and developing countries. In developed countries, this increase has been driven by internal demands from various industries (namely pharmaceuticals, entertainment, computer programs and semiconductors), whereas in developing countries, the driving force has been coercion and pressure exerted by foreign governments and industries rather than being the result of local demands (Sell 2007).

One of the principal tools employed to obtain increases in the levels of IP protection in developing countries has been the inclusion of detailed chapters on the subject in free trade agreements (FTAs) in exchange for the promise—often unrealized—of increased foreign direct investment and technology transfer[1] as well as an improved trade balance with the developed countries' partners in the FTAs.[2] The IP provisions in FTAs may contribute to an increase in inequality both between and within countries because they limit the capacity of governments to regulate commercial conduct that may have adverse economic and social effects. The Max Planck Institute for Intellectual Property and Competition Law (MPI) issued a set of principles that includes the following caution:

> Continuous extension of IP protection and enforcement increases the potential for law and policy conflicts with other rules of international law that aim to protect public health, the environment, biological diversity, food security, access to knowledge and human rights. At the same time, such extension often counters, rather than facilitates, the core IP goal of promoting innovation and creativity. (Principles for Intellectual Property Provisions in Bilateral and Regional Agreements, 2015)

IP provisions in FTAs may have implications for a wide range of public policy areas. For instance, anticircumvention and technological protection measures in the field of copyright may drastically reduce the scope of generally admissible exceptions, such as fair use (Samuelson, Reichman, and Dinwoodie 2008). The obligation to join the International Union for the Protection of New Varieties of Plants (UPOV) as revised in 1991 introduced undesirable rigidities in the seed supply systems, particularly by banning farmers' practices of saving and exchanging seeds (Correa 2015). A vast academic literature has addressed the "flexibilities" available under the Agreement on Trade-Related Aspects of Intellectual Property Rights (TRIPS) and the negative impact of FTAs in relation to access to medicines (Velasquez, Correa, and Seuba 2012). Several UN documents have also addressed this impact (UNAIDS 2012). For example, the Special Rapporteur on the Right of Everyone to the Enjoyment of the Highest Attainable Standard to Physical and Mental Health noted that the TRIPS agreement and FTAs have had an adverse impact on prices and availability of medicines, making it difficult for countries to comply with their obligations to respect, protect, and fully implement the right to health. It has recommended that developing countries and least developed countries (LDCs) review their laws and policies and amend them to make full use of the flexibilities available to them (United Nations 2009). UNDP and UNAIDS have argued:

> Countries at minimum should avoid entering into FTAs that contain TRIPS-plus obligations that can impact on pharmaceuticals price or availability. Where countries have undertaken TRIPS-plus commitments, all efforts should be made to mitigate the negative impact of these commitments on access to treatment by using to the fullest extent possible, remaining public health related flexibilities available. (2012)

Goal 10 of the Sustainable Development Goals adopted by United Nations Development Programme in 2015 is to reduce "inequality within and among countries." In defining this goal, the UN members recognized that despite some reduction in income inequality between countries, large disparities remain in "access to health and education services and other assets." Moreover, inequality within countries has risen.

In this paper, I explore the extent to which the recommendation to use "to the fullest extent possible, remaining public health related flexibilities available" may be effectively implemented in the context of FTAs. Bilateral and regional FTAs do limit the policy space of governments to address national inequalities. The basic question addressed in this paper is whether contracting parties to FTAs can mitigate their adverse effects through interpretation and implementing regulations. I first present a possible taxonomy of IP obligations ensuing from FTAs and the room for maneuver they leave to contracting parties. Second, I consider the so-called certification process unilaterally undertaken by the U.S. government. Third, I describe the interpretative framework for obligations regarding IP. Finally, I provide examples of how FTA's provisions may be interpreted that would reduce their likely negative impact on equality for FTA's contracting parties, particularly in developing countries. The examples address two areas of significant relevance for access to medicines and public health: data exclusivity and patent/drug approval "linkage" provisions.

2. TAXONOMY OF IP OBLIGATIONS

A significant number of countries have entered into FTAs that generally confirm the applicability of the TRIPS agreement's obligations regarding IP and incorporate additional obligations not provided for in that agreement. As a result, a contracting party to an FTA that includes a specific IP chapter is subject to standards that may be classified and that takes their relationship with the TRIPS agreement into account. The TRIPS agreement enforcement mechanism has become the most important international treaty in the area of IP.[3] The IP provisions in FTAs may be placed in the following categories.

TRIPS-minimum: National laws must implement the minimum standards of protection provided for in relation to the availability and enforcement of IP rights, as contained in the TRIPS agreement (article 1.1). For instance, article 34 reads that the term of protection for patents "shall not end before the expiration of a period of twenty years counted from the filing date." This means that patents might be granted for a term different from twenty years but not shorter than this period.

TRIPS-plus: Most of the provisions contained in FTAs belong to this category. TRIPS-plus provisions expand existing obligations under the TRIPS agreement by either extending the term of protection of patents to compensate for delays in regulatory approvals, applying border measures to exports (the TRIPS agreement mandates them for imports), or obliging the contracting parties to protect new uses or methods/processes relating to a known product (article 18.37.2 of the Trans-Pacific Partnership (TPP)). TRIPS-plus provisions also restrict the use of certain safeguards or "flexibilities," such as when parallel imports (such as in the U.S.-Morocco FTA) or the grounds to grant compulsory licenses are restricted (such as in the U.S.-Jordan FTA).

TRIPS-extra: This category contains the TRIPS-plus provisions but also introduces issues not addressed by the TRIPS agreement, such as the liability of Internet service providers (Lerman 2015), the settlement of domain name disputes (Kennedy 2015), and data exclusivity for biological products as provided for in the TPP. A further example is the so-called linkage between drug registration and patent protection, which is absent from the TRIPS agreement. Under linkage provisions, national health authorities are bound to refuse marketing approval to a generic version of a product if a patent thereon is in force without the consent or acquiescence of the patent owner. Interestingly, the obligation imposed on those authorities in some U.S. FTAs sets a standard higher than the one applicable in the United States. The Food and Drug Administration (FDA) is only required to inform patent holders about generic producers' applications; patent holders must take direct responsibility to prevent marketing approval through judicial procedures.[4]

TRIPS ceilings: Although World Trade Organization (WTO) members have long believed that they may increase the level of IP protection at their discretion, the broader protection that may be granted in accordance with article 1.1 of the TRIPS agreement is subject to the proviso that "such protection does not contravene the provisions of this Agreement." Provisions in some TRIPS-plus agreements may impede legitimate trade or erode safeguards recognized in favor of users of IP rights. Examples of these "ceilings" are the conditions established for seizure of goods in transit (Baker 2012), the idea/expression dichotomy in article 9.2 of the TRIPS agreement, and the citation right found in article 10 (2) of the Berne Convention (Grosse Ruse-Khan and Kur 2008). Some FTAs contain a number of provisions that may fall under this category.

TRIPS-minus: Some FTAs contain provisions that may be deemed below the TRIPS standards. For instance, the TRIPS agreement includes a nondiscrimination clause that applies in all fields of patented technologies (article 27.1). However, many FTAs do not reproduce this clause[5] and discriminate in favor of pharmaceutical companies. For instance, the Dominican Republic-Central America FTA (CAFTA-DR) requires a "restoration of the patent term to compensate the patent owner for unreasonable curtailment of the effective patent term resulting from the marketing approval" with respect to pharmaceutical products only (article 15.9.6(b)).[6] Other regulated products (such as agrochemicals) do not benefit from this extension.

Clearly, most of the provisions in FTAs correspond to the categories of TRIPS-plus and TRIPS-extra. The standards contained in the TRIPS agreement forced a large number of developing countries to introduce massive changes in their IP legislation. The prescribed standards of IP protection, which are generally inadequate for the level of development of those countries, have the potential to dramatically increase inequalities, particularly in the area of public health. First, implementation of the TRIPS agreement exacerbates the lack of access to medicines, particularly in low- and middle-income countries.[7] Second, it does not contribute to solving the problem of lack of sufficient R&D on the diseases prevailing in developing countries (Pedrique et al. 2013) because large pharmaceutical companies continued to focus on commercially attractive treatments (Correa 2016). Third, no evidence shows that higher standards of IP protection have led to increased technology or foreign investment flows generally or in relation to particular sectors, such as pharmaceuticals.[8]

The FTAs' expanded and tightened standards of IP protection can only aggravate the inequalities created by the "one-fits-all" model established under the TRIPS agreement. Although these standards are unlikely to have a significant impact on enhancing local innovation,[9] technology transfer, and foreign (or local) investment, rights holders may be able to block competition and to charge high prices in monopolistically controlled markets. This may lead to particularly serious effects in the area of public health (Abbott 2012) where unsustainably high prices have become an issue of global concern ('tHoen 2016, 107). During the past fifteen years, the average price of cancer drugs in the United States has increased five- to tenfold, to more than $120,000 by 2014 (Kantarjian 2015). Fifteen cancer drugs introduced in the past five years cost more than $120,000 a year; a cholesterol-lowering treatment for those with a certain rare genetic disorder costs $311,000 a year; a cystic fibrosis medicine developed partly with funding from a charity costs $300,000 annually, and the examples go on (Langreth 2014). Similar trends toward unsustainable prices are found in developing countries whenever generic competition is delayed or blocked ('tHoen 2016).

3. THE "CERTIFICATION" PROCESS

The conclusion of an FTA with TRIPS-plus and TRIPS-extra provisions often does not put an end to the demands for further expansion and strengthening of IP rights: "what appears to be the experience of countries that have negotiated FTAs is that the process of negotiations does

not conclude with the signing of the agreement" (Roffe 2007). U.S. partners, in particular, may be forced to make additional concessions in the
process of the so-called certification required under U.S. law. This process
is explained by the International Trade Administration as follows:

> Before an FTA enters into force, U.S. legislation approving the Agreement
> requires that the President determine that the FTA partner has taken mea-
> sures to bring it into compliance with its FTA obligations as of day one of
> the agreement. The Office of the U.S. Trade Representative (USTR) and
> other agencies . . . review the relevant laws, regulations, and administra-
> tive practices (measures) of the FTA partner.
>
> The FTA partner is advised of any shortcomings in its laws and other
> measures, and the Administration consults with the FTA partner on the
> issue. If requested, assistance is provided to help a trading partner imple-
> ment its commitments. (2007)

This process is based on unilateral judgments by the U.S. government
and is used as a mechanism to put pressure on trade partners (often eager
to show their citizens that they have successfully concluded an FTA with
the United States) to limit any gaps or flexibilities that they may have
preserved under the signed FTA. It has been noted in this regard that:

> The U.S. has faced criticism for putting forward expectations for domestic
> reforms from their negotiating partners that go beyond the actual FTA
> text, and for using the implementation process as a vehicle to continue the
> negotiation of the final agreement. Indeed, Members of Congress criti-
> cized the USTR in the case of the U.S.-CAFTA-DR for: expanding the
> scope of what is defined as a new product that is subject to data protection
> rules; increasing the regulatory requirements for generic entry into the
> market; and allowing for patent or data protection of a new application of
> an existing product. (Vivas-Eugui and von Braun 2016)

The implementation of the U.S.-Peru FTA provides another telling
example of the reduction of the policy space kept in the FTA. This example
is particularly informative because Peru (as well Colombia and Panama)
benefited in their negotiations with the United States from a bipartisan
agreement reached in June 2007 between the Republican administration
and Democratic leaders in the U.S. Congress to mitigate FTA's obligations
relating to public health.[10] Despite the room opened by this agreement,
in the process of implementing the IP chapter, broader obligations were
introduced in relation to data exclusivity that expanded the rights conferred to the "originator" pharmaceutical companies (Roca 2009).

In the context of the TPP negotiations, those companies expressed their dissatisfaction with regard to the term of protection of data exclusivity for biologicals (five to eight years) agreed upon by the U.S. government. The industry's ambition was to impose on all TPP contracting parties a twelve-year period of exclusivity as recognized under U.S. law (Biologics Price Competition and Innovation Act). In response to the criticism received, the USTR implicitly referred to the certification process as a means to fulfill industry's desires, signaling that they were listening to calls from business groups and some members of Congress to address their complaints with TPP through the way it is implemented, as well as other avenues. "At this stage, we're talking with stakeholders, members of Congress, and we're looking at the various stages that TPP goes through, including, once it's approved, there's a period of time between approval and entry into force, to look at how it's implemented."[11] The certification process is likely to increase the imbalance in rights and obligations inherent to FTAs' provisions on IP and thereby deepen the inequality gap between developed and developing countries' partners, as well as within the latter. For this reason, the Max Planck Institute principles referred to earlier stated that "IP-demanding countries should not employ unilateral certification or other assessment processes in order to influence the implementation of IP obligations."[12]

In addition to the certification process, it is worth noting that the United States has attempted to further increase the levels of protection accorded in FTAs' partners through unilateral pressures, such as those exerted through the USTR reports and the classification of countries in the "watch lists" elaborated under the Special Section 301 of the U.S. Trade Act. For example, Chile implemented the "linkage" obligation established by the FTA with the United States through the provision of information to the patent owner about a third party intending to commercialize a product with similar characteristics to one already patented.[13] The U.S. government viewed this implementation as insufficient to comply with the FTA. The USTR Report on Special Section 301 keeps Chile on the "Priority Watch List" and refers to "linkage" as one of the "longstanding IPR issues under the United States-Chile Free Trade Agreement" and "urges Chile to implement an effective system for addressing patent issues expeditiously in connection with applications to market pharmaceutical products" (2016, 49). Chile's stand on this issue is rather exceptional; generally, FTAs' partners implement the TRIPS-plus and TRIPS-extra obligation through reforms of national laws to avoid the threat of retaliations under the FTAs' dispute settlement provisions.[14]

4. THE INTERPRETATIVE FRAMEWORK

FTAs reproduce some TRIPS provisions and include additional provisions on IP. An important question is under which principles those provisions are to be interpreted and, particularly, whether there are interpretative frameworks that may mitigate the inequality generated by FTA rules.

A. TRIPS AGREEMENT

The TRIPS agreement contains specific obligations that may affect access to medicines (notably, the requirement to grant patents in all fields of technology) but allows WTO members to introduce some measures, such as the "Bolar exception," compulsory licenses, and parallel imports, that may attenuate to some extent the inequalities generated by the high prices of patented medicines (Correa 2017; Calboli and Lee 2016). In addition, the Preamble and articles 7 and 8 of the TRIPS agreement provide elements for the interpretation of its provisions and other measures that governments may adopt to pursue public policy objectives. Also important, the Doha Declaration on the TRIPS Agreement and Public Health (hereinafter "the Doha Declaration"),[15] adopted in 2001, confirmed the right to adopt measures to protect public health (Correa and Matthews 2011).

The Preamble to the TRIPS agreement states that "measures and procedures to enforce intellectual property rights" should not themselves "become barriers to legitimate trade." It also recognizes "the underlying public policy objectives of national systems for the protection of intellectual property rights including developmental and technological objectives." WTO panels and the Appellate Body have relied on several occasions on the Preamble in WTO disputes relating to alleged violations of the TRIPS agreement, particularly to define its object and purpose (Yusuf 2016).

Article 7 of the TRIPS agreement, adopted on the basis of a proposal originally submitted by developing countries,[16] reflects the prevailing justification for granting IPRs in technology-related fields as a tool for the promotion of innovation, but also the developing countries' concerns about shortcomings in the transfer and dissemination of technology and, more generally, on the "balance of rights and obligations" necessary to ensure that intellectual property works "to the mutual advantage of producers and users of technological knowledge and in a manner conducive to social and economic welfare." The inclusion of article 7 in Part I of the TRIPS agreement, and not in the Preamble, suggests that it is not a mere hortatory provision. Its applicability to interpret the agreement's provisions has been reinforced by the explicit reference made to the objectives and principles in the Doha Declaration.[17]

Article 8 of the TRIPS agreement is also an important provision for framing national laws that respond to particular public health and other public interests. It makes clear that measures may be adopted to prevent or remedy abuses of intellectual property rights.

Although article 7 has specific wording on the objectives of the TRIPS agreement and is incorporated into its normative part, it has been mentioned less frequently by WTO panels and the Appellate Body, perhaps because most disputes have taken place among developed countries (Yusuf 2016). However, the panel report in *Canada–Patent Protection for Pharmaceutical Products* (relating to the so-called Bolar exception) states the following:

> Obviously, the exact scope of Article 30's authority will depend on the specific meaning given to its limiting conditions. The words of those conditions must be examined with particular care on this point. Both the goals and the limitations stated in Articles 7 and 8.1 must obviously be borne in mind when doing so as well as those of other provisions of the TRIPS Agreement which indicate its object and purposes.[18]

In summary, article 7 (jointly with article 8) of the TRIPS agreement provides important elements for the interpretation and implementation of the rights and obligations under the agreement with a view toward respecting WTO members' policy space to pursue their own public policy objectives.

B. FTAs' PROVISIONS

Some FTAs contain wording inspired or reflecting articles 7 and 8 of the TRIPS agreement. The FTA between the EU and Colombia, for instance, states the following:

> The Parties recognize the need to maintain a balance between the rights of intellectual property holders and the interest of the public, particularly regarding education, culture, research, public health, food security, environment, access to information and technology transfer (article 196.3).[19]

Moreover, the TPP[20] reproduces in articles 18.2 and 18.3, *mutatis mutandis*, the provisions of articles 7 and 8 of the TRIPS agreement, thereby suggesting that the same interpretive framework would apply.

FTAs oblige the contracting parties to comply with the obligations specifically prescribed by them but also with those under the TRIPS agreement. Therefore, the Preamble and articles 7 and 8 of the TRIPS agreement apply even if not explicitly mentioned in the FTA. As a result, a country party to an FTA may invoke, under the FTA dispute-settlement system, application of the elements contained in the Preamble and article 7 and 8 in relation to both obligations directly imposed by the TRIPS agreement as well as to any TRIPS-plus obligation established by the FTA.

The adoption of the Doha Declaration created the expectation that it could serve as a barrier against the ratcheting up of IP protection through FTAs and other processes (such as the accession to WTO). Many FTAs contain specific references recognizing the "principles"[21] or the "importance"[22] of the Doha Declaration. Although it has not prevented developed countries from imposing higher levels of IP protection for pharmaceuticals, it may be credited with some effects, notably the inclusion of no limitations to the grounds for granting compulsory licenses of patents, as provided for in pre-Doha Declaration FTAs (Correa and Matthews 2011). In the case of the U.S. FTAs with Peru, Colombia, and Panama, notwithstanding the requirements regarding data exclusivity, the FTAs provide that "a Party may take measures to protect public health in accordance with" the Doha Declaration.[23] The extent to which this provision may lessen the requirement for data protection is unclear. The Doha Declaration confirms certain "flexibilities" in the TRIPS agreement, but it does not create exceptions nor does it refer to the issue of data protection. However, this may facilitate "a pro-public health interpretation of the provisions on regulated products, as well as other sections of the FTA" (Roffe and Vivas-Eugui 2007).

The provisions in FTAs referring to the TRIPS objectives and principles and references to the Doha Declaration suggest that these agreements have generally preserved some (limited) space for contracting parties to protect their public interests, notably in the area of public health. The interpretation of the TRIPS-plus provisions contained in such agreements should be conducted with reference to the TRIPS agreement and subsequent developments under the Doha Declaration (Xiong 2012).

It must be borne in mind, however, that the effect of articles 7 and 8 (and the Doha Declaration) in interpreting the obligations under an FTA may be limited to situations in which the content or scope of the established obligations are ambiguous. They may not help to overcome or mitigate clearly worded TRIPS-plus obligations. A deliberate objective of FTAs as proposed by developed countries has been to increase IP protection beyond the levels required by the TRIPS agreement. Disputes settlement bodies under FTAs may give primacy to IP rules in case of conflict with national measures adopted pursuant to public interests such as the protection of public health or the environment (Correa 2013a). Notwithstanding that the interpretive rules of the Vienna Convention on the Law of Treaties (VCLT) may be applied under the FTAs dispute settlement systems,[24] such bodies may be prone to expansive interpretations of the adopted obligations, for instance, through the principle of "evolutionary interpretation" (Bjorge 2014) based on new developments or subsequent agreements. This may generate broader understandings of the obligations than those that should be admissible under the WTO dispute-settlement mechanism.[25] In addition, the procedures are different: there is no possibility of a review of the legal arguments as may currently be done by the Appellate Body of the WTO (Mehmet 2008), and third parties may not be permitted to express their views as allowed under article 10 of the WTO Dispute Settlement Understanding.[26]

Moreover, FTAs may allow for a choice of forum between the WTO and the particular FTA dispute-settlement system,[27] provided that the subject of the dispute is regulated under the substantive provisions of WTO agreements and the particular FTA. This opens the door for "forum shopping": the complaining party is likely to choose the forum most likely to provide a judgment favorable to its own position. One important issue is, therefore, the extent to which the interpretations of TRIPS provisions incorporated in FTAs that are heard by FTA dispute-settlement bodies may substantially differ from those of a WTO panel or Appellate Body, and whether such interpretations may subsequently influence WTO jurisprudence.[28] Interestingly, the TPP contains a provision aimed at recognizing WTO jurisprudence in relation to obligations established by WTO agreements:

> With respect to any obligation of any WTO agreement that has been incorporated into this Agreement, the panel shall also consider relevant interpretations in reports of panels and the WTO Appellate Body adopted by the WTO Dispute Settlement Body (Article 28.11).[29]

To sum up: FTAs have as a clear objective the expansion and strengthening of intellectual property rights, thereby providing an inherently biased context for interpretation of substantive and enforcement obligations. Although this may favor commercial over public interest considerations, FTAs dispute settlement bodies would in any case be bound by the Preamble and articles 7 and 8 of the TRIPS agreement, as well as by other specific provisions contained in the FTAs requiring a balance of rights and obligations. Although these provisions may help to attenuate the negative impact of those FTAs obligations likely to increase inequalities, they would not be sufficient to redress the imbalance created by the high standards of IP protection embedded in those agreements.

C. THE LIMITED IMPACT OF "SIDE LETTERS"

In response to the concerns raised by health authorities and nongovernmental organizations (NGOs) about the impact of a number of FTAs' IP standards on access to medicines, some FTAs signed by the United States included "side letters" or "understandings" that allude to the contracting parties' ability to protect public health. For instance, the United States and Morocco exchanged letters in June 2004 indicating that:

> The obligations of Chapter Fifteen of the Agreement do not affect the ability of either Party to take necessary measures to protect public health by promoting access to medicines for all, in particular concerning cases such as HIV/AIDS, tuberculosis, malaria, and other epidemics as well as circumstances of extreme urgency or national emergency. In recognition of the commitment to access to medicines that are supplied in accordance with the Decision of the General Council of 30 August 2003 on the Implementation of Paragraph Six of the Doha Declaration on the TRIPS Agreement and public health (WT/L/540) and the WTO General Council Chairman's statement accompanying the Decision (JOB(03)/177, WT/GC/M/82) (collectively the "TRIPS/health solution"), Chapter Fifteen does not prevent the effective utilization of the TRIPS/health solution.[30]

The wording of the first sentence of this side letter is ambiguous and its legal effect uncertain. One possible interpretation is that measures "necessary" to protect public health may be adopted even if they imply a derogation or limitation to the existing obligations under the FTA. Another interpretation is that the contracting parties understand that the adoption of such measures would not give them a right to ignore their treaty obligations, as they would be presumed to be neutral or entirely consistent with the protection of public health.

The General Counsel of the USTR sent a letter to a member of the U.S. Congress on the U.S.-Morocco FTA in which he stated:

> As stated in the side letter, the letter constitutes a formal agreement between the Parties. It is, thus, a significant part of the interpretive context for this agreement and not merely rhetorical. According to Article 31 of the Vienna Convention on the Law of Treaties, which reflects customary rules of treaty interpretation in international law, the terms of a treaty must be interpreted "in their context," and that "context" includes "any agreement relating to the treaty which was made between all the parties in connection with the conclusion of the treaty."[31]

The USTR General Counsel went further and argued that if circumstances ever arise in which a drug is produced under a compulsory license, and it is necessary to approve that drug to protect public health or effectively utilize the TRIPS/health solution, "the data protection provision in the FTA would not stand in the way."

However, side letters or understandings to limit FTAs obligations are likely to be of limited use and provide only contextual elements for interpretation. As noted in a U.S. congressional report:

> In the event that a brand name drug company challenges a decision to approve a generic drug produced under a compulsory license, the Bush Administration has acknowledged that the conflict will only be "informed" by the letter and will have to be "resolved on the merits of a particular case." (Waxman 2005, 13)

A side letter or understanding may be deemed, in fact, as noted by the USTR General Counsel, a "subsequent agreement between the parties regarding the interpretation of the treaty or the applications of its provisions" that should "be taken into account together with the context."[32] Hence, side letters may give the false impression that they are able to effectively address the public health concerns generated by the TRIPS-plus and TRIPS-extra obligations provided for by FTAs, whereas their actual role in reducing the inequalities they generate may be limited.

5. FLEXIBILITIES WITHIN FTAs

A vast literature has addressed the flexibilities that WTO members may utilize in implementing the TRIPS agreement (Velasquez et al. 2012) and has observed the limitations developing countries have faced to effectively apply them (Deere 2009). Most analyses on FTAs have focused on how they increase the TRIPS agreement's standards and further limit the contracting parties' space to design IP systems consistent with different levels of development and public policy objectives. Given this situation, is it still possible to articulate implementing laws, regulations, and practices to pursue such objectives? The following sections examine the (limited) extent to which it is possible to do so in relation to two regulatory areas that may significantly increase inequalities between and within FTAs' partners. These suggestions also may be applied by WTO members that accepted TRIPS-plus obligations in the process of accession to the WTO, as is the case for China (Correa and Abbott 2009).

A. TEST DATA PROTECTION

FTAs signed by the United States and the EU systematically include *sui generis* protection (generally called "data exclusivity") applicable to the outcome of clinical studies conducted to demonstrate the efficacy and safety of a drug or agrochemical product. This TRIPS-plus protection can have a significant impact on the prices of medicines,[33] and the extent and modalities of the protection conferred varies among different FTAs.[34] It is not possible to make specific suggestions for implementing the obligations with a pro–public health perspective that would be applicable to all FTAs. The options discussed here regarding drugs are not exhaustive, but they may be relevant for all or most FTAs.

How protection is acquired: Data exclusivity generally is the corollary of the registration of a medicine incorporating a new chemical entity (see below). However, protection does not need to arise automatically as a result of such registration. It may be granted by the competent authority[35] upon determination that an application has been duly made and that the legally prescribed conditions have been met. As in the case of other titles, an initial fee and annual maintenance fees may be established. Competent authorities may be bound to publish the products for which protection is granted, and third parties may be permitted to request the revocation of the grant.

Period to seek protection: National regulations may provide periods within which marketing approval should be requested after the first approval in the world of a medicine in order to obtain data exclusivity protection. This period may be, for instance, six months or one year (as established for the Paris Convention in relation to the priority right).[36]

Covered products: The exclusive protection of test data is generally conferred under FTAs only in relation to products that contain "new" entities; that is, active principles not included in a product approved previously in the same country. Hence, products that contain salts, esters, or variants of active principles already incorporated in approved products are excluded from such protection. Moreover, national regulations may limit the protection to cases in which there is a new "active moiety," as provided for under U.S. legislation.[37] The adoption of this concept would imply that protection should not be granted to test data relating to products containing chemical entities with a functional unit contained in a previously approved product, such as when marketing approval is applied for a pro-drug for an already registered drug.

Undisclosed data: In line with article 39.3 of the TRIPS agreement, FTAs require the protection of *undisclosed* test data. Whenever the test data for a particular product has been made publicly available, data exclusivity may not be obtained or would cease to exist. National laws may determine that public availability of a summary of clinical studies or of information in scientific literature is sufficient to consider the test data as disclosed. Interestingly, many drug regulatory authorities are moving in the direction of making available all test data related to an approved drug. For instance, in accordance with a policy applied since January 2015 by the European Medicines Agency, the information about clinical studies generally cannot be considered "commercial confidential information." This information is to be published on the Internet (European Medicines Agency 2013). The "clinical reports may not be used to support a MAA [marketing authorization application]/extensions or variations to a MA nor to make any unfair commercial use of the clinical reports" (European Medicines Agency 2013), but this restriction does not change the nature of the information as *disclosed* to the extent that it is publicly available.

Scope of exclusive rights: The right granted under data exclusivity protection only covers *commercialization* of the protected product in the territory where marketing approval has been obtained. Hence, the rights holder cannot prevent third parties from importing or manufacturing and distributing the product without commercial purposes, for example, distribution made in public hospitals or with a humanitarian purpose.[38] Likewise, commercialization is only impeded in the territory where data protection was obtained, and data exclusivity cannot be enforced against manufacturing and exportation of the covered products, even if made with commercial purposes.

Early working: If a product were subject to data exclusivity, a generic company could nevertheless produce or import samples to undertake the studies required for marketing approval. Thus a generic company could initiate the procedures during the data exclusivity term of protection so commercialization can begin immediately after expiry of that term. If the product were on patent, the possibility of undertaking the required studies would depend on the recognition of a Bolar exception (Correa 2017).

Exclusion of protection: Exceptions may be provided for data exclusivity protection, such as for cases of emergency, public health reasons, or when duplicating the test data would be unethical. As noted previously, the EU–Colombia–Peru FTAs state that "in interpreting and implementing the rights and obligations under this Title, the Parties shall ensure consistency with this Declaration" (article 197:2). In the case of the Chilean regulation, for instance, the hypothesis of exclusion included anticompetitive practices and reasons of public health, national security, public noncommercial use, national emergency, or other circumstances of extreme urgency established by a supreme decree of the Ministry of Health that justifies termination of the protection, or lack of commercialization of the protected product within twelve months of its approval for marketing (article 9 (a) and (b), Decree 107/2010).

Compulsory licenses/government use: A data exclusivity regime could be an obstacle for the execution of a compulsory license or government use of a patent. Hence it may be necessary to waive the rights conferred under data exclusivity to allow a compulsory licensee to obtain marketing approval of the licensed product.[39] National regulations may provide that data exclusivity shall have no effects against a compulsory licensee granted for any of the grounds established under the applicable patent law, nor against persons authorized to undertake a governmental noncommercial use of the patented product.

Termination of protection: National laws may provide for a number of grounds for terminating data exclusivity protection, such as:

- when the rights holder or a person authorized by him does not commercialize the approved product in a way sufficient to supply the demand within a period (for example, twelve months) from the date of approval for commercialization or when the commercialization is interrupted, for more than x consecutive months (for example, six months), except in cases of *force majeure* or governments' acts that prevent such commercialization.

- for public interest reasons such as national security, emergency, or circumstances of extreme urgency that justify the termination of the period of exclusivity.

- when, as a result of administrative or judicial procedures, it is determined that the rights holder has abused his rights, for example, through practices declared as anticompetitive.

B. PATENT/DRUG APPROVAL LINKAGE

U.S. FTAs typically require the contracting parties to create a "linkage" between patent protection and drug marketing approval,[40] thereby stretching the patent owner's exclusive rights by blocking regulatory approval for marketing competing generic products.[41] This linkage obscures the fact that the objectives of these two areas of regulation differ completely. Patent protection rewards new and inventive contributions to the state of the art, whereas drug approval regulations seek to ensure that only drugs with proven efficacy and safety are commercialized. As noted by a commentator, "the newly delegated role of the regulatory authority as an 'enforcer' of a private right is therefore a significant benefit to the rights holder" (Mercurio 2006). By significantly delaying the marketing approval for generic drugs, linkage provisions may limit states' actions aimed at progressively realizing the human right to health, as required by the International Covenant of Economic, Social, and Cultural Rights.[42]

The USTR (2016) has championed the adoption of linkage provisions in FTAs and has systematically threatened unilateral sanctions under Special Section 301 of the U.S. Trade Act against countries that do not implement some form of drug-patent/registration linkage. Paradoxically, the modality of linkage imposed on developing countries by the United States in some FTAs is more restrictive than that applied in the United States (Abbott 2006). The U.S. drug regulatory authority only provides information to the patent owner to enable the owner to initiate judicial proceedings against potential infringers,[43] so the linkage is based on the limited intervention ability of the Food and Drug Administration (FDA).[44] Disputes arising from the marketing approval of a generic product are settled by the courts. In many FTAs, however, it is the drug regulatory authority itself—rather than the patent owner—who is obliged to deny an application of marketing approval of a generic product. As a result of this "administrative linkage," it is the state that may be bound to assume

responsibility for unduly refusing an application for marketing approval of
a generic medicine when the patents were invalid or not infringed.

A major problem with the administrative linkage is that drug regulatory authorities have no legal capacity to determine whether a particular
patent is infringed and whether it would overcome a challenge of inva-
lidity. This is aggravated when patent offices and courts allow for the
proliferation of pharmaceutical patents on marginal developments aimed
at evergreening basic patents as a result of deficient examination or the
application of low standards of patentability and various legal fictions
(Correa 2015). In these situations, marketing approval might be denied,
for instance, if there were patents over a particular salt or formulation of
a drug, even when the drug itself may be off patent.

An exhaustive study conducted in Canada, where linkage came into
force in 1993, has shown how pharmaceutical companies have strategically used linkage provisions and evergreening to delay the market entry
of generic products. Canadian data revealed a "strong and increasing use
of linkage regulations by pharmaceutical firms to restrain generic competition" (Bouchard et al. 2010, 220). In particular, it showed that firms
were obtaining the most extensive patent protection through the linkage
provisions "on drugs with the least innovative value" as such provisions
were "primarily utilized only for follow-on drugs" (220) and

> that private firms may be obtaining extended patent protection for weakly
> inventive products while at the same time generic competition is chilled
> and public are deprived of reasonably priced pharmaceuticals raises the pos-
> sibility that the *quid pro quo* of the traditional patent bargain is breached,
> yielding a result that would be at odds with legislative intent. (222)

They concluded:

> Together, the results reported here show that the combination of con-
> ventional patent law, emerging linkage regulation regimes and existing
> drug approval framework provide a powerful mechanism for multina-
> tional pharmaceutical firms to efficiently and effectively identify attractive
> new and follow-on drug candidates for market exclusivity. The linkage
> regulation regime in particular has proven to be an excellent vehicle for
> firms to obtain extended legal protection on drugs at all stages of develop-
> ment, including drugs about to come off patent protection, drugs moving
> through the regulatory approval stage, and drugs that are currently in
> development. (227)

An administrative type of linkage in which the drug regulatory authority should take action on its own to refuse an application for marketing of a generic product creates an almost absolute presumption of validity for pharmaceutical patents. The U.S. Federal Trade Commission (FTC), however, has held that the circumstances under which a patent is granted "suggest that an overly strong presumption of a patent's validity is inappropriate," and that it "does not seem sensible to treat an issued patent as though it had met some higher standard of patentability" (2003, 8–10). In dealing with preliminary injunctions, U.S. courts do not recognize a presumption of validity when the patent is challenged by the alleged infringer. In *New England Braiding* (1992), for instance, the court stated that "unless the alleged infringer undertakes to challenge validity with evidence, the patentee need do nothing to establish its rights under the patent. . . . However, the presumption does not relieve a patentee who moves for a preliminary injunction from carrying the normal burden of demonstrating that it will likely succeed on all disputed liability issues at trial, even when the issue concerns the patent's validity." A bill was introduced to the U.S. Congress in April 2007 that proposed a reduction in the threshold to obtain the invalidation of a patent (by establishing a "preponderance of the evidence" and not "a clear and convincing evidence" standard), but the America Invents Act adopted in 2011 provided that during the procedures before the USPTO Patent Trial and Appeal Board (PTAB) the patent has no presumption of validity.[45]

The vulnerability of patents is also recognized in other jurisdictions. In India, for instance, it is settled law that an injunction would not be granted in an action for infringement of a patent if the validity of the patent itself has been questioned and a revocation petition has been filed.[46] In Argentina, a reform introduced pursuant to a complaint by the United States under the WTO dispute-settlement rules provides that in dealing with applications for a preliminary injunction the judge needs to consider whether a patent will be deemed valid if challenged by the alleged infringer (article 83).

The negative impact of linkage provisions on public health[47] may be attenuated by indirect and direct measures. Indirect measures include:

1. A rigorous examination of patent applications to ensure patents are granted only when genuine inventive contributions have been made. Calibration of patentability standards to make them compatible with national policies (in the area of public health, industrial policy,

environmental protection, food security, and so forth) is one of the most important flexibilities allowed by the TRIPS agreement.[48] FTAs have not generally reduced the room for maneuver left to contracting parties in this regard.[49]

2. Limiting the presumption of validity of patents to the compliance with legal procedures rather than substantive requirements.
3. Reducing the room for pharmaceutical companies' abuse of preliminary injunctions (Correa 2007). To prevent the risk of such abuse, national laws and regulations could provide that the grant of such measures by judicial authorities should be subject to an evaluation by the court of several admissibility factors: would the patentee likely prevail if the validity of the patent were challenged, would there be an "irreparable harm" if an injunction were not granted, would the balance of equities tip in the patentee's favor, and would granting the preliminary injunction be in the public interest?[50] In addition, such measures may not be granted without providing the alleged infringer with an opportunity to articulate its defense.[51]

Direct measures to mitigate the negative impact on the accessibility of medicines are discussed in the following section.

C. SCOPE OF PATENT CLAIMS

Where allowed by national laws, regulations, and practices, the pharmaceutical industry often applies for and obtains patents on derivatives and other developments (such as salts, formulations, and uses) of existing drugs to artificially extend a monopolistic position with regard to particular drugs. This evergreening strategy has been documented in developed (European Commission 2009) as well as in developing countries (Correa 2013b). A Chilean study showed that "72 percent of active ingredients that were protected by a single patent were in fact protected by a secondary patent. Among the drugs that were protected by several patents, in most cases they were protected by only secondary patents or a combination of primary and secondary patents" (Abud, Hall, and Helmers 2015, 12). Another study reinforced this finding:

If the future looks like the past (and the patent landscape in other countries like that in the U.S.) a conservative estimate is that eliminating secondary patents could free up 36 percent of new medicines for generic production, since only 64 percent of drugs in our sample had patents with chemical compound claims. Additionally, for those drugs that still come under patent because a chemical compound claim exists, exclusions on secondary patents could limit the duration of patent protection by 4–5 years. (Kapczynski, Park, and Sampat 2012)

The effects of evergreening could be drastically limited if linkage provisions are applied in respect of patents in force only on the *active ingredients*, excluding those covering other subject matter. This distinction may be crucial to preserving a competitive market when the active ingredients are off patent. In the case of sofosbuvir, for instance (an exorbitantly highly priced drug),[52] in addition to the patent on the active ingredient, in many countries Gilead has obtained a patent on the most thermodynamically stable polymorphic form of sofosbuvir (WHO 2016). If the patent on the active ingredient is not granted or has expired, the polymorph patent might be used to refuse the marketing approval of a generic product.

The extent to which the scope of the linkage obligations may be limited will ultimately depend on their wording in the respective FTAs and implementing legislation. For instance, the TPP refers to a "patent claiming the approved product or its approved method of use" (article 18.53(1)(a)). In this case, a patent covering a particular polymorph, salt, or formulation may not be invoked to prevent a generic product from being approved for marketing unless the "approved product" has been characterized as a specific polymorph, salt, or formulation.

INFRINGEMENT

Drug regulatory authorities lack the capacity to assess whether the infringement of a patent might occur. Patent claims are interpreted in a number of ways. Various theories and methodologies are applied by courts (Cotropia 2005) with regard to what is protected and eventually infringed. The same claims may be read as covering or not covering a certain product. In addition, an infringement may be "literal" or by "equivalence." There is no harmonized doctrine to determine when a product or process not identical to the one patented is infringing (Westin 1998). This creates a great deal of uncertainty and allows for discretion in determining when a patent is infringed.

In view of these circumstances, regulations should stipulate that linkage provisions would be applied only when a patent in force would be literally infringed by the product whose registration is sought. In the case of sofosbuvir, for instance, the linkage provisions should not apply if generic companies developed a different stable molecular dispersion, liquid, or amorphous form and have taken care of preventing conversion of the developed product to the stable polymorphic form covered by the patent (WHO 2016).

LISTING PATENTS

Countries subject to linkage obligations could establish that a patent may be invoked to refuse the marketing approval of a generic product only when the patent was previously included in a publicly available database similar to the U.S. Orange Book.[53] Patent listings may be subject to deadlines (within a certain period after grant) and to some exclusions. For instance, under the FDA's Orange Book regulations, no metabolite, intermediate, or packaging patents may be listed. Patents having only method of making (process) claims, those claiming formulations that do not cover the marketed drug product, and methods of use covering unapproved indications cannot be listed (Hemphill and Sampat 2012). If a patent covers a polymorph, the patentee may be required to submit test data within a given period demonstrating that a drug product containing the polymorph will perform the same (bioequivalence) as the drug product described in the National Drug Administration (NDA).

SETTING DEADLINES

As suggested previously, some terms may be provided to trigger the application of linkage provisions. This may refer to listing patents, submitting test data (when required), and bringing an infringement action. Under FDA regulations in the United States, such an action must be initiated within forty-five days after receiving notice about an application for marketing approval of a generic product.[54]

Patent litigation may last for years. Delays in reaching final decisions may be due to an inefficient or overburdened judicial system, the technical complexity of issues to be addressed, as well as to dilatory tactics by the parties. Hence, if a provisional measure that prevents the drug regulatory agency from approving a generic drug was obtained, the exclusion of the market may last for years, even when there was no justification for it. For this reason, implementing regulations may provide for a maximum period of suspension. In the case of the United States, the approval of a generic product may be made effective thirty months after the date of the receipt of the notice of certification regarding the application for a generic product "unless the court has extended or reduced the period because of a failure of either the plaintiff or defendant to cooperate reasonably in expediting the action."[55]

DAMAGES

If linkage provisions are unduly used to exclude generic products from the market, the patentee should be liable for damages and other penalties might be imposed as well. Australia has provided a remedy when baseless litigation by a pharmaceutical company takes place. In accordance with Section 26D of the Therapeutic Goods Act 1989, if a provisional measure was granted and the infringement proceedings are subsequently discontinued or dismissed, or they had no reasonable prospect of success, the court may award compensation to the applicant as well as to the government for losses sustained as a result of the injunction (Correa 2014). Of course, this would not apply if the drug regulatory authority acted *ex officio*. Implementing regulations may ensure that action is only taken upon formal request of the patent owner, even in the case of administrative linkage, thereby making the patent owner liable in the case of wrongful suspension or refusal of the marketing approval of a generic product.

PUBLICLY AVAILABLE INFORMATION

In accordance with some FTAs, contracting parties must put in place "a transparent system" to provide notice to a patent holder that another person is seeking to market an approved pharmaceutical product during the term of a patent covering the product or its approved method of use.[56]

One way of complying with linkage provisions without an excessive burden on the drug regulatory agencies is to make information on all filings for marketing approval publicly available on a website. Companies that believe their patents might be infringed could—within a given period—initiate legal actions before the courts.

COMPULSORY LICENSES

The administrative linkage, as implemented under FTAs, may make compulsory licenses and noncommercial government use impractical because generic companies would be unable to get approval to market their generic products, even if permitted under the patent law.

It is unclear whether a compulsory license may be issued to provide entry of generic drugs where the law does not allow registration prior to the expiration of the patent. This potential impediment is caused by the fact that a manufacturer granted authority to produce under compulsory license still must be registered by the national drug regulatory authority. Thus, if the regulatory authority is prohibited from registering generics until the patent expires, the compulsory license will be prevented from coming to fruition. (Mercurio 2006, 226)

To avoid a possible limitation on compulsory licenses and government use of patents derived from linkage provisions, specific safeguards may be provided for in implementing regulations to ensure that marketing approval is granted for the products to be marketed under such authorizations.

6. CONCLUSIONS

IP provisions contained in FTAs are likely to aggravate current inequalities among and within countries, particularly low- and middle-income countries. Those agreements normally contain a set of obligations that increase the level of IP protection beyond what is required under the TRIPS agreement, and what would be adequate to developing countries that have signed those agreements. Moreover, the certification process conducted by the U.S. government may expand the obligations agreed upon under particular FTAs, thereby enhancing the potential benefits of FTA provisions for foreign rights holders without any positive impact for the U.S. partner countries. Some provisions in the TRIPS agreement and FTAs that broadly refer to welfare implications of IP protection may attenuate the negative implications of such agreements in vital areas, such as public health, but the room for interpretation in the public interest is limited. This also applies to side letters incorporated into some FTAs, which would not allow a contracting party to ignore unambiguously defined treaty obligations.

There is some space, however, to explore options for the implementation of IP obligations imposed by FTAs with the aim of limiting their potential negative impact. In two areas (data exclusivity and linkage) of particular importance for access to medicines, contracting parties could introduce a number of conditions for that purpose. Such space may be fully exploited by countries that have preserved the freedom to implement FTA obligations. It is more limited when a contracting party is subject to the certification process. Nevertheless, some measures—such as limiting the presumption of validity of patents and applying rigorous standards to examine patent applications—may be implemented in any case to mitigate the impact of linkage provisions, which in essence are incompatible with the independence of functions performed by patent offices and drug regulatory agencies, and to ensure that patents are not used as a tool to limit legitimate competition.

NOTES

1. There is a dearth of empirical evidence on the general economic and social impact of FTAs in developing countries, but a recent report concluded that "there is limited evidence that FTAs can encourage investment, technology transfer and firm upgrading, which is valuable because of the importance of supply capacity" (Stevens et al. 2015).

2. However, in accordance with estimates by the U.S. International Trade Commission, FTAs entered into by the United States are reported to have "had a significant positive effect on U.S. bilateral trade balances. The agreements increased U.S. bilateral trade surpluses or reduced bilateral trade deficits by $4.4 billion per country per year on average, and by $87.5 billion per year in total (59.2 percent) in 2015" (Lawder 2016).

3. Unlike other IP international treaties, noncompliance with the obligations set out by the TRIPS agreement may lead to trade retaliations. See Kennedy (2015).

4. For this and other examples of FTAs provisions that go beyond U.S. law, see Abbott (2006).

5. For instance, article 15.9 of CAFTA-DR reproduces the first sentence of article 27.1 but omits the second one about nondiscrimination ("patents shall be available and patent rights enjoyable without discrimination as to the place of invention, the field of technology and whether products are imported or locally produced").

6. This extension delays the entry of generic competitors. For instance, the anticancer drug Gleevec "received a patent term extension in the U.S., from 28 May 2013 to 4 January 2015. Extensions have also been obtained in major European markets to 2016 . . . Thus generic competition, with the consequent falls in price, is delayed by two or three years in major markets beyond expiry of the original patent. Introduction of similar provisions in developing countries will have the same delaying effect" (Clift 2007, 22).

7. See Global Commission on HIV and the Law (2012, 5). The commission recommended, inter alia, that the WTO "suspend TRIPS as it relates to essential pharmaceutical products for low- and middle-income countries" (14).

8. On this issue, see WHO (2011).

9. Inequality may negatively affect the incentive to innovate via a price and a market size effect (Foellmi and Zweimüller 2016).

10. http://www.hktdc.com/info/mi/a/baus/en/1X0078EY/1/Business-Alert-%E2% 80%93-US/Congress—Administration-Announce-Trade-Policy-Agreement.htm.

11. Quoted in Palmedo (2016).

12. Quoted in Palmedo (2016), para. 29.

13. September 2, 2002, the Quinta Sala from the I Corte de Apelaciones (I Court of Appeals, Fifth Chamber) of Chile ruled that the Instituto de Salud Publica, which issues sanitary registries, "had no power whatsoever to either deny a marketing approval or to acknowledge rights derived from a patent" (Cadillo Chandler 2010).

14. However, dispute settlement has been rarely used under FTAs (Vidigal, 2017).

15. In the case of the EU–Colombia–Peru FTA, a reference to the importance of the Doha Declaration is complemented by a provision stating that "in interpreting and implementing the rights and obligations under this Title, the Parties shall ensure consistency with this Declaration" (article 197:2).

16. See document MTN.GNG/NG11/W/71, 19 May 1990.

17. Paragraph 5(a): "In applying the customary rules of interpretation of public international law, each provision of the TRIPS Agreement shall be read in the light of the object and purpose of the Agreement as expressed, in particular, in its objectives and principles." See also Yu (2009, 999).

18. Report of the panel, WT/DS114/R (2000), para 7.26.

19. Available at http://trade.ec.europa.eu/doclib/docs/2011/march/tradoc_147704 .pdf.

20. This agreement has not entered into force, pending ratification by the negotiating parties.

21. See U.S.–Chile FTA, Preamble.

22. See E.U.–CARIFORUM Economic Partnership Agreement (EPA), article 147(b).

23. Article 16.10.2.(e)(i) (Peru, Colombia) and article 15.10.2.(e)(i) (Panama).

24. See Part III, article 18 of the E.U.-CARIFORUM EPA.

25. However, some WTO rulings have relied on an "evolutionary interpretation." In Section 110(5) of the U.S. Copyright Act, the WTO panel incorrectly considered the World Intellectual Property Organization (WIPO) Copyright Treaty as a subsequent development, even though it has neither come into force nor been ratified by either party. See Frankel (2005) and Marceau (2001).

26. The TPP provides for the participation of third parties in disputes (article 28.14).

27. See article 28.4 of the TPP.

28. Rulings in the context of FTAs have influenced WTO jurisprudence in some cases. For instance, in *Brazil-Tyres* the WTO panel referred to a MERCOSUR ruling in support of its finding that Brazil's exemption for MERCOSUR imports was not "arbitrary" within the meaning of Article XX of the General Agreement on Tariffs and Trade (GATT) of 1994. See *Brazil—Measures Affecting Imports of Retreaded Tyres* (DS332), http://www.wto.org/english/tratop_e/dispu_e/cases_e/ds332_e.htm.

29. The wording "shall also consider," however, may leave room to deviate from those interpretations.

30. A similar statement is contained in an "Understanding regarding certain public health measures" made between the signatories of CAFTA on August 5, 2004, and in an exchange of letters with Bahrain.

31. Letter from USTR General Counsel John K. Veroneau to Congressman Levin dated July 19, 2004, Congressional Record, V. 150, PT. 13, July 22, 2004 to September

14, 2004, 17294. http://www.who.int/intellectualproperty/topics/ip/en/Morocco. FTA.letter.pdf.

32. Article 31.3 (a) of the Vienna Convention on the Law of the Treaties.

33. For instance, a study found that "of all the current forms of intellectual property protection in Jordan, the provision for data protection has the most significant effect on the price of medicines" (Abbot 2012). In Colombia, data exclusivity was estimated to increase annual pharmaceutical spending by US$ 43.8 million between 2003 and 2011(Gamba, Buenaventura, and Serrano, 2012). In Argentina, a more recent study estimated that the introduction of data exclusivity would have entailed an annual increase in the spending on pharmaceuticals of US$ 192 million (Cont, Panadeiros and Urbiztondo 2018).

34. For instance, CAFTA-DR provides that a Party "may require" that the original firm applies for approval within five years after having obtained approval for commercialisation in the other territory, a condition absent in other FTAs.

35. A certificate of protection may be issued, separately or as an integral part of the certificate of approval for commercialisation or sanitary registration.

36. See, article 4.4, Decree 107/2010 of Chile. http://www.ispch.cl/ley20285/t _activa/marco_normativo/7c/DS_MINSAL_107-2010.pdf.

37. See Section 505(b) of the US Federal Food, Drug, and Cosmetics Act; article 4.2(i) of the Malaysian Directive on Data Exclusivity, 2011. http://npra.moh.gov.my /images/reg-info/DataEx/Directive_on_DE.pdf.

38. It should be noted that there will be no "commercial purposes" merely because a price is charged for the product. The title holder cannot prevent acts of use, production, or importation of the product that do not imply commercialization.

39. See article 10 (c) of Decree 107/2010 of Chile. http://www.ispch.cl/ley20285/t _activa/marco_normativo/7c/DS_MINSAL_107-2010.pdf.

40. This section is substantially based on Correa (2008).

41. The patent-registration linkage is not required in the EU where there is complete independence between intellectual property protection and drug registration— nor under the FTAs signed by the EU.

42. See, for example, Seuba (2016), Hazan and Chastonay (2004), and Yamin (2003). See also Cullet (2003).

43. The TPP seems to allow for this possibility. The linkage mechanism may provide that notice be given to a patent holder, or to allow for a patent holder to be notified, prior to the marketing of a pharmaceutical product that another person "is seeking to market that product during the term of an applicable patent claiming the approved product or its approved method of use" (article 18.53(1)(a)). TPP contracting parties may opt to provide for "judicial or administrative proceedings" (article 18.53(1)(c)).

44. In *Alphapharm PTY v. Tommy G. Thompson* (Secretary of Health and Human Services) (DDC 2004) (CA 03–2269), the District Court in Washington, D.C. ruled that United States law does not require the FDA "to police the listing process by analyzing whether the patents listed by NDA (New Drug Application) applicants actually claim the subject drugs or applicable methods of using those drugs." See Chael (2004).

45. P.L. 112–29, the Leahy-Smith America Invents Act (2011).

46. See http://spicyipindia.blogspot.com/2007/05/bilcare-decisions-by-delhi-high -court.html.

47. Negative impacts of the administrative linkage provisions, such as those originally adopted in the FTAs with Peru and Panama (similar to those in DR-CAFTA), and the excessive burden put on states' regulatory agencies were recognized in the bipartisan agreement reached in June 2007 referred to above. Those provisions were consequently revised and more flexibility allowed for their implementation.

48. See Max Planck Institute for Intellectual Property and Competition Law (2014) and Correa (2016).

49. One exception is the TPP obligation to grant patents on "at least one of the following: new uses of a known product, new methods of using a known product, or new processes of using a known product" (article 18.37.2).

50. These are the factors generally considered by U.S. courts. The irreparable harm is not to be presumed. See AIPPI National Group: United States, "Injunctions in Cases of Infringement of IPRs." https://www.aippi.org/download/commitees/219/GR219usa.pdf.

51. Note that the TRIPS agreement leaves judicial authorities discretion regarding granting preliminary measures *inaudita altera parte* (article 50). This also seems to be the situation under FTAs. For instance, the TPP provides that "each Party's authorities shall act on a request for relief in respect of an intellectual property right *inaudita altera parte* expeditiously in accordance with that Party's judicial rules" (article 18.75.1). The reference to the "Party's judicial rules" leaves the door open for different policies on the matter, subject to what is provided for under national laws.

52. This drug is priced at US$ 2,500 per gram in some high-income countries, whereas it can probably be manufactured for US$ 2–4 per gram (UNITAID 2016, 8). Although Pharmasset, the company that originally developed sofosbuvir, had initially considered a price of $36 000, "Gilead ultimately set $84 000 as its market list price after internal deliberation over multiple factors, including an evaluation of the high prices of previous drugs and how much health systems could bear" (Roy and King 2016).

53. Under U.S. FDA regulations, drug makers are required to list any patent containing at least one claim that covers the drug's active ingredient, its formulation, or any method of use pertaining to an approved indication, issued before NDA approval (Hemphill and Sampat (2012).

54. CFR—Code of Federal Regulations Title 21, Sec. 314.107(3).

55. CFR—Code of Federal Regulations Title 21, Sec. 314.107(3).

56. See, for example, article 16.10.3 (c) of the US-Peru FTA.

REFERENCES

Abbott, Frederick M. 2006. "Intellectual Property Provisions of Bilateral and Regional Trade Agreements in Light of U.S. Federal Law." UNCTAD—ICTSD Project on IPRs and Sustainable Development. ICTSD Issue Paper No. 12, February.

Abbott, Ryan. 2012. "Access to Medicines and Intellectual Property in Jordan." Intellectual Property Watch, July 23. http://ssrn.com/abstract=2116096.

Abud, Maria J., Bronwyn Hall, and Christian Helmers. 2015. "An Empirical Analysis of Primary and Secondary Pharmaceutical Patents in Chile." PLOS | One https://doi.org/10.1371/journal.pone.0124257.

Baker, Brook K. 2012. "Settlement of India/EU WTO Dispute re Seizures of In-Transit Medicines: Why the Proposed EU Border Regulation Isn't Good Enough." PIJIP Research Paper No. 2012-02. Washington, DC: American University Washington College of Law.

Bjorge, Eirik. 2014. "The Evolutionary Interpretation of Treaties." Oxford Scholarship Online.   https://www.ilsa.org/jessup/jessup15/Second%20Batch/EirikBjorgeCh3 .pdf.

Bouchard, Ron A., Richard W. Hawkins, Robert Clark, Reider Hagtvedt, and Jamil Sawani. 2010. "Empirical Analysis of Drug Approval-Drug Patenting Linkage for High Value Pharmaceuticals." *Northwest Journal of Technology and Intellectual Property* 8 (2): 174–227.

Cadillo Chandler, Dhanay M. 2010. "Pharmaceutical Patents and Marketing Approvals Within the U.S.—Chile Free Trade Agreement Context: A Brief Analysis." *In Search of New IP Regimes*, 201–18. IPR University Center. http://ssrn.com /abstract=1602883.

Calboli, Irene, and Edward Lee, eds. 2016. *Research Handbook on Intellectual Property Exhaustion and Parallel Imports.* Cheltenham, UK: Edward Elgar.

Chael, Mark. 2004. "Court: FDA's Role Is Not to Analyze Patent Claims." Patent-lyo (blog), August 23. http://www.patentlyo.com/patent/2004/08/court_fdas_role .html.

Clift, Charles. 2007. "A Guide to Assessing the Impact of TRIPS-Plus Provisions on Drug Prices in Developing Countries." ICTSD Programme on IPRs & Sustainable Development. Geneva: International Centre for Trade and Sustainable Development.

Cont, W., Panadeiros, M., and Urbiztondo, S. 2018. "Acuerdo de Comercio Mercosur—Unión Europea: Impacto Sobre el Gasto en Medicamentos Adquiridos en Farmacias y por PAMI en Argentina." FIEL. http://www.fiel.org/publicaciones /Documentos/DOC_TRAB_1517423760907.pdf.

Correa, Carlos. 2007. "TRIPS and TRIPS-Plus Protection and Impacts in Latin America." In *Intellectual Property, Trade and Development: Strategies to Optimize Economic Development in a TRIPS Plus Era*, ed. Daniel Gervais. Oxford: Oxford University Press.

——. 2008. "Expanding Patent Rights in Pharmaceuticals: The Linkage Between Patents and Drug Registration." In *The Development Agenda: Global Intellectual Property and Developing Countries*, ed. Neil Netanel, 247–64. Oxford: Oxford University Press.

——. 2013a. "The Impact of the Economic Partnership Agreements on WTO Law." In *EU Bilateral Trade Agreements & Intellectual Property For Better or Worse*, ed. Joseph Drexl, Henning Grosse Ruse-Khan, and Souheir Nadde-Phlix, 87–107. New York: Springer.

——. ed. 2013b. *Pharmaceutical Innovation, Incremental Patenting and Compulsory Licensing.* Geneva: South Centre.

——. 2014. "Tackling the Proliferation of Patents: How to Avoid Undue Limitations to Competition and the Public Domain." South Centre Research Paper No. 52, August. http://www.southcentre.int/research-paper-52-august-2014/.

——. (with Sangeeta Shashikant and Francois Meienberg). 2015. *Plant Variety Protection in Developing Countries. A Tool for Designing a Sui Generis Plant Variety Protection System: An Alternative to UPOV 1991.* Geneva: APBREBES.

——. 2016. "The Current System of Trade And Intellectual Property Rights." *European Yearbook of International Economic Law 2016*, vol. 7: 175–97.

——. 2017. "The Bolar Exception: Legislative Models and Drafting Options." In *Contemporary Issues in Pharmaceutical Patent Law: Setting the Framework and Exploring Policy Options*, ed. Bryan Mercurio. New York: Routledge.

Correa, Carlos, and Frederick Abbott. 2009. "The Accession Process and Its Legal Consequences." In *The WTO and Accession Countries*, ed. Carlos A. Primo Braga and Olivier Cattaneo. London: Edward Elgar.

Correa, Carlos, and Duncan Matthews. 2011. "The Doha Declaration Ten Years on and Its Impact on Access to Medicines and the Right to Health." UNDP Discussion Paper, December 20. http://www.undp.org/content/dam/undp/library/hivaids/Discussion_Paper_Doha_Declaration_Public_Health.pdf.

Cotropia, Chrisopher A. 2005. "Patent Claim Interpretation Methodologies and Their Claim Scope Paradigms." *William & Mary Law Review* 47 (1): 49–133.

Cullet, Phillipe. 2003. "Patents and Medicines: The Relationship Between TRIPS and the Human Right to Health." *International Affairs* 79 (1): 139–60.

"Declaration on Patent Protection. Regulatory Sovereignty Under TRIPS." 2014. Max Planck Institute for Intellectual Property and Competition Law. https://www.mpg.de/8132986/Patent-Declaration.pdf.

Deere, Carolyn. 2009. *The Implementation Game—The TRIPS Agreement and the Global Politics of Intellectual Property Reform in Developing Countries.* Oxford: Oxford University Press.

European Commission. 2009. *Final Report, Pharmaceuticals Sector Inquiry.* http://ec.europa.eu/competition/sectors/pharmaceuticals/inquiry/staff_working_paper_part1.pdf.

European Medicines Agency. 2013. "European Medicines Agency Policy on Publication of Clinical Data for Medicinal Products for Human Use." http://www.ema.europa.eu/docs/en_GB/document_library/Other/2014/10/WC500174796.pdf.

Foellmi, Reto, and Joseph Zweimüller. 2016. "Is Inequality Harmful for Innovation and Growth? Price Versus Market Size Effects." *Journal of Economic Issues* 41: 529–37.

Frankel, Susy. 2005. "WTO Application of the Customary Rules of Interpretation of Public International Law to Intellectual Property." *Virginia Journal of International Law* 46: 365–90.

Gamba, Miguel, Buenaventura, Francisco, and Serrano, Mayra. 2012. *Impacto de 10 Años de Protección de Datos en Medicamentos en Colombia.* Bogota, Colombia: IFARMA.

Global Commission on HIV and the Law. 2012. "HIV and the Law: Risks, Rights & Health." http://www.hivlawcommission.org/index.php/report.

Grosse Ruse-Khan, Henning, and Annette Kur. 2008. "Enough Is Enough—The Notion of Binding Ceilings in International Intellectual Property Protection." Max Planck Institute for Intellectual Property, Competition & Tax Law Research Paper Series No. 09–01. http://dx.doi.org/10.2139/ssrn.1326429.

Hazan, Yaël R., and Philippe Chastonay, eds., 2004. *Santé et droits de l'homme*. Geneva: Ed. Medecine & Hygiene.

Hemphill, C. Scott., and Bhaven N. Sampat. 2012. "Weak Patents Are a Weak Deterrent: Patent Portfolios, the Orange Book Listing Standard, and Generic Entry in Pharmaceuticals." http://www.nber.org/chapters/c13215.pdf.

International Trade Administration. 2007. "Free Trade Agreement Compliance." U.S. Department of Commerce. http://trade.gov/fta/compliance.asp.

Kantarjian, Hagop. 2015. "High Cost of Cancer Drugs Goes Beyond the Price." *Modern Healthcare*, April 3. http://www.modernhealthcare.com/article/20150404/MAGAZINE/304049978.

Kapczynski, Amy, Chan Park, and Bhaven Sampat. 2012. "Polymorphs and Prodrugs and Salts (Oh My!): An Empirical Analysis of 'Secondary' Pharmaceutical Patents." PLOS | One 7(12). http://doi.org/10.1371/journal.pone.0049470.

Kennedy, Mathew. 2015. *WTO Dispute Settlement and the TRIPS Agreement: Applying Intellectual Property Standards in a Trade Law Framework*. Cambridge: Cambridge University Press.

Langreth, Robert. 2014. "Big Pharma's Favorite Prescription: Higher Prices." *Businessweek*, http://www.businessweek.com/articles/2014-05-08/why-prescription-drug-prices-keep-rising-higher.

Lawder, David. 2016. "New U.S. Study Shows Some Positive Effects from Free Trade Deals," *Reuters*, June 29. http://www.reuters.com/article/us-usa-trade-study-idUSKCN0ZG083.

Lerman, Celia. 2015. "Impact of Free Trade Agreements on Internet Policy, a Latin America Case Study." Internet Policy Observatory. http://repository.upenn.edu/internetpolicyobservatory/12.

Marceau, Gabrielle. 2001. "Conflicts of Norms and Conflicts of Jurisdictions. The Relationship Between the WTO Agreement and MEAs and Other Treaties." *Journal of World Trade* 35 (6): 1081–1131.

Mehmet, Karli. 2008. "Assessing the Development Friendliness of Dispute Settlement Mechanisms in the Economic Partnership Agreements & an Analytical and Comparative Guide to the Dispute Settlement Provisions in the EU'S FTAs." European Studies Centre, University of Oxford. The Global Trade Ethics Programme, Occasional Paper, August. https://www.oxfam.org.nz/sites/default/files/oldimgs/whatwedo/mtf/mtf%20in%20pacific/dispute%20settlement%20in%20epas.pdf.

Max Planck Institute for Intellectual Property and Competition Law. n.d. 2015. "Principles for Intellectual Property Provisions in Bilateral and Regional Agreements." http://www.ip.mpg.de/fileadmin/ipmpg/content/forschung_aktuell/06_principles_for_intellectua/principles_for_ip_provisions_in_bilateral_and_regional_agreements_final1.pdf.

——. 2014. "Declaration on Patent Protection. Regulatory Sovereignty Under TRIPS." https://www.mpg.de/8132986/Patent-Declaration.pdf.

Mercurio, Byran. 2006. "TRIPS-Plus Provisions in FTAs: Recent Trends." In *Regional Trade Agreements and the WTO Legal System*, ed. Lorand Bartels and Federico Ortino, 215–37. Oxford: Oxford University Press.

New England Braiding Co., INC. and Seal Company of New England, Inc., v. A.W. Chesterton Company (970 F.2d 878, 23 U.S.P.Q.2d 1622, July 28, 1992).

http://openjurist.org/970/f2d/878/new-england-braiding-co-inc-v-aw-chesterton
-company.

Palmedo, Mike. 2016. "USTR Identifies TPP Implementation Process as Opportunity to Address Industry Concerns with Final Text." Infojustice.org (blog), January 25. http://infojustice.org/archives/35661.

Pedrique, B., N. Stub-Wourgaft, C. Some, P. Olliavo, P. Trouiller, N. Ford, B. Pécoul, and J. Bradol. 2013. "The Drug and Vaccine Landscape for Neglected Diseases (2000–11): A Systematic Assessment." *The Lancet Global Health* 1 (6): e371–e379. http://dx.doi.org/10.1016/S2214-109X(13)70078-0.

Roca, Santiago. 2009. "Demócratas, salud pública y propiedad intelectual en el APC Perú-EE.UU." *Puentes* 10 (2): 5–7. http://www.ictsd.org/bridges-news/puentes /news/dem%C3%B3cratas-salud-p%C3%BAblica-y-propiedad-intelectual-en-el -apc-per%C3%BA-eeuu#_edn4.

Roffe, Pedro. 2007. "Intellectual Property, Bilateral Agreements and Sustainable Development: The Challenges of Implementation." CIEL, January. http://www .ciel.org/Publications/FTA_ImplementationPub_Jan07.pdf.

Roffe, Pedro, and David Vivas-Eugui. 2007. "A Shift in Intellectual Property Policy in US FTAs?" *Bridges* 11 (5). http://www.ictsd.org/bridges-news/bridges /news/a-shift-in-intellectual-property-policy-in-us-ftas.

Roy, Victor, and Lawrence King. 2016."Betting on Hepatitis C: How Financial Speculation in Drug Development Influences Access to Medicines." BMJ 354: i3718. https://doi.org/10.1136/bmj.i3718.

Samuelson, Pamala, Jerome H. Reichman, and Graeme Dinwoodie. 2008. "How to Achieve (Some) Balance in Anti-Circumvention Laws." *Communications of the ACM* 51 (2): 21–25. http://scholarship.law.berkeley.edu/facpubs/2367.

Sell, Susan. 2007. "TRIPS-Plus Free Trade Agreements and Access to Medicines." *Liverpool Law Review* 28 (1): 41–75.

Seuba, Xavier. 2016. "On the Right to Health as a Human Right, Human Rights and Intellectual Property Rights." In *Intellectual Property and International Trade: The TRIPS Agreement*, 3rd ed., ed. Carlos M. Correa and Abdulqawi A. Yusuf. Norwell, MA: Wolters Kluwer.

Stevens, Christopher, Muhammad Irfan, Isabella Massa, and Jane Kennan. 2015. *The Impact of Free Trade Agreements Between Developed and Developing Countries on Economic Development in Developing Countries: A Rapid Evidence Assessment*. London: Overseas Development Institute.

'tHoen, Ellen. 2016. *Private Patents and Public Health: Changing Intellectual Property Rules for Access to Medicines*. Amsterdam, Netherlands: Health Action Network.

UNAIDS. 2012. "The Potential Impact of Free Trade Agreements on Public Health." Issue Brief. Geneva: UNAIDS. http://www.unaids.org/sites/default/files/media _asset/JC2349_Issue_Brief_Free-Trade-Agreements_en_0.pdf.

UNDP and UNAIDS. 2012. "The Potential Impact of Free Trade Agreements on Public Health." Issue Brief. http://www.unaids.org/sites/default/files/media_asset /JC2349_Issue_Brief_Free-Trade-Agreements_en_0.pdf.

UNITAID. 2016. "An Economic Perspective on Delinking the Cost of R&D from the Price of Medicines." Discussion Paper. https://unitaid.eu/assets/Delinkage_ Economic_Perspective_Feb2016.pdf.

United Nations. 2009. "Report of the Special Rapporteur on the Right of Everyone to the Enjoyment of the Highest Attainable Standard of Physical and Mental Health." United Nations General Assembly, 11th Session, Agenda Item 3, A/HRC/11/12. New York: United Nations.

United Nations Development Programme. 2015. "Sustainable Development Goals." New York: United Nations. http://www.undp.org/content/dam/undp/library /corporate/brochure/SDGs_Booklet_Web_En.pdf.

U.S. Federal Trade Commission. 2003. "To Promote Innovation: The Proper Balance of Competition and Patent Law and Policy." http://www.ftc.gov/os/2003/10 /innovationrpt.pdf.

USTR. 2016. "Special 301 Report." Office of the United States Trade Representative, April. https://ustr.gov/sites/default/files/USTR-2016-Special-301-Report.pdf.

Velásquez, Germán, Carlos Correa, and Xavier Seuba. 2012. *IPR, R&D, Human Rights and Access to Medicines—An Annotated and Selected Bibliography*. Geneva: South Centre.

Vidigal, Geraldo. 2017. "Why Is There So Little Litigation Under Free Trade Agreements? Retaliation and Adjudication in International Dispute Settlement." *Journal of International Economic Law* 20 (4): 927–50. https://doi.org/10.1093/jiel/jgx037.

Vivas-Eugui, David, and Johanna von Braun. 2016. "Beyond FTA Negotiations— Implementing the New Generation of Intellectual Property Obligations." http:// infojustice.org/wp-content/uploads/2016/01/vivas-and-von-braun.pdf.

Waxman, Henry. 2005. "Trade Agreements and Access to Medications Under the Bush Administration." Washington, DC: United States House of Representatives. http://democrats.reform.house.gov/Documents/ 20050609094902–11945.pdf.

Weston, Ray D., Jr. 1998. "A Comparative Analysis of the Doctrine of Equivalents: Can European Approaches Solve an American Dilemma?" *IDEA: The Journal of Law and Technology* 39: 35.

WHO. 2011. *Trends in Local Production of Medicines and Related Technology Transfer*. Geneva: World Health Organization. http://apps.who.int/medicinedocs/documents /s19063en/s19063en.pdf.

WHO. 2016. "Patent Situation of Key Products for Treatment of Hepatitis C-Sofosbuvir." WHO Working Paper. http://www.who.int/phi/implementation/ip_trade /sofosbuvir_report.pdf?ua=1.

Xiong, Ping. 2012. "Patents in TRIPS-Plus Provisions and the Approaches to Interpretation of Free Trade Agreements and TRIPS: Do They Affect Public Health?" *Journal of World Trade* 46 (1): 155–86.

Yamin, Alicia E. 2003. "Not Just a Tragedy: Access to Medications as a Right Under International Law." *Boston University International Law Journal* 21 (2): 325–71.

Yu, Peter. 2009. "The Objectives and Principles of the TRIPS Agreement." *Houston Law Review* 46: 797–1046.

Yusuf, A. 2016. "Chapter 1." In Intellectual Property and International Trade: TRIPS Agreement, 3rd ed., ed. Carlos Correa and Abdulqawi Yusuf. Norwell, MA: Wolters Kluwer.

CHAPTER 8

The Frustrated TPP and New Challenges for the Global Governance of Trade and Investment

Osvaldo Rosales

1. INTRODUCTION

The Trans-Pacific Partnership (TPP) was the first of a new generation of trade negotiations of a vast scope, known as mega-regional agreements. TPP would have created the largest free trade area in the world measured by its members' joint gross domestic product (GDP), and the second largest, after the European Union, by total trade among its members. The members of the TPP were Australia, Brunei Darussalam, Canada, Chile, Japan, Malaysia, Mexico, New Zealand, Peru, Singapore, the United States, and Vietnam. These countries cover around 38 percent of world GDP, 24 percent of global trade, and a market of 800 million of people.

TPP was expected to eliminate the vast majority of tariffs on the goods traded among its members, but it was also designed to increase access to services markets, investment, and government procurement. It also set rules on matters that World Trade Organization (WTO) agreements have regulated to a limited extent, such as intellectual property rights (IPR), or not at all, such as e-commerce, state-owned enterprises, regulatory coherence, several labor and environmental matters, and some commitments to supporting small and medium enterprises.

The strategic and explicit aim of the United States in the TPP was to write new rules for global trade and investment over the coming decades, not only in the trans-Pacific area but potentially at the global level, particularly as a counterbalance China's influence in the Asian Pacific, the most dynamic economic area in the world today and probably over the next decades. Following the formal withdrawal of the United States from this agreement, the other eleven governments expressed their willingness to remain in the agreement and are assessing the adjustments that will have to be made once the main partner has retired.

A widespread conclusion of many critics is that the TPP reduced the policy space for the management of capital flows, affecting macroeconomic stability and the possibility of using countercyclical policies. They also underscore the fact that it posed a certain threat to different levels of social and environmental regulations and imposed significant restrictions on access to new drugs and biological drugs, as well as to affordable seeds and agricultural chemicals needed to raise agricultural productivity. They also claim that these agreements limit tax autonomy, particularly to further progressive taxation and to combat "tax havens."

The novelty of the TPP is that it offered more flexibility to governments than the previous U.S. free trade agreements (FTAs) in these areas, resulting in greater control of external capital flows, investment, and intellectual property. The policy space was, therefore, larger than was allowed in the previous U.S. FTAs.

The reasons for such flexibility were both internal to the United States and related to a dynamic negotiation process with more complex interactions between the United States and its eleven partners, including the big economies of Australia, Canada, and Japan. The domestic reasons were the desire of President Obama to conclude negotiations during his tenure, forcing increased flexibility by the United States to close the deal in the shortest time possible, and the need to incorporate explicit flexibilities in the chapters on IPRs and investor-state dispute settlements (ISDS) according to precise mandates delivered by the Congress and particularly by legislators from the Democratic Party (U.S. Congress, 2015). Several experiences of foreign investors' lawsuits against the United States led the Democrats to introduce amendments that reduced the space for foreign investors to sue states in defense of their investment or IPRs.[1] In turn, the fact that the TPP was a multinational negotiation opened the space to alliances with variable geometry between two or more partners in specific subjects, thus reducing the bargaining power of the largest economy when compared with bilateral negotiations.

FTAs today have little support in the United States. The effect of the financial crisis of 2008 has placed inequality and job creation at the heart of the debate. In this context, typically, trade liberalization is seen as a major cause of job losses, lower wages, and reductions in the welfare of the working and middle class. This reduces the support for these agreements or promotes provisions demanding the protection of labor or environmental rights.[2]

However, the pharmaceutical industry, the financial industry, Internet companies, and Hollywood businesses have managed to lobby for clauses in FTAs that protect their interests beyond regulations that facilitate free trade. One of these excesses has been establishment of ISDS agreements that skew the playing field in favor of the external investor and against the ability of the state to regulate important aspects of public policies, such as environment and health. Using bilateral investment treaties (BITs) or the investment chapter of FTAs, U.S. corporations and individuals have filed 117 cases at the International Center for Settlement of Investment Disputes (ICSID). There are also five cases of foreign corporations against the United States, all of them Canadian firms. These lawsuits against the United States in the North American Free Trade Agreement (NAFTA) context have induced a marked reaction in environmental groups[3] and in legislators from the Democratic Party who resent the reduced policy autonomy generated by such investment agreements. Following the older authorizations for negotiating trade agreements (such as the "fast track" negotiating authority vested in the U.S. president from 1975–1994 and the Trade Promotion Authority [TPA] vested to the U.S. president in 2002), Democratic lawmakers have managed to introduce clauses seeking to preserve the government's authority to regulate public welfare issues.

The great influence of financial deregulation in the subprime crisis in the United States also has generated a significant current of opinion in academia, international organizations such as the International Monetary Fund (IMF) and the World Bank, and Congress that are aimed at correcting the excesses of financial deregulation. This was reflected in the negotiations of financial issues in the TPP with regard to previous FTAs. In fact, the respective TPP chapter offers more flexibility to governments to control financial flows than did previous U.S. FTAs.

A negotiation between several actors also introduces more restrictions to the principal negotiator in active negotiations with a large number of participants. In this sense, one of the purposes of TPP was to isolate China, so it was essential for the United States to be receptive to Japanese demands. The agreement also aimed to reduce the growing trade and economic dependence Australia had been developing with China. This was perceived by the Australian negotiators, who particularly used that as leverage in the negotiations of biological medicines, as a position that Chile and Peru also supported. Finally, those countries that already had FTAs with the United States (Australia, Canada, Chile, Mexico, Peru, and Singapore) understood the dynamics of negotiating with the country, the relations between negotiators and the U.S. Congress, and the difficulties that each of them had faced in their own parliaments at the time of legislative approval. This experience was fundamental for the TPP to exclude additional requirements on complex issues already addressed in their respective FTAs.

In short, the evolution of the U.S.'s negotiations showed a double trend. On one hand, there was strong pressure from the U.S. business lobbies seeking financial deregulation; high protection for intellectual property rights in pharmaceuticals, software, Internet, and digital issues; and strong investor rights and an ISDS mechanism. On the other hand, negotiating instructions from Congress sought to defend the regulatory space of public policies in areas such as health and the environment, thus limiting the ability of multinational corporations to demand policies or decisions from states in these areas that adversely affected their investments. The net effect of such conflicting pressures and criteria was an important dose of ambiguity in the final texts. This was useful for those governments that negotiated with the United States because they could reach agreements using exactly this ambiguity, which prevented them from assuming commitments that restricted their policy space to a much lesser extent than in past negotiations.

Also, in contrast to patents and public health issues, the United States was more successful in imposing binding positions on issues related to the Internet due to the absence of a multilateral agreement. Thus flexibility for the contracting parties is scarce in technological measures, such as the liability of Internet service providers and legal protections for program-carrying signals transmitted by satellite.

2. DIFFERENCES BETWEEN THE TPP AND PREVIOUS FTAS

The novelty of the TPP was that it dealt with new issues not yet included in the WTO agenda. Table 8.1 shows a synthesis of these novelties. The first column shows the classic issues of a trade agreement covered by WTO. The second column shows issues covered by WTO but only in a very partial way and with few of its members. The third column indicates the subjects that are not present in the WTO agenda. This analysis maintains its validity in the new agreement that excludes the United States, the CPTPP (Comprehensive and Progressive Agreement for Trans-Pacific Parnership).

In the case of the trade of goods, the negotiation goals defined by the U.S. Congress for the trade agreements (including TPP) in the Trade

Table 8.1   Thematic Coverage of Mega-Regional Negotiations, 2014*

Traditional Topics	"Second Generation" Topics	Topics Not Regulated by WTO
Tariffs	Trade in services	Regulatory convergence
Quotas	Intellectual property	E-commerce and digital trade
Customs valuation	Government procurement	State-owned enterprises
Antidumping duties		Investment
Safeguards		Competition policies
Technical norms		Temporary entry of business
Sanitary and phytosanitary		persons
norms		Cross-border data flows
Dispute settlement		Copyright and the Internet
		Export taxes
		Energy trading
		Labor standards
		Conservation of forests,
		fisheries, and protected
		species
		Trade and climate change

* Transatlantic Trade and Investment Partnership, Trans-Pacific Partnership and Regional Comprehensive Economic Partnership

Source: Economic Commission for Latin America and the Caribbean (ECLAC).

Promotion Authority (TPA) established that the main new objective was the connection between global value chains (GVC) and trade liberalization. The liberalization of trade in services is also linked with the GVC, highlighting the role of services in the efficiency of the GVC, on one hand, and the linkage between this liberalization and the plurilateral Trade in Services Agreement (TiSA), on the other.

In turn, the TPA opened the door for the digital trade of goods and services and cross-border data flows. The goal was "to ensure that governments refrain for implementing trade related measures that impede digital trade in goods and services, restrict cross-border data flow, or require local storage or processing of data" (reference to localization requirements).

Another new issue with the TPP was the introduction of "regulatory practices" to stimulate regulatory convergence between members of the TPP. Here the principal objectives proposed by the U.S. Congress were to increase transparency in rules, legislation, and law; eliminate redundancies in testing and certification; and stimulate convergence and regulatory compatibility through harmonization, equivalence, or mutual recognition of different regulations, and the use of international standards.

State-owned and state-controlled enterprises (SOEs) were novelties of the TPP. In this case, the goals were to eliminate and prevent trade distortions and unfair competition that favored SOEs, ensuring engagement based solely on commercial considerations. Another new issue was "localization barriers," and the goal was to prevent and eliminate localization practices and prohibit indigenous innovation wherein a country seeks to develop local technology by the enforced use of domestic standards or local content.

On labor, the TPA stipulated that "each party must adhere to and put in practice the core international labor standards, such as freedom of association, collective bargaining, elimination of forced labor and child labor, elimination of discrimination." On environment, the instruction was to "ensure that enforceable labor & environmental standards are subject to the same dispute settlements mechanism as other enforceable provisions of the agreement and withdrawal of trade concessions until the dispute is resolved."

Finally, on currency issues, the negotiation objective was to "avoid manipulation of the exchange rate in order to prevent the effective balance of payments adjustment or to gain unfair competitive advantage over other parties."

In summary, the merits of the TPP lay in its significant economic weight, particularly after accessions by Canada, Mexico, and Japan. The TPP also addressed multiple issues linked to GVCs, such as the regionalization of exchanges; connectivity, logistics; complexity of cross-border flows; increasing links between trade of goods, services, and investment; disciplines related to property rights of tangible and intangible assets; legal certainty for multinational companies to move GVC segments to developing countries; and digital trade and regulatory convergence. Thus it was much closer to the demands of emerging value chains than the provisions of the stalled multilateral trade system. And herein lies the particular importance of regulatory convergence.

The controversies around TPP lay in the many relevant issues unrelated to trade. The most relevant issues are excessive IPR protections, with strong patent term extension, data exclusivity, and patent linkage; more protection of business interests (such as those of the pharmaceutical industry) than free trade; and an investment chapter with an abusive system of ISDS, with a bias in favor of foreign investors that means a huge imbalance of rights and obligations between investors and state. Another relevant issue concerned the treatment of capital controls and the balance of payments exceptions in previous FTAs wherein the United States did not recognize certain interventions on the capital account that were allowed by the General Agreement on Trade in Services (GATS) and IMF's Articles of

Agreement. Finally, disciplines to regulate SOEs may be too stringent for countries with a high presence of enterprises, particularly in Asia.

The main U.S. goals in the TPP were to create rules to govern the increasingly complex interaction of production activities, trade, and investment within GVCs. But, of course, there are also geopolitical objectives, such as recovering lost competitiveness of U.S. firms from the Chinese and other Asian competitors; limiting the expansion of Chinese firms in East Asia through binding and demanding rules (IPRs, SOEs, Labor & Environment); neutralizing the China-Japan-Korea FTA and Regional Comprehensive Economic Partnership (RCEP) by incorporating Japan and potentially later on Korea into the TPP; and seeking to export TPP commitments into the multilateral framework. In my opinion, the main mistake of the design of the TPP was leaving out China and conceiving the TPP as a game of "all against China." For the world economy and for the best governance of global trade and investment, the best scenario would have been a less ambitious agreement on critical issues, with the ability to engage China in it, forcing a reasonable upgrade of China's trade and investment policies. An agreement of this kind could be easily projected to the multilateral space, providing significant stimulus to the ailing world economy.

3. INTELLECTUAL PROPERTY RIGHTS (IPR)

A. TRIPS AND IPR CHAPTERS IN U.S. FTAS

The main criticisms of the developing countries to the WTO's Agreement on Trade-Related Aspects of Intellectual Property Rights (TRIPS) are: (i) less flexibility to develop public policies in health in general, and in particular, in the case of medicines, given the higher costs of them, when patents on these medicines are introduced; (ii) expansion in the coverage of copyright protection; (iii) limited protection of living matter, genetic resources, and traditional knowledge; and (iv) strong mechanisms of enforcement and dispute settlements. However, TRIPS allowed different timelines for its implementation depending on countries' levels of development.[4]

These flexibilities were much more limited in FTAs, particularly in those promoted by the United States. FTAs limited the flexibilities of the TRIPS agreement in several areas: (i) limitation on the use of compulsory licenses; (ii) restrictions on the freedom to implement systems of exhaustion of rights and, consequently, resorting to parallel imports;[5] (iii) extension of protection to second uses; (iv) expansion of the protection of test data on safety and efficacy of products, which is transformed into a prohibition of use of this information for at least five years after adoption of the pharmaceutical product and ten years after adoption of agrochemicals; and (vi) the possibility to prohibit the marketing of products to third parties before the expiry of the patent protection, except with the consent of the owner.

Abbot (2007) has suggested that the major controversy surrounding the Internet protocol (IP) chapters in U.S.-negotiated FTAs has focused on pharmaceutical-related provisions, including patents and marketing exclusivity requirements. Although country-to-country results vary, the U.S. template has included: (i) extending the scope of patent protection to cover new uses of known compounds, and plants and (on occasion) animals; (ii) providing patent term extensions to offset regulatory delay; (iii) limiting the scope of permissible exceptions to patent rights; (iv) providing fixed periods of marketing exclusivity for a broad class of previously unapproved products based on submission of regulatory data, or reliance on foreign marketing approval or foreign submission of regulatory data; (v) prohibiting the effective granting of marketing approval by the health regulatory authority during the patent term without the consent or acquiescence of patent holders ("linkage"); (vi) authorizing nonviolation nullification or impairment dispute-settlement claims; and (vii) prohibiting parallel importation in some cases (Abbot 2007).[6]

The conclusion of FTAs negotiated by the United States is usually followed by intensive intervention by the USTR (and the U.S. private sector) in the national implementation process as a precondition to bringing the FTA into force. In some cases, the implementation phase has proved to be even more difficult than the treaty negotiation because the USTR's demands may exceed those explicitly enumerated in the FTA, and because these implementation negotiations tend to be "nontransparent" (Abbot 2007). These provisions strengthen the position of originator-patent holder pharmaceutical enterprises on national markets and may impose substantial obstacles to the introduction of generic pharmaceutical products.

The Democratic Party majority in the U.S. Congress in 2007 obtained modification of the pharmaceutical-related provisions in the FTAs with the Executive Branch (USTR 2007) and also required changes to signed but not yet ratified agreements with Colombia, Panama, and Peru. The proposed changes included limiting the granting of marketing exclusivity in some cases to a period contemporaneous with that obtained in the

United States; eliminating provision for patent term extension based on approval delay; eliminating the express linkage between patents and marketing approval; and incorporating an express provision for compulsory licensing notwithstanding existing marketing exclusivity. These changes are a clear improvement and have been extremely important in the evolution of negotiations, including the TPP. However, it must be noted that additional TRIP-plus obligations have been proposed to reduce the magnitude of the changes.[7]

B. TPP'S IPR CHAPTER: HARD PROVISIONS BUT AN IMPORTANT LEVEL OF AMBIGUITY

The relevance of the IPR issue in the TPP may be exemplified by citing the extent and breadth of the treatment given to this subject in the text of the TPP agreement: the chapter covers 74 pages, 83 provisions, 159 footnotes, and 6 annexes. But one of the most important conclusions of this chapter is its high level of ambiguity. Along with drastic provisions aimed at protecting the rights of producers and innovators, other equally precise paragraphs address the need to preserve the space for public policy.

Such a mixture of hard-binding provisions and precise references to respect the main international agreements in matters of public health and dissemination of technologies and similar issues can only generate a final product with a high degree of ambiguity and many loopholes. This ambiguity is the result of contradictory pressures within the United States between big business and some Democratic lawmakers and in negotiations between the United States and its counterparts.

For example, there is a trend in the USTR to align the TRIPS agreement more closely with the interests of big business and to go further in each agreement to create precedents for the next agreement. However, at the same time, the TPA approved by the Congress in 2003 expressed the need to ensure full implementation of the TRIPS agreement. Moreover, in revising the FTA with Colombia, Congress forced the USTR to unilaterally change its negotiating stance, indicating that intellectual property rights obligations should not preclude or prevent a party from taking necessary measures to protect public health.[8] Moreover, for the first time, Congress explicitly stated that if the TRIPS is modified the parties shall consult to introduce corresponding changes in the respective FTAs. This tension between TRIPS and pressures from the powerful pharmaceutical industry provides some flexibility for exclusions in the agreement and the implementation process. In fact, despite the hardness of the provisions, the United States has never used the dispute settlement chapter of its FTAs to invoke patent infringement.

I. IPR CHAPTER IN THE TPP: AN INTRODUCTION STRONGLY COMMITTED TO INTERNATIONAL AGREEMENTS

An interesting novelty in the IPR chapter of the TPP was located in the introductory chapter, which outlines the objectives (18.2), principles (18.3), and agreements with respect to this chapter (18.4). Making the objectives and principles explicit at the beginning of the chapter is important because it provides the context for implementing the agreement and, therefore, should guide discussions in any future controversy on these issues.

The hard provisions protecting the rights of inventors or content producers is included in the agreement alongside calls to abide by international standards and commitments that protect the rights of persons and governments against corporate interests. Several articles provide examples in which the protection and enforcement of IPRs should contribute to, or be compatible with, the promotion of technological innovation and the transfer and dissemination of technology (article 18.2: Objectives); protecting public health and nutrition; preventing the abuse of intellectual property rights by rights holders or the resort to practices that unreasonably restrain trade or adversely affect the international transfer of technology (article 18.3: Principles); promoting innovation and creativity; facilitating the diffusion of information, knowledge, technology, culture, and the arts; and fostering competition and open and efficient markets (article 18.4: Understandings in Respect of this Chapter). Of course, in all cases, these measures should be consistent with the provisions of the chapter.

In other words, the IPR protection can only occur in the context described, which provides a wide range of freedom to governments that eventually may be subject to dispute by application of IPR's chapter. As this is also a state-to-state controversy, the probability of its occurrence is smaller. The inclusion of these provisions is a joint achievement of pressure exerted by the U.S. Congress, on one hand, and the countries that negotiated with the United States, on the other. According to negotiators from several of the participating countries of the TPP, the resulting treaty is a robust defense against future demands on this issue.

This commitment to international agreements is reinforced regarding public health in article 18.6, which protects public health, promotes access to medicines for all, and allows the necessary space to deal with a national emergency or other circumstances of extreme urgency. The pressure of Democrats was consistent on this issue. For example, on May 25, 2016, a group of fifteen House Democrats sent a letter to USTR Michael Froman urging the administration to clarify its position on compulsory licensing for generic medicines in Colombia. The letter said:

> As you know, the issuance of compulsory licenses is permissible under U.S. trade agreements and the WTO Agreement. . . . We therefore find it deeply troubling that U.S. officials may not be respecting the Doha Declaration. . . . There are growing concerns about the very high and increasing costs of pharmaceuticals in the United States and in other nations. And the annual price of this medicine in Colombia is almost twice as much as the average annual income per person in Colombia. As policymakers struggle to address this issue, we should not seek to limit the existing, agreed upon flexibilities public health authorities have to address these concerns. We ask that you clarify the position the Administration has taken in meetings with Colombian officials on this important issue as soon as possible.[9]

II. TPP'S IPR CHAPTER: AN ASSESSMENT

As a preliminary conclusion, the IPR chapter in the TPP includes standards of protection more demanding than that in other TRIPS areas, such as expanding the scope for patentability of an invention; expanding patent terms; data exclusivity; patent linkage; and expanding the scope for trademarks (for sound and smell). However, when comparing the end of negotiations with the initial aspirations of the USTR in terms of strengthening IPR, it is also clear that important goals were not achieved.[10] As previously noted, these demanding provisions coexist with precise references to multilateral commitments that expand the policy space to states. This coexistence can impose additional restrictions on governments, however, due to the high political and economic cost involved when rights holders push to impose more restrictive clauses that eventually pave the way for controversies. Bringing these controversies to the multilateral space would help to develop precedents in the WTO that can apply to members of the WTO with which the United States does not have bilateral agreements, and it would help to put the treatment of such issues on the agenda of an upcoming multilateral round of trade negotiations.

Finally, as Abbot synthesizes:

> U.S. law reflects a balance between the interests of IPRs holders and consumers. Most U.S. IPRs' rules are formulated in terms of general principles and exceptions to them. The FTAs negotiated by the United States largely reflect the general rules of application, though not in all cases. What the FTAs do not adequately reflect is the interplay between rule and exception that establishes the balance. This is of special importance in areas such as public health regulation where incomplete familiarity with the flexibility inherent in the U.S. system may lead its trading partners to conclude that restrictive implementation of the FTAs is required. (2006, 20)

If so, the message is clear: (i) during the negotiating process, developing countries should carefully consider whether the capacity of their domestic legal and regulatory system will permit them to balance interests, as does the U.S. legal system, and avoid accepting commitments that would strain domestic capacity and that could lead to the application of rules in a more restrictive manner than the agreements require; (ii) if commitments are accepted, developing countries should pay careful attention to implementing the agreements in a way that properly reflects the domestic public interest; and (iii) appeals to TRIPS standards and to the successive pronouncements of the U.S. Congress on this topic can be very useful.

4. GLOBAL GOVERNANCE OF INVESTMENTS AND FTAS

The measures of liberalization, promotion, and facilitation of investment are crucial issues for developing countries: improving their position in international value chains, balancing the rights of investors with the legitimate space for public policies, and framing the policy of domestic and foreign investment in a sustainable development approach (UNCTAD 2015). This undeniable fact, however, is still not taken seriously by developing countries, which often fail to treat these issues urgently in international forums. In the absence of these forums, the agenda of the governance of international investment tends to be filled by the messy explosion of bilateral investment agreements or free trade agreements, which include as one of their provisions the criticized ISDS mechanisms.

Widespread criticism of international investment agreements (IIA), and in particular the ISDS scheme, require developing countries themselves to mobilize to propose reforms. Moreover, the difficulties that ISDS have generated in negotiating the Transatlantic Trade and Investment

Partnership (TTIP) between the United States and the EU reveals the possibility of a partnership between developing countries and the EU to create an International Tribunal on Investments that can correct the many failures of the ISDS system.

A. INVESTMENTS IN TRADE AGREEMENTS

WTO agreements have gradually begun to incorporate matters relating to investments, which reflects the growing complementarity between trade in goods and services and investment. Indeed, the phenomenon of value chains has reinforced this link, increasing the relevance of services in the competitiveness, innovation, and transmission of technological in value chains.

However, the multilateral framework has lagged significantly in this area, leaving the field open to bilateral agreements. These bilateral agreements not only grant legal protection to investments but incorporate rules detailing how to treat these investments. The opening of investment schemes has become a key objective of FTA negotiations (Rosales and Sáez 2010). Protecting investments in FTAs consolidates existing provisions and adds new topics such as the prohibition of anticompetitive practices, intellectual property protection, the liberalization of investment approval procedures, and the liberalization of trade in services. Disciplines on investment incentives and tax normally are not included (Sauvé 2006).

This type of agreement seeks to reduce the use of instruments that limit the entry of foreign investment, such as a performance requirement and discrimination in favor of national investment. Most of the controversy revolves around the ISDS mechanism, which is skewed in favor of the external investor and prevents the state from bringing investors to trial. This mechanism also reduces the regulatory public policy space due to the high level of ambiguity in the definitions and procedures. States may face costly lawsuits in their attempts to regulate various aspects of public policies.

Given the widespread debate regarding investor bias in these agreements, promoted mainly by the United States, the FTAs of the United States have been the source of many of these criticisms. An important focus is the concept of "indirect expropriation." In the North American Free Trade Agreement (NAFTA), chapter 11 (investment) prohibited both direct and indirect expropriation, with certain exceptions, but it did not provide a precise definition of this concept. This gave rise to a series of demands based on this ambiguity, including frivolous claims. In the U.S.-Chile FTA, indirect expropriation was defined as "an act or series of acts of a party which have an effect equivalent to a direct expropriation without formal transfer of title or the right of domain" (Chile-U.S. 2003, Annex 10-D, Expropriation, point 4b). The same text clarifies that:

> Except in rare circumstances, nondiscriminatory regulatory actions by a Party that are designed and applied to protect legitimate public welfare objectives, such as public health, safety, and the environment, do not constitute indirect expropriations.

Governments of developing countries are aware of these threats and, as Sauvé (2006) points out, value the exceptions and reservations provided in these agreements, both with respect to existing or future measures and to periods of transition with regard to key disciplines. If these exceptions and reservations are well handled, states can maintain a greater degree of freedom in public policy areas. However, some of these exceptions are limited with respect to what a multilateral investment regime could provide (possibly as part of the multilateral trading system). The challenge remains to develop the negotiating skills necessary to provide adequate handling for exceptions, reservations, and deadlines for implementation in line with medium- and long-term public sector objectives.

Due to the lag in providing multilateral governance for international investments, FTAs have been including investment topics and the ISDS system remains as a potential threat to state deployment of public policies. Developing countries have made a mistake in refusing to discuss a multilateral scheme of investment regimes. The TPP represents progress toward greater balance and more space for public regulation. However, the playing field remains unbalanced, and multilateral governance of the international investment regime is increasingly important.

B. TPP: THE INVESTMENT CHAPTER

The investment chapter of the TPP expanded the regulatory space reserved to states beyond that previously provided in FTAs with the United States, both in environment, public welfare, and health (article 9.16) and in financial regulation (article 29.3; Annex 9-G), where temporary financial safeguards in "exceptional circumstances" are allowed (article 29.3).

For example, article 9.16 states that "none of the provisions of this chapter can be interpreted as a limitation to a state from adopting, maintaining, or enforcing any measure that it considers appropriate to ensure that investment in its territory is conducted in a manner that is sensitive to the environment, health or other regulatory objectives." It is a reaffirmation of the right to regulate that preserve the states, to the extent that regulations are nondiscriminatory.

The following sections present cases in which investment provisions in the TPP were more flexible than previous FTAs signed by the United States.

INVESTORS' EXPECTATIONS

The TPP text talked about "reasonable and unambiguous expectations." The fact that expectations must be clear and unequivocal sets a much more demanding yardstick for any investor seeking to claim that its expectations have been "interfered with" by the government. In addition, the TPP explained what should be understood by "clear and reasonable" (footnote 36), putting the burden of proof on the investor and strengthening the position of the government when applying the measure. In addition, "public interference" can only be claimed when a violation of any provision of the treaty causes a pecuniary loss to the investor. In other words, it is not "any" public interference; public interference in itself is not enough to trigger a sanction. On the contrary, the sanction can only result from an arbitration procedure that establishes the existence of a "violation" of the treaty accompanied by "property damage" to the investor. The "claim" itself does not imply imposition of a "penalty."

In an arbitration procedure, arbitrators should consider factors other than interference, such as "the economic impact of the same" and the "character" of government action. The mere fact that a measure "interferes" with "reasonable and unambiguous expectations" is not sufficient to establish a violation of the treaty nor to initiate arbitral proceedings. This is a clear advance with respect to previous formulations in FTAs.

MINIMUM STANDARD OF TREATMENT

In this area, we also have more accurate and balanced precepts. For example, article 9.6.4. states: "For greater certainty, the mere fact that a Party takes or fails to take an action that may be inconsistent with an investor's expectations does not constitute a breach of this Article, even if there is loss or damage to the covered investment as a result."

> For greater certainty, whether an investor's investment-backed expectations are reasonable depends, to the extent relevant, on factors such

as whether the government provided the investor with binding written assurances and the nature and extent of governmental regulation or the potential for government regulation in the relevant sector. (footnote 36)

Finally, article 9.22.7 delivers a clear statement that in alleging a violation of the minimum standard treatment (MST) the investors bear the burden of proof on all elements.

EXPROPRIATION AND COMPENSATION

Article 9.8 and annex 9-B established that nondiscriminatory regulatory acts of a party that are designed to protect legitimate objectives of public welfare, such as public health, safety, and the environment, do not constitute indirect expropriation. They clarify, in addition, that protection of public health includes measures regarding regulation, price, and supply as well as reimbursement of pharmaceutical products (including biologics, diagnostics, vaccines, medical devices, therapies and genetic technologies, supports and apparatus related to health and blood, or blood-related products). This standard is relevant in light of previous investors' claims that certain regulations have constituted an indirect expropriation.

IMPLEMENTATION OF THE ARBITRATION

Article 9.23 (6) and (7) establish that the tribunal must consider whether the plaintiff's claim or the objection of the respondent is frivolous. Parties to the dispute must be granted reasonable opportunity to present their comments. Also, if an investor submits a claim, the investor has the burden of proof for all elements of the claim in a manner consistent with the general principles of international law applicable to the arbitration. This provision seeks to prevent the use of the dispute-resolution mechanism without information with respect to the breach of an obligation. In short, the outcome is a proper balance between protection of foreign investments and the sovereign right of states to regulate.

Recent literature provides different points of view with respect to the TPP's investment chapter. Hodgson (2015) argues that it widens the regulatory space reserved to states, which is exemplified by the greater flexibilities in environment, health, and public welfare, as well as with flexibilities in financial regulation and the tobacco exception. In broader terms, in his view, "the long controversial coverage of investment agreements and authorizations have been restricted, both in substance and with respect to ISDS." But Johnson and Sachs (2015) believe the changes to investment rules are marginal, contained ambiguous language, and do not address the fundamental concerns about ISDS such as the right to regulate, the burden of proof, investors' expectations, dismissal of frivolous claims, arbitrator ethics, and clarifying rules of nondiscrimination. Also, some "improvements" were expressly or implicitly included in previous agreements.

On investment, the TPP was a step forward when compared with previous FTAs. The bias in favor of external investors was lessened but it persists. This bias was compensated for by the inclusion of several provisions that widen the regulatory space assigned to governments. Reform of the international system of investment governance is still needed that includes a neutral, independent, and efficient dispute-settlement mechanism (DSM). In the new global context of value chains, climate change, and sustainable development, international investment law must enable host governments and investors to maintain a fruitful relationship in the long term.

C. REFORMING THE INTERNATIONAL SYSTEM OF INVESTMENT GOVERNANCE

The great paradox for IIAs and investment chapters in FTAs is that partners may confront demands in ISDS that seek to influence the "undisciplined countries"—those without FTAs. It is important to recognized that countries with IIAs, including those with ISDS mechanisms, do not necessarily receive more foreign direct investment (FDI).

Academic and NGO criticisms of ISDS systems are sufficiently large and well-known (Schill 2015; Johnson, Sachs, and Sachs 2015). Core objectives for reform include: (i) congruence with principles of constitutional law, democracy, and the rule of law; (ii) congruence with human rights; (iii) compatibility with sustainable development; (iv) neutral, transparent, predictable, independent, and efficient dispute settlements; (v) sufficient policy space for host states to regulate in the public interest (updating regulations based on scientific evidence); and (vi) dispute-settlement mechanisms that are accessible to small and medium-sized investors (Schill 2015).

The challenge for developing countries is to build an attractive package for foreign investors that addresses the legitimate crisis of the current system but also promotes and facilitates investment by effectively expanding

DSMs in IIAs to attract responsible investment that will have a positive impact on sustainable development (UNCTAD 2015). While this process advances, governments in developing countries' must be supported by a minimum institutional infrastructure able to identify, track, and manage investment conflicts. This task is part of the state modernization challenge; there is a critical need for coordination between domestic agencies linked to investment, international trade, capital movement and financial issues, regulatory offices, and different geographical levels of government.

The investment issue is of growing importance for developing countries. The current challenge is not only to define the best policies for attracting FDI but to support international expansion of their own firms, including legal stability for multinational enterprises (MNEs) from developing countries, such as the "translatinas."

D. TPP AND TAXATION MEASURES

Free trade agreements in the style of the FTAs signed by United States are said to affect the capacity of governments to act with autonomy with regard to their tax policies. It is argued that these agreements prevent modifying the tax burden or impose new taxes, which limits progressive tax reforms or the establishment of royalties for the exploitation of natural resources. Strictly speaking, that is not correct. Normally tax issues are exempted from the application of the regulations of the FTAs, and that is recorded in the so-called exceptions to the agreement. The only restriction is that any tax changes must be nondiscriminatory in nature, which could mean, for example, that changes meet the criteria of national treatment (NT) and most favored nation (MFN) treatment.

TPP did not display innovations in this area. Chapter 29 addresses tax measure exceptions and specifies the exclusion of tax regulations from the TPP (article 29.4.2); it also validates the countries belonging to various international tax conventions, specifying the primacy of these conventions on the provisions of the TPP (article 29.4.3), and validates NT and MFN commitments on tax policy. Additionally, article 29.4 paragraphs (e), (f), and (g) validate nonconforming tax measures, which are those explicitly left outside the disciplines of the agreement.

The provisions of article 29.4(h) allows adoption of new measures or tax reforms to raise taxes or to improve their progressive structure, subject to the NT and MFN nature of these measures. Finally, article 29.4.8

(Expropriation and Compensation) described the obstacles foreign investors face when pleading expropriation in cases in which tax measures are nondiscriminatory.

5. BALANCE OF PAYMENTS AND REGULATIONS TO CAPITAL FLOWS

Negotiations on trade in financial services in the TPP and in the CPTPP include measures related to financial institutions, investments in financial institutions, cross-border trade in financial services, and the rights of financial regulators to take action to ensure stability in financial markets.

The fourth category—the rights of financial regulators to take action to ensure stability in financial markets—centers mostly on capital controls. Initially, the United States sought to use the language of the U.S.-Korea FTA (KORUS) as a template for the TPP. A reading of the plain language of the financial services chapter (in conjunction with the investment chapter) of the KORUS seemed to indicate that capital controls would not be allowed. Although a "prudential exception" to this limitation exists, it is rather narrow and appears to apply to financial institutions and not to macroeconomic policies applied by governments to address systemwide risks.

This raised concerns in Congress, and a May 2012 letter addressed to Secretary of the Treasury Timothy Geithner and signed by Representatives Barney and Levin requested an official written statement from the Obama administration clarifying the U.S. policy in FTAs and BITs regarding capital controls (both past and present).[11] They sought assurance from the administration that parties to an FTA will have the ability to deploy capital controls on the inflow or outflow of capital without being challenged by private investors. The rationale is that this policy space must be preserved to manage volatility and for long-term controls to avoid a financial crisis like that of 2008–09, a position firmly supported by the IMF and that reflects the emerging challenges of trade in financial services.

Until very recently, the USTR and the U.S. Treasury were dominated by the neoliberal framework addressing the link between opening capital accounts and economic growth. In the opinion of both entities, this openness facilitated access to new sources of savings, improved resource allocation, and favored economic growth. In their view, more financialization was always, and in all places, good for growth and development. Thus they refused financial regulation, stressing that the best financial regulation was self-regulation of the sector. The subprime mortgage crisis sent these policy options into the dustbin and prompted policy changes in the approach of the IMF and the World Bank.

A. CAPITAL FLOWS: NEW ACADEMIC PERSPECTIVES ON TRADE AGREEMENTS

Recent work by the IMF speaks of the need to differentiate capital flows of a short-term character that may be partly speculative from FDI flows that can facilitate technology transfer. Long-term capital flows seem to stimulate economic growth, whereas the impact of short-term flows is less certain and may increase volatility and the frequency of crises (Ostry, Loungani, and Furceri 2016, 581).

> Since 1980, there have been about 150 episodes of surges in capital-inflows in more than 50 emerging market economies and about 20 percent of the time, these episodes end in a financial crisis, and many of these crises are associated with large output declines. (Ghosh, Ostry, and Qureshi 2016)

TPP members have addressed capital controls in a variety of ways in agreements between one another (see table 8.2). For example, Chile, Peru, and Singapore tried to obtain greater flexibility to impose capital controls in their FTAs with the United States, but they were only able to get a special dispute-settlement procedure that includes an additional six-month cooling off period before investors can file a case and that limits damages. The Australia-Singapore FTA and the Malaysia-New Zealand FTA both allow either party to adopt restrictions on transfer of payments related to investment in the event of serious balance of payments and external financial difficulties or threat thereof.

B. BALANCE OF PAYMENTS, CAPITAL MOVEMENTS: EVOLUTION IN U.S. APPROACHES

In the FTAs negotiated by the EU with Latin American countries, the balance of payments chapter applies to "all current payments and capital movements between the Parties," forcing them to allow payments and transfers in freely convertible currency and in concordance with the IMF Articles of Agreement.[12] The chapter also allows exceptions and has safeguards for exceptional circumstances.[13] In such a case, it is possible to apply measures beyond the obligations of the treaty. Those measures may last one year but can be extended if the exceptional circumstances

Table 8.2 Treatment of Capital Controls in FTAs and BITs

Treatment of Capital Controls	Coverage in Existing Agreements
Capital controls are prohibited, but there are special procedures for disputes related to certain types of controls. These include an extended cooling off period before investors can file claims and have limits on damages.	U.S.-Singapore FTA
	U.S.-Chile FTA U.S.-Peru FTA
Capital controls are prohibited, but a safeguard with some special restrictions allows for the use of capital controls in the event of serious balance of payments and external financial difficulties or threat thereof	Australia-Chile FTA
	Australia-Malaysia FTA Australia-New Zealand FTA Australia-Singapore FTA New Zealand-Singapore FTA
Capital controls are prohibited, no ISDS.	Australia-Malaysia FTA Australia-New Zealand FTA
Capital account liberalization is encouraged, but agreements defer to national law.	Malaysia-Chile BIT
	Malaysia-Peru BIT Malaysia-Viet Nam BIT Singapore-Peru BIT Singapore-Viet Nam BIT Chile-New Zealand BIT Chile-Peru BIT Chile-Viet Nam BIT Australia-Chile FTA Australia-Viet Nam BIT

Source: Boston University Pardee Center (2013).

continue. These provisions are similar to those contained in articles 59 and 60 of the Maastricht Treaty.

In contrast, the United States refused to accept capital-controls measures and balance-of-payments (BoP) exceptions in FTAs negotiated with Latin American countries (Sáez 2010). The mandate given by Congress to the USTR did not allow for use of these measures, which are accepted by GATS and the IMF Articles of Agreements. The FTA with Chile was the first one to use this approach, and the issue was finally resolved at the highest political level through an annex applicable to measures adopted by Chile that could be subject to dispute settlement by U.S. investors.

According to this annex, a U.S. firm may claim damages if it believes Chile is breaching an obligation when applying a restriction on payments and transfers.[14] The claim can be submitted only one year after the measure is adopted and can refer only to the reduction in the value of transfers, not subsequent effects on profits, showing a distinction between volatile and nonvolatile capital flows. This reflects Chile's use in the past of unremunerated reserve requirements on capital to address the volatility of short-term inflows in the 1990s and its willingness to keep open the possibility of reusing this policy instrument in the future.[15]

In the case of BoP, the TPP showed a significant change from previous U.S. FTAs, enshrining the balance-of-payments provisions of both GATT 1994 and the IMF rules in annex 29.3 (Exceptions of Balance of Payments). In previous FTAs, the United States had refused to pick up these provisions, accentuating the emphasis on financial deregulation. Provisions in the TPP and in the CPTPP allow governments to restrict payments and transfers, both current and capital, "in the event of serious balance of payments and external financial difficulties or threats thereof." These measures "shall not exceed 18 months in duration"; "however, in exceptional circumstances, a Party may extend such measure for additional periods of one year." These measures are subject to the requirements of NT, MFN, and expropriation and compensation provisions, and they must be consistent with the IMF agreement and article 12 of GATT 1994 and the Understanding on the Balance of Payments Provisions.

6. FINAL REFLECTIONS: FTA AND DEVELOPMENT

A. REASONS TO NEGOTIATE

The best scenario for trade negotiations for developing countries is on the multilateral stage. For example, an updated WTO, with trade agreements of comprehensive coverage and depth, would be the best-case scenario, as it could deal with the challenges of technological change; value chains; the growing link between trade in goods, services, and investments; e-commerce; and the challenges of intellectual property in this new context. Unfortunately, the WTO is far from able to address these issues today.

With the weakening of the WTO, regional integration emerges as second best, and the EU is the best example of this. However, this route requires leadership and political consensus, which is not always present in developing countries. Failure of integration in Latin America is one example of this. For small and open economies in this region, the weakness of multilateral and regional options has influenced several countries, particularly Chile, Colombia, Mexico, and Peru, to engage in bilateral trade agreements with extra-regional economies, particularly with major trading partners such as the United States, the EU, and China. There is an important "domino effect" associated with these negotiations. When the United States or the EU negotiates an FTA with a developing country, nearby countries without trade agreements may experience a competitive disadvantage in those markets with major products. To overcome this disadvantage, these countries also may seek bilateral trade negotiations with these partners.

FTAs by themselves do not assure dynamism or export diversification; nor do they guarantee greater FDI flows. It is indeed a naïve view that a free trade agreement will automatically trigger an important increase in exports. In an extreme case, this could happen if Country A, which has a great competitive potential, negotiates an FTA with Country B, which has high tariffs and nontariff barriers to products for which Country A is very competitive. If those countries are geographically close and transportation costs are small, and if the FTA effectively addressed the trade barriers, including the nontrade barriers, the FTA will quickly favor exports from Country A in the direction of Country B.

In real life, however, the results are more complex because now there is an extensive network of trade agreements and there are many competitors who have trade agreements with the major economies. Tariffs have fallen in a systematic way, and nontrade barriers can be as or more important than tariffs and may not be well covered in trade agreements. In addition, the link of goods-services-investment is increasingly important, and that link is well treated only in a small number of trade agreements. Finally, to be effective, the benefits derived from trade agreements must be accompanied by domestic advances in infrastructure, logistics, and transport, and this does not always happen.

Why, then, do developing countries seek to negotiate FTAs with the United States or the EU? They negotiate because there are trade and nontrade benefits. Among the various reasons given to justify North-South free trade negotiations are these: (i) attracting investment with high standards; (ii) accessing new technologies; (iii) facilitating participation in value chains linked to main trading partners; (iv) through these processes, enhancing business modernization; and (v) facilitating additional higher-standard FTAs with other trade partners.

The market access advantages available in the FTAs do not lie only in the reduction or elimination of tariffs. In the case of FTAs with the United States, for example, these additional benefits help to consolidate GPS access, compensate tariff advantages of competitors, eliminate tariff peaks, eliminate tariff escalation that blocks export diversification, and avoid trade barriers based on sanitary and phytosanitary measures or technical barriers. For countries in the region far from the United States but with a network of FTAs, such as Chile or Peru, other benefits of these agreements have been improved competitiveness by raising the quality and timeliness requirements of national companies; more opportunities for business and technological alliances with partners of the industrialized world; and growth of an entrepreneurial culture oriented to seize opportunities in the global economy.

Other benefits that justify these agreements include stimulating the presence of small and medium enterprises (SMEs) in trade, stimulating productivity and innovation, and increasing export diversification (Gervin 2015). However, these objectives are not achieved automatically; FTAs are only part of the equation. These FTAs can afford to take advantage of commercial opportunities to the extent that investments in infrastructure, logistics, and transport are made and workers' skills are strengthened. But with or without FTAs, the key tool is active industrial policies that foster innovation and productivity and strengthen linkages between exports and the rest of the economy.

Stimulating productivity, innovation, and export diversification is a challenge not related to the FTAs. It is defined by the domestic adoption of appropriate policies. Countries with FTAs but that lack industrial policies cannot achieve these objectives, whereas countries with active industrial policies but without FTAs may move forward on these important challenges. Several countries in the region failed because they thought of FTAs as a substitute for policies to diversify the productive structure. Without robust policies that support the SMEs in the use of FTAs, benefits will be limited, possibly generating advantages only for traditional exporters. If this is the outcome, FTAs will not help to reduce inequalities.

B. DEALING WITH THE COSTS OF NEGOTIATIONS

Depending on the institutional framework and the quality of the negotiation, there may be significant costs. Of course, each country must make its own cost-benefit analysis to make the appropriate decision. This must

be framed in a strategy of long-term development that adequately balances the internal and external challenges and defines precise areas to
improve the quality of the international insertion. It may be convenient
to negotiate FTAs with some of these economic giants, but these negotiations can affect important areas of economic policy. It is, therefore,
essential to develop negotiating strategies to realize medium-term objectives and to detect issues that may affect the strength of the long-term
development strategy.

A negotiating strategy has a variety of possible instruments. The first
tool defines areas (sectors, themes, or activities) that will be out of the
agreement and, therefore, will not form part of the negotiation. This is
referred to in negotiating jargon as exclusions or nonconforming measures (NCMs). For example, there are the NCMs of annex I in the TPP
(Present Measures) and annex II (Futures Measures), wherein the state
parties of the agreement reserve the right not to respect NT or MFN
clauses, or other sectors specifically defined.[16]

A second tool is to exploit the internal differences of the other party,
if they exist. We saw that important differences of opinion existed in
American society regarding issues in these agreements. It is important to
manage relationships with the various actors of the negotiating counter-
part (the legislature, administration, business, academics), collect legal
precedents, and understand academic and legislative arguments that can
aid in outlining your negotiating strategy.

Take a lesson from the American practice and maintain close contact
with national members of the legislature, explain how they can place
limits on excessive concessions or emphasize the offensive objectives in
the negotiation. Use the legislature as an esquire protection similar to
what U.S. negotiators do: explain the limits the legislature places on the
agreement and avoiding further discussion on certain subjects. Finally,
the ambiguity in final texts is extremely useful when there is not an auspi-
cious field for precise agreements.

C. POLICY SPACE AND COMPLEMENTARY POLICIES

In economics, there is consensus favoring the impact of trade on economic
growth, technology diffusion, and best business practices. However, it is
clear that not everyone benefits equally. Increases in trade and open markets may require difficult adjustments, particularly for firms with lower
productivity levels and for workers with lower skills. Hence it is important

to accompany trade agreements with explicit policies that support firms and workers with financial assistance and retraining and to train workers who will eventually be displaced due to the higher level of imports.

WTO and FTAs have limited some instruments, such as export subsidies or FDI performance requirements. But important policy space remains in several critical areas: (i) support for innovation and research and development policies; (ii) preferences for SMEs in public procurement; (iii) support for "green" goods and services; (iv) selective attraction of FDI; (v) possible use of production clusters and other policies for local development; (vi) support for development of specialized suppliers; (vii) specialized human capital programs and training programs for workers; and (viii) certification of competencies and quality certification.

Normally, the problem with executing these policies lies not in conflict with the FTAs but in limited resources for them, which reduces their impact on the productive and export structure. A further limitation is that the hallmark of modern industrial policy that inspires some public agencies is not necessarily shared by other areas of the government, resulting in lack of coordination affecting the overall effectiveness of the policy. Open economy industrial policies that stimulate innovation, productivity, and entrepreneurship are not limited by the FTAs. Other limitations on the policy space may lie in the poor design of policies, lack of coordination between the various public agencies, or in the short life of programs due to changes with each government cycle.

In any case, the TPP contains rules that can effectively reduce the space of policies for developing countries when compared with WTO regulations. This is true for IPR, investment, balance of payments, financial services, and capital flows. What is new, however, is that the TPP breaks with the USTR's tradition of a permanent increase in the intensity of the requirements of each FTA. The reasons for this were explained in the text: (i) the novelty of negotiating with the other eleven countries, including two members of the G7 (Canada and Japan) and four members of the G20 (Australia, Canada, Japan, and Mexico); and (ii) internal differences in the U.S. Congress with regard to issues such as labor, environment, ISDS, and IPR.

D. THE TPP IS DEAD, LONG LIVE THE NEW TRANSPACIFIC DEAL

President Trump had excluded the United States from the TPP, and a new era seems to have begun. In any case, some major business associations did not support the TPP because three key issues were not addressed:

(i) the provisions on biologic drugs needed to be strengthened to provide the pharmaceutical sector with a level of protection similar to that in the U.S. market (twelve years); (ii) two specific provisions on financial services were missing: lack of application to financial services of language prohibiting governments from requiring data to be stored on local servers,[17] and a provision that allows Malaysia to maintain a screening mechanism under which it can block foreign investment in financial services if it deems them not in the best interest of the country; and (iii) language in the TPP allowing government to block investor-state challenges of their antitobacco policies. USTR had pointed out that these objections can be addressed through side letters or through the implementation plans of the agreement.

This unilateral pressure from the United States was breaking the plurilateral nature of the TPP and the delicate balance between the twelve members. The United States (61.4 percent) and Japan (17.2 percent) comprised 78 percent of the total GDP of the TPP, so without the endorsement of the United States and Japan, the agreement would not enter into force.[18]

A new opportunity is opening in the area of trade negotiations. In fact, the TPP was reinvented without the United States and the name of the new deal of the eleven countries is Comprehensive and Progressive Agreement for Transpacific Partenership. In the meantime the Free Trade Area of the Asia-Pacific (FTAAP)— a free trade agreement in the Asia-Pacific Economic Cooperation (APEC) forum driven by China—will continue its slow but persistent advance. The Regional Comprehensive Economic Partnership promoted by China in Asia and the "One Belt, One Road" initiative are other relevant issues that have to be followed carefully.

The antiglobalization climate is stronger in the United States and the EU today than it is in developing countries. There is growing support in developing countries for measures to increase the regulation of financial flows and to reduce the investors' space to sue states. It is, therefore, an opportune moment for developing countries to adopt a more proactive stance on reforming the governance of trade and global investments rules.

Latin America, for example, should seek partnerships with the EU and China to promote the reform and modernization of the WTO, the establishment of an International Tribunal of Investments, correcting the bias of the current ISDS system. It could also promote new international arrangements to update and deepen the TRIPS agreement, preserving developing economies interests and supporting the EU in its attempts to enlarge the regulatory space for financial flows. It could also reinforce the link with academics and U.S. legislators who are committed to these issues. If Latin America hopes to play a more relevant role in the new architecture of the new institutional building of twenty-first century trade, then the convergence of the Pacific Alliance and Mercosur is more urgent.

Questioning the mega-trade agreements without considering alternatives has not been a good strategy for developing countries. The vacuum tends to be filled by FTAs promoted by the United States or the EU. Taking advantage of the new political stance in the developed countries, with greater resistance to the impacts of globalization, developing countries could begin to design new forms of globalization. This would require adoption of new policy schemes: open economies, countercyclical macroeconomic policies, control of short-term capital inflows, macroprudential regulations, modern industrial policies with an emphasis on innovation, and meeting the demands of climate change. Overcoming the marked inequalities of the twentieth century will not be possible without confronting these requirements. Developing countries should not be content to play a secondary role in the design of a twenty-first century global scenario.

NOTES

I appreciate the effective collaboration of Tania García-Millán in the preparation of this text.

1. Previously, the Democratic Party had pressured the U.S. Trade Representative (USTR) to reformulate several points already negotiated in the FTA with Colombia, giving more flexibility to Colombia in the field of intellectual property that protects the pharmaceutical industry.

2. This explains the remarkable support for antiestablishment presidential candidates in the 2016 U.S. election, as well as the fact that the two major candidates opposed TPP, and once in power President Trump announced that the United States would not sign the agreement.

3. The vast majority of the demands of the United States against other states correspond to mining or energy companies claiming breach of bilateral investment agreements.

4. This section borrows from Rosales and Sáez (2010).

5. Parallel imports are goods brought into a country without the authorization of the patent, trademark, or copyright holder after these goods have been put in circulation elsewhere. The TRIPS agreement recognizes the right of each country to have its own regulations on parallel imports.

6. Of course there are differences between different FTAs negotiated by the United States. For example, FTAs with Latin American countries have not limited the use of compulsory licenses as did those with Morocco and Singapore. The same is the case of

parallel imports, as opposed to those undersigned by the United States with Australia and Morocco. In the case of "second applications," the FTA with Chile specifies that marketing permissions relate to "new chemical entities," which were not collected in the CAFTA-DR.

7. Patents and marketing exclusivity are to be expressly de-linked, but signatories will be obligated to provide transparent and expeditious mechanisms for initiating patent infringement litigation. Direct patent term extension will be eliminated, but obligations will be added to ensure expeditious processing of applications for patents and marketing approval. Although marketing exclusivity obligations may be limited, in some cases to periods contemporaneous with those running in the United States, the basic requirement of marketing exclusivity remains a substantial TRIPS-plus obligation (Abbot 2007).

8. The complete reference is: "The obligations of this Chapter do not and should not prevent a Party from taking measures to protect public health. Accordingly, while reiterating their commitment to this Chapter, the Parties affirm that this Chapter can and should be interpreted and implemented in a manner supportive of each Party's right to protect public health and, in particular, to promote access to medicines for all. Each Party has the right to determine what constitutes a national emergency or other circumstances of extreme urgency, it being understood that public health crises, including those relating to HIV/AIDS, tuberculosis, malaria and other epidemics, can represent a national emergency or other circumstances of extreme urgency" (TPP Chapter 18, article 18.6).

9. The letter was led by Ways and Means Committee Ranking Member Sander Levin (D-MI) and also signed by Reps. Jim McGovern (D-MA), Jim McDermott (D-WA), Jan Schakowsky (D-IL), Eddie Bernice Johnson (D-TX), Peter Welch (D-VT), Rosa DeLauro (D-CT), John Lewis (DGA), Barbara Lee (D-CA), Chris Van Hollen (D-MD), Peter DeFazio (D-OR), Lloyd Doggett (D-TX), David E. Price (D-NC), Carolyn B. Maloney (D-NY), and Sam Farr (D-CA).

10. Some objectives of the USTR not enshrined in the final agreement include the following: (i) responsibility of ISP to replicate the U.S. system of notification of copyright infringement and automatically drop content; (ii) technological protection measures that sanction infringement independent of whether or not the infringement is linked to a copyright; (iii) patenting surgical procedures, patenting animals (genetic sequences or similar), and patenting plants; (iv) treble damages in patent infringement (fines three times the damage); (v) more precise patentability criteria (novelty, inventive step, and industrial application) and more flexibility in implementation; (vi) payment of reasonable royalties for patent infringement; (vii) "linkage" so health authority cannot grant sanitary permits to generic pharmaceutical products until expiration of the patent; (viii) protection of undisclosed information for biological pharmaceutical products (twelve years); and (ix) definition of biological pharmaceutical products (including proteins, vaccines, and blood derivatives). This information was provided by the Chilean negotiators of the TPP.

11. This is a novel approach. Traditionally treaty law allow parties to make interpretations of language through letters exchanged contemporaneously with negotiations with the intent that they are binding.

12. In the NAFTA model of negotiation, capital movements appear in the invest-ment chapter (through ISDS), in the services chapter (article 10.12: Payments and Transfers), or in the exceptions chapter, which is similar to the TPP. See Sáez (2010).

13. These safeguards describe "exceptional circumstances, payments and capital movements between the Parties [that] cause or threaten to cause serious difficulties for the operation of monetary policy or exchange rate policy of either Party."

14. "A claimant may submit any such claim only after one year has elapsed since the events giving rise to the claim" (Annex 10-C, Special Dispute Settlement Provi-sions, 1a); "the claimant may, on behalf of the enterprise, only seek damages with respect to the shares of the enterprise for which the claimant has a beneficial interest" (Annex 10-C, Special Dispute Settlement Provisions, 1b); and "loss or damages arising from restrictive measures on capital inflows shall be limited to the reduction in value of the transfers and shall exclude loss of profits or business and any similar consequential or incidental damages" (Annex 10-C, Special Dispute Settlement Provisions, 1c).

15. In the same spirit, claims can be immediately submitted when restrictions affect transfers related to FDI and payments pursuant to a loan or bond issued in a foreign market, provided that such payments are made in accordance with the maturity date agreed on in the loan or bond agreement.

16. For example, in the TPP, Chile's annex I has 38 pages and annex II has 24 pages. They cover issues as varied as health care and child care; education; social services, social security; environmental services; construction services; mining; energy; hunting; domestic and international transportation; communications; arts and cultural indus-tries; entertainment, audiovisual and broadcasting services; and the rights or prefer-ences of socially or economically disadvantaged minorities, or indigenous peoples.

17. In the U.S. House, sixty-three bipartisan lawmakers are urging the USTR to ban the local server requirement for the financial sector in the TPP and in future FTAs.

18. In fact, the TPP will enter into force once approved in their parliaments by all the members within a period of up to two years of signing the agreement, which took place in February 2016. If all members have not passed it legislatively in two years, the TPP shall enter into force sixty days after the expiry of this period if at least six of the original signatories, which together account for at least 85 percent of the combined gross domestic product of the original signatories in 2013, have approved it.

REFERENCES

Abbot, Frederick M. 2006. "IP Provisions of Bilateral and Regional Trade Agreements in Light of U.S. Federal Law." UNCTAD/ICTSD Project on IPR and Sustainable Development. Geneva: UNCTAD/ICTSD.

Abbot, Frederick M. 2007. "The Problems of Intellectual Property in Latin America and How to Address Them." ECLAC Project Document, December. Santiago: ECLAC.

Boston University Pardee Center. 2013. "Capital Account Regulations and the Trading System: A Compatibility Review." BU Pardee Center Task Force Report.

Chile-United States. 2003. "Chile-United States Free Trade Agreement." https://ustr .gov/trade-agreements/free-trade-agreements/chile-fta/final-text.

Gervin, Ed. 2015. "The TPP and Small Business: Boosting Exports and Inclusive Growth." Progressive Policy Institute Policy Brief, November. Washington, DC: Progressive Policy Institute.

Ghosh, Alish, Jonathan Ostry, and Mahvash Qureshi. 2016. "When Do Capital Inflow Surges End in Tears." *American Economic Review* 106 (5): 581–85.

Hodgson, Mélida. 2015. "The Trans-Pacific Partnership Investment Chapter Sets a New Worldwide Standard." Columbia FDI Perspectives No. 160. New York: Columbia Center on Sustainable Investment.

Johnson, Lise, and Lisa Sachs. 2015. "The TPP's Investment Chapter: Entrenching, Rather Than Reforming, a Flawed System." CCSI Policy Paper, November. New York: Columbia Center on Sustainable Investment.

Johnson, Lise, Lisa Sachs, and Jeffrey Sachs. 2015. "Investor-State Dispute Settlement, Public Interest and U.S. Domestic Law." CCSI Policy Paper, May. New York: Columbia Center on Sustainable Investment.

Ostry, Jonathan, Prakash Loungani, and Davide Furceri. 2016. "Neoliberalism: Oversold?" *Finance and Development* 53 (2): 38–41.

Rosales, Osvaldo, and Sebastián Sáez. 2010. "Temas controversiales en las negociaciones comerciales Norte-Sur." In *Temas controversiales en negociaciones comerciales Norte-Sur*, Libros de la CEPAL No. 106. Santiago: Economic Commission for Latin America and the Caribbean (ECLAC).

Sauvé, Pierre. 2006. *Trade and Investment Rules: Latin American Perspectives*. Serie Comercio Internacional No. 66. Santiago: Economic Commission for Latin America and the Caribbean (ECLAC).

Sáez, Raul. 2010. "Trade in Financial Services: The Case of Chile." In *Financial Services and Preferential Trade Agreements, Lessons from Latin America*, ed. Mona Haddad and Constantinos Stephanou. Washington, DC: World Bank.

Schill, Stephan. 2015. "Reforming Investor-State Dispute Settlement (ISDS): Conceptual Framework and Options for the Way Forward." E15 Task Force on Investment Policy, The E15 Initiative, Strengthening the Global Trade and Investment System for Sustainable Development, July. Geneva: ICSTD, WEF.

UNCTAD. 2015. "World Investment Report. Reforming International Investment Governance." Geneva: United Nations.

USTR. 2007. "Bipartisan Agreement on Trade Policy: Intellectual Property, May 2007, Trade Facts." https://ustr.gov/sites/default/files/uploads/factsheets/2007/asset_upload_file127_11319.pdf.

U.S. Congress. 2015. "Bipartisan Congressional Trade Priorities and Accountability Act of 2015." Section 2: Trade Negotiating Objectives. https://www.congress.gov./bill//114th-congress/senate-bill/995/text.

CHAPTER 9

The Effects of International Tax Competition on National Income Distribution

Valpy FitzGerald and Erika Dayle Siu

1. INTRODUCTION

Globalization involves increasing freedom of capital movement: both for firms from industrialized countries investing in developing countries and for financial asset owners in developing countries themselves. Standard principles of international taxation suggest that the tax burden should fall most heavily on those factors of production that are least mobile to maximize government income and minimize the disincentives to economic growth. As global market integration has deepened, tax competition has driven down taxes on mobile factors of production (capital and highly skilled labor) and thus tends to both increase taxation on immobile factors (not only land and natural resources but also unskilled labor and those outside the labor force) and reduce government expenditure—or raise indirect taxation—thereby worsening income distribution.

The long-term trend toward lower rates of both corporate income tax (CIT) and personal income tax (PIT) is clear. CIT rates have declined by about one-third in all country groups over the past three decades (figure 9.1), and the top marginal PIT rate has declined in almost all countries by a similar proportion (table 9.1). Both forms of income taxation are in fact dominated by capital income—directly in the case of CIT and indirectly in the case of PIT, where higher incomes are mainly dividend returns and asset gains. The downward trend in statutory rates and the pressure on the taxable base itself is the result of countries competing to attract investment by foreign investors and retain that of domestic wealth holders able to move their capital abroad.

Because governments must maintain expenditure levels, an important consequence of the downward trend of the rates of both types of income

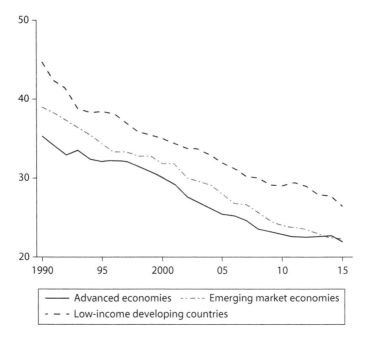

Figure 9.1   Average Corporate Income Tax Rate 1990–2015 (percent).
Source: **IMF (2017).**

tax has been a shift toward consumption taxes over the past three decades (figure 9.2). Consumption taxes are essentially taxes on labor incomes; therefore, the effect of this changing balance is to increase income inequality in both developed and developing countries.

This downward pressure on income tax rates (both CIT and PIT) is derived from domestic political pressures as well as from international

Table 9.1   Top Personal Income Tax Rates 1981–2010

	1981	1990	2000	2010
Australia	60	47	47	45
Canada	43	29	29	29
France	60	57	53	40
Germany	56	53	51	45
Italy	72	50	49	43
Japan	75	50	37	40
United Kingdom	60	40	40	50
United States	70	28	40	35

Source: OECD (2011, table 9.9).

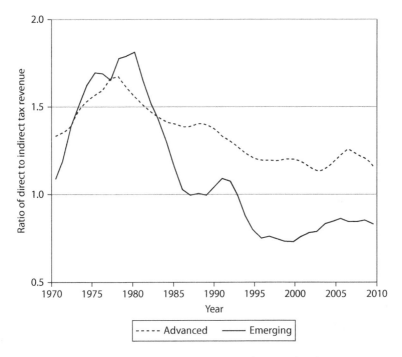

Figure 9.2   Long-term trend in balance between direct and indirect taxation as sources of government revenue. *Source*: IMF (2013).

competition and reflects a shift away from the post-WWII consensus on the welfare state in developed countries, market transitions from socialism, and the end of planned economic development in poor countries. In effect, the two drivers are mutually reinforcing, but it is reasonable to assume that in larger economies domestic political pressures will predominate, whereas in smaller emerging economies international competition will do so.

That these changes pose a serious equity issue is without doubt, as the Organisation for European Economic Cooperation and Development (OECD) points out:

It is generally assumed that choices related to corporate taxation are most affected by globalisation because of the ease with which multinational enterprises can move the location of at least some of their activities. However, highly skilled workers are also becoming more mobile and some countries are taking this into account in designing their personal tax systems.

In contrast, the taxation of lower-skilled workers and of consumption is seen as being less affected by globalisation because these tax bases are less mobile. . . . a shift in the tax structure from mobile income taxes to less mobile taxes, such as consumption taxes, would reduce progressivity since consumption taxes are in general less progressive than income taxes.

Therefore, such tax shifts imply a trade-off between growth enhancing tax reforms and equity. (OECD 2010a, 20)

This "new orthodoxy" espoused by international organizations (including the IMF) differs from the traditional position of neoclassical economists who argue, assuming full employment, that lower profit taxes will raise the capital-labor ratio and thus wages as well, so that there is no such trade-off. In other words, lower profit taxation will increase growth and reduce inequality. However, as we shall see, even belief in the existence of a "trade-off" of this nature—based on the idea that lower profit taxes increase investment rates and thus growth—however intuitive, is not really justified on either empirical or theoretical grounds.

The erosion of the direct tax base through tax avoidance and evasion has been a major concern for the advanced economies for over two decades (OECD 1998). Corporations mainly engage in tax avoidance (within the letter if not the spirit of the law), and high-net-worth individuals mainly engage in tax evasion by not declaring their overseas assets to the relevant authorities in their country of tax residence. Profit tax revenue is even more important for developing countries that host major international investments with beneficial ownership resident abroad.

However, current international taxation arrangements clearly require strategic enhancement to effectively address tax competition given the difficulties in acquiring the potential fiscal resources generated by both foreign and domestic transborder firms and the consequences for both capital flight and social equity of the inability to tax residents' overseas assets. That is, the problem is not only one of the tax *rate* applied but also—and more important—of the tax *base* to which these rates are applied.

This tax base is increasingly undermined by aggressive avoidance schemes and "offshore" asset structures. Competition to attract such investments merely on the basis of preferential taxation leads to global welfare losses, which are exacerbated by secrecy protections for beneficial owners. Nonetheless, the global network of offshore financial centers, which promotes tax avoidance and evasion and generally impedes financial regulation, is vast.

To address these issues, in this chapter we examine both the direct impact of international tax competition on income distribution through tax incidence and the indirect effect through fiscal adjustment. Section 2 summarizes the evidence on the nature, scale, and consequences of international tax competition, focusing on corporation tax for which most evidence is available. The effect of PIT evasion on domestic income distribution is less researched, but fortunately it is uncomplicated in its immediate impact on inequality.

Section 3 addresses the economics of profit taxation in terms of its effect on wages, investment, and growth, on one hand, and on fiscal balances and income distribution, on the other. It is shown that profit taxes do have a positive redistributive effect through their various channels of impact and thus that international tax competition has the effect of increasing inequality at the national level. Section 4 explores the implications for developing countries in particular with regard to effective international tax coordination because in relative terms at least they are the main victims of international tax competition. Section 5 examines the evolution of international tax cooperation and the improvements necessary to increase fiscal income and replace the failing system of official development assistance. We conclude with some observations on the changes in intergovernmental institutions that would be required for the international tax regime to contribute to reduced inequality at the national level.

2. THE NATURE AND CONSEQUENCES OF INTERNATIONAL TAX COMPETITION

All countries levy CIT, largely because it is easier to collect from registered and regulated companies than from individual shareholders, many of whom may reside (or pretend to reside) abroad. Indeed, many shareholders may not reside in the host country, especially in developing host countries, so taxing only personal wealth would remove the ability of host countries to tax the income of corporations operating within their borders. Furthermore, CIT effectively taxes earnings that companies retain, which are hard to tax at the personal level. Similarly, if there was no corporate tax, small businesses could escape tax by incorporating and labeling their earnings as capital income.

Nonetheless, since the 1980s, statutory CIT rates have declined from an average of some 45 percent of (declared) profits after allowed deductions to around 25 percent in developed countries. In high- and middle-income developing countries ("emerging markets") the average rate has fallen from 40 percent to 25 percent; and in low-income developing countries from 45 percent to 30 percent (IMF 2014). There are domestic reasons for this shift, including changing attitudes toward the private sector and the decline of organized labor, but with increasing capital mobility worldwide, the competition between countries to attract foreign firms (and to retain their own) has been a major driver (Leibrecht and Hochgatterer 2012).

In fact, as table 9.2 shows, *effective* CIT rates—that is, the amount of tax corporations actually pay as a proportion of profits (World Bank 2016)—are much lower than the statutory rates depicted in figure 9.1 due to the large allowances made to firms in domestic tax legislation. Indeed, such deductions from the taxable base are a key form of international tax competition. In high-income OECD countries, the effective rate is now only 13 percent of profits, and in developing countries it varies by region—from 11 to 20 percent—with an average of around 16 percent. Worldwide, the World Bank estimates that the CIT burden is only 14 percent of (declared) profits. In other words, about one-half of the statutory rates, which have themselves declined steadily over past decades.

Multinational enterprises (MNEs), furthermore, pay an even lower effective rate because a large part of their profits is reported in offshore financial centers (which gives them an unfair advantage over domestic firms). At the same time, the importance of CIT revenue to developing countries is much greater and has been rising over time: in the 1980s it represented about 12 percent of fiscal revenue and now about 16 percent.

Table 9.2   Corporate Income Tax (CIT) Paid, as a Percentage of Corporate Profits

Region	CIT as % of Profits
East Asia	17
Europe and Central Asia	11
Latin America and the Caribbean	20
Middle East and North Africa	13
South Asia	15
Sub-Saharan Africa	18
Subtotal Developing*	**16**
OECD (high income)	13
World*	**14**

*Subtotal and world weighted by GDP.

Source: World Bank (2016).

In developed countries, it has remained at around 8 percent (albeit rising and falling during the recent boom).

The key issue, in consequence, is not so much the CIT *rate* (which appears to be converging worldwide at around 25 percent apart, of course, from tax havens) but rather the CIT *base*, which is eroded both by excessive allowances to firms and shifting profits to lower-tax jurisdictions. A recent survey (Reidel 2014) of econometric work on this issue shows quantitative estimates varying across approaches and studies, but it suggests that MNEs as a whole transfer 30 percent or more of their income earned at high-tax affiliates to lower-tax entities. The United States, for instance, suffered estimated losses in 2004 and 2008 of $60 billion and $90 billion, respectively, or about 30 percent of CIT revenues (Clausing 2011).

The OECD "conservatively" estimates that base erosion and profit shifting (BEPS) causes revenue losses worldwide of between $100 and $240 billion annually—equivalent to 4 to 10 percent of global revenues from CIT. Given developing countries' greater reliance on such revenues, estimates of the impact on these countries, as a percentage of GDP, is even higher. These sums are of a similar order of magnitude to the total flow of international development assistance (OECD 2015).

The rising ratio of CIT revenue as a proportion of GDP, despite this reduction in rates, implies that the corporate tax base of developing countries has in fact been growing despite profit shifting abroad by large firms. This appears to be due to two factors: the growing share of profits in national income in response to structural adjustment programs (liberalization, privatization, wage restraint, and so forth); and improved tax administration and market formalization of micro-, small-, and medium-sized firms. In the Latin America region, in particular, although natural resource exports have experienced a sustained boom, fiscal income from their tax and royalties have actually declined. On average for twelve Latin American countries (excluding Venezuela), resource revenues have dropped from 5.4 percent of GDP in 2010 to 2.3 percent in 2016 (OECD, 2018). Against this backdrop of decreasing fiscal space, there are enormous competitive pressures from foreign investors and foreign governments to lower CIT rates and extend further concessions in the form of tax holidays, tax-free zones, investment treaties, and acceptance of corporate ownership structures designed to facilitate tax avoidance.

The IMF identifies two separate "spillovers" from this de facto regime built up from different and competitive national systems and a patchwork of double taxation treaties that permit increased MNE tax avoidance. Tax-base erosion by profit shifting incentives ("base spillover") means that according to the Fund's estimates a 1 percentage point increase in a country's CIT rate will reduce its CIT tax base by about 0.6 percent of GDP. Tax policy response to other countries ("strategic spillover") means that a 1 point CIT rate reduction in all other countries induces a 0.5 point rate cut, with a slightly larger response to rates in "haven" countries and with larger countries' tax policies having a stronger effect (IMF 2015).

In consequence, the IMF argues:

> Base erosion, profit shifting and international tax competition really matter for developing countries . . . at least as much as for the advanced economies. Base spillovers from others' tax rates may be noticeably stronger for non-OECD countries than for OECD countries, and statistically more significant. And the signs are that these may operate less through effects on real investment decisions than through profit shifting. The revenue losses through avoidance activities associated with tax havens (are) in the order of something over one point of GDP in the long run—a large amount, far larger relative to their total tax take than is the case in OECD members, and harder for them to replace from other sources. (Crivelli, de Mooij, and Keen 2015, 23)

The absolute size of tax losses for developing countries is large, according to the OECD:

> Data on revenues lost by developing countries from offshore non-compliance is unreliable. Most estimates, however, exceed by some distance the level of aid received by developing countries—around USD 100 billion annually. (2010, 6)

The IMF derives sensible policy recommendations from its research such as this: "For the *corporate income tax*, quantify and review tax expenditures, resisting further inappropriate base erosion and pressure to cut statutory rates; reduce the tax bias toward debt finance" (de Mooij and Keen 2015, 49). Yet IMF operational advice and conditionality seems unaffected: a recent ILO study of IMF Article IV reports in 183 countries over 2005 to 2015 finds that tax measures are discussed in 138 cases, but are all restricted to extending or collecting consumption taxes—VAT in particular (Ortiz et al. 2015).

Unbridled competition between countries to attract foreign firms by lowering statutory rates and extending allowances creates "winners" and "losers," but overall such coordination failure leads to a welfare loss worldwide. No evidence supports the theory that international tax competition makes governments more efficient. The welfare losses arise from the externalities generated by one country's tax rate setting on the welfare of other countries (Zodrow 2010; Wilson 1999). A lower tax rate in other countries moves capital out and reduces tax revenue and public spending; whether the best response is to raise or lower the tax rate depends on the marginal value of public spending. In terms of the game theory underlying the literature, the Nash equilibrium is Pareto inefficient: that is, all countries would benefit from a uniform increase in tax rates. This is the central result in the argument against unconstrained international tax competition. This conclusion is strongly reinforced where (a) CIT resources are used to enhance productivity and (b) income distribution has an effect on growth.

The fact that international tax competition is focused on the location of financial assets rather than on productive capital itself (which is predominantly attracted by labor skills, local markets, natural resources, and infrastructure) increases the opportunities for offshore financial centers to offer extremely low tax rates to corporations and individuals while maximizing their own fiscal income as free riders. However, such facilities are only meaningful when combined with secrecy, which shields owners from their own revenue authorities (Slemrod and Wilson 2009). Ironically, such secrecy must be combined with strong property rights, and thus these jurisdictions are invariably within or effectively underwritten by major financial centers. Furthermore, such secrecy on beneficial ownership not only encourages criminal behavior by companies but also impedes domestic financial regulators from ascertaining the balance sheet position of multinational corporations.

In sum, tax competition between jurisdictions not only has lowered income tax rates but also has encouraged aggressive tax avoidance by large firms and the marketing of tax evasion schemes to high-net-worth individuals, which has had serious global economic and social consequences. It is vital for developing countries to be able to protect their corporate tax base and to levy a reasonable tax rate on large firms, whether foreign or domestically owned, with international policy support. In this regard, information exchange and agreed rules for determining the CIT base would benefit both developed and developing countries, and these actions would be a significant step toward global fiscal coordination.

3. THE ECONOMICS OF PROFIT TAXATION: INVESTMENT, GROWTH, AND INCOME DISTRIBUTION

So far we have seen how tax competition reduces profit taxes (whether CIT on corporate profits or PIT on dividends) and thus directly increases inequality whether expressed as the wage-profit split or the distribution of household income. Indeed, the two are equivalent to the extent that corporation tax is in effect a "withholding tax" on dividends otherwise payable to shareholders (Stiglitz 1976), affecting both the current income and accumulated wealth of shareholders. In other words, CIT is a tax on the rich who are the main owners of corporations—directly or through pension funds.

This immediate redistributive effect is not disputed (among economists at least): the controversy arises from the difficulty of determining the final incidence of profit taxes because this depends on their indirect effect through the impact on investment and thus growth and employment, on one hand, and the fiscal adjustment with its macroeconomic and welfare outcomes, on the other.

Some economists have long argued that the final outcome of CIT in terms of tax incidence—who ultimately bears the real burden of a tax— is quite different from what it appears to be at first sight (Harberger 1962). The premise is that CIT leads to lower investment and thus a lower capital-labor ratio; as labor productivity falls (this model assumes full employment), so do wages. Thus workers, not shareholders, bear the real incidence of the corporate income tax; and it is more efficient to tax workers directly (for example, through a VAT), so the optimal corporate income tax rate is zero.

This concept is theoretically underpinned by Mirrlees (1976) who argued that the efficiency losses (mainly investment incentives) from capital taxation—losses borne by labor in the long run due to lower productivity growth and thus lower wages—are so great that in effect capital incomes should not be taxed at all.

By extension, the traditional view of capital income taxation in small open economies is that residence-based taxes reduce the after-tax return on domestic savings by driving a wedge between the rate of return on world financial markets and the after-tax rate of return received by residents—in other words, a tax on the ownership of capital or "savings."

In contrast, source-based taxes raise the required rate of return on domestic investment above the rate of return on world financial markets and thus amount to taxes on the location of capital—that is, on investment. In consequence, the traditional literature suggests that a small open economy should not apply any source-based capital income taxation at all, adopting only residence-based systems (Burgess and Stern 1993).

If these residence-based taxes cannot be collected effectively (due to lack of fiscal information, administrative capacity, or international cooperation), then capital income taxation would be undesirable. In sum, the traditional result from the optimal tax literature is *still* that "small open economies should adopt no source-based taxes and that capital income taxes should be eliminated altogether if countries cannot enforce residence-based taxes" (Bovenberg 1994, 118).

Similarly, for the small open economy, it is suggested that firms must take as given the *after*-tax rate of return on investment because investors (foreign and domestic) will move their capital abroad if they earn less than this rate; so if CIT rises, capital moves abroad and the *before*-tax rate of return rises, leaving dividends unchanged, but the outflow leads again to a lower capital-labor ratio, lower labor productivity, and thus lower wages. In sum, because capital tends to be much more mobile than workers, a significant share of the burden of corporate tax tends to get shifted to labor (Auerbach 2006).

Nonetheless, there is remarkably little empirical evidence for this fundamentalist position. A recent systematic review of the empirical literature finds "*some* evidence that suggests that corporate taxation may lower wages, but the *preponderance* of evidence does not suggest any wage effects from corporate taxation . . . there is no robust evidence that corporate tax burdens have large depressing effects on wages" (Clausing 2012, 468).

Moreover, the link between higher CIT rates and lower growth—however attractive intuitively—is far from solid empirically. Econometric studies recently surveyed by the IMF are ambiguous on the size and even the direction of the effect of increased CIT on growth; although their own estimates do find modest negative effects, these are small and statistically not very significant (IMF 2015). Specifically, in relation to foreign investment, the IMF finds evidence that CIT rates affect capital flows into developing countries but that these rates do not in fact contribute to gross private fixed capital or economic growth (Klemm and van Parys 2009).

The standard theory of the negative effect of profits tax on growth is invalid for several reasons, which may in turn help explain the unconvincing empirical evidence. First, the textbook causality runs from lower savings (corporate savings—retained earnings—reduced by a profit tax, and private savings reduced by progressive income tax) to lower investment and thus growth, employment, and wages. This conclusion requires the assumption of full-factor employment and complete wage-price flexibility, neither of which hold in practice. Moreover, savings are not determined in this simplistic way and may well be raised by rent-iers cutting consumption or by corporations borrowing from banks to fund planned investment. Indeed, the Keynesian view is that investment causes savings rather than the other way around, with macroeconomic adjustment to aggregate investment generating the required savings level, assuming government adopts an accommodating fiscal and monetary pol-icy. Moreover as Kalecki argued eight decades ago, raising the capital tax "does not tend to lower the net profitability of investment (which covers the risk) or to raise the rate of interest." If the investor borrows, her net (taxable) capital does not increase, and if she uses her "own means," then she would be taxed anyway. "Thus," says Kalecki, "the net profitability of investment is unaffected by capital taxation" (1937, 449).

Second, corporate investment decisions are complex and rely on the fact that external finance (for example, from banks) is always an alterna-tive to retaining profits, so tax levels will influence funding structures (the use of debt in particular) rather than the level of investment as such (Stiglitz 1976). Evidence suggests that the adverse effects, if they exist, are much less than is commonly alleged, especially by politicians and corpo-rations. Almost all countries provide tax exemption for interest. Because, at the margin, a very large fraction of investment is financed by debt, the reduction in return is commensurate with the reduction in cost: there is no adverse effect. Indeed, most countries provide depreciation allowances greater than true economic depreciation (that is, that would correspond to the true decline in market value), so higher tax rates can be associated with greater investment (Stiglitz 1973).

Third, intergenerational distribution is central to the neoclassical model (although its founder Ramsey himself wanted to weight all generations equally and was thus opposed to a social rate of discount) even though *intra*generational distribution is not. As Kalecki (1937) points out, capital-ists do not accumulate for their own future consumption nor for future consumption of their heirs: rather, their aim is to increase capital and leave it to their heirs so the latter can continue their own work. More recently, Uhlig and Yanagawa (1996) show that increasing capital income tax can lead to faster growth even in a standard overlapping-generations model if there is endogenous growth: capital income taxation affects the old, but it stimulates young workers to save and learn. The net effect on savings is positive if the interest elasticity of savings is relatively low, which it appears to be.

Fourth, the standard neoclassical model assumes that government expenditure itself is a deadweight loss in terms of output and growth (although there may be redistributive welfare gains to particular household groups), but this assumption is also inconsistent with modern endogenous growth theory. As Aghion and Howitt (1998) show, when public expenditure is used for human capital investment with strong externalities (and where markets will not fund education through credits), taxing higher incomes to pay for the public education of the poor leads to higher levels of aggregate income.

Fifth, in a similar direction, FitzGerald (2012) shows that if the profit tax revenue is spent—all or in part—on infrastructure provision, this will raise capital productivity within a standard growth model so that the optimal profits tax rate is positive. This rate is a function of the relative marginal productivities of public and private capital and is, in fact, independent of the international tax rate—there are no gains from tax competition. Moreover, capital taxation "has all the merits of financing state expenditure by borrowing, but is distinguished from borrowing by the advantage of the state not becoming indebted" (Kalecki 1937, 450).

Sixth, and last but not least, there is growing evidence (and policy consensus) for the positive effect of reduced inequality directly on growth, whether through enhanced social stability (and thus reduced investor risk) or through greater family investment in health and education (Ostry, Berg, and Tsangarides 2014).

Of course, as orthodox economists point out frequently, redistributive goals can be met by an appropriate composition of welfare expenditure targeted toward the poor. Although this may reduce poverty, it still implies that in the absence of higher profit taxes the cost of increased poverty reduction will be borne by middle-income groups. Specifically, it implies that raising the income of unemployed and retired citizens will be funded by employed workers. In this limited sense, inequality will in principle be reduced in the lower half of the distribution but increased in the upper half. In fact, both empirically and as the result of public choice, middle-income groups tend to enjoy roughly neutral fiscal incidence. Raising the share of poorer groups in national income can only be achieved democratically by increasing the tax burden on the wealthy.

The empirical case for the impact of profit taxes on reducing inequality is positive but has mixed results across regions. In Latin America, for the period 2013–14, personal income tax contributed to a 2 percentage point reduction of the Gini coefficient, whereas personal income tax in the European Union achieved a 12 percentage point reduction in the same period (ECLAC 2017). The lower redistributive impact for Latin America may be explained by several factors: a narrow tax base, high levels of evasion and avoidance, and low contribution of the middle class to the personal income tax base (ECLAC 2017).

Finally, in the wider macroeconomic context, it is worth noting that in economies where there is a balanced budget rule (or a binding rule for the fiscal deficit or public debt) the effect of raising profit taxes and increasing public expenditure on infrastructure or welfare will lead to an increase in output and employment. This, in turn, will further reduce income inequality. The increase in overall national income will mean that the absolute level of net profits (and thus investment) will not fall even though the share of the rich declines.

Some of these policy considerations are at last being taken on board by the IMF, which now recommends:

> Lowering the tax wedge and improving the design of labor taxes and social benefits can strengthen work incentives and induce a positive labor supply response; reforming capital income taxes to tax rents reduces distortions and encourages private investment; well-targeted tax incentives can stimulate private investment and enhance productivity through research and development (R&D); efficient public investment, especially in infrastructure, can raise the economy's productive capacity; more equitable access to education and health care contributes to human capital accumulation, a key factor for growth. If growth-friendly reforms require fiscal space, revenue measures should focus on broadening the tax base and minimizing distortions; and expenditure measures should aim at rationalizing spending and improving efficiency. (IMF 2015, 1)

Even so, the IMF apparently cannot bring itself to enunciate the logical consequence of its argument—higher profit taxation. The orthodox argument against capital taxation (for both corporations and individuals) continues to be enormously influential—no doubt in part because it has suited the interests of both the shareholders in, and the executives of, large corporations. Indeed, the neoclassical notion that higher profit taxes are bad for the poor ironically implies that tax avoidance and evasion by the wealthy might even be motivated by altruism!

4. THE IMPLICATIONS OF TAX COORDINATION FOR DEVELOPING COUNTRIES

In the absence of official estimates (or reliable unofficial ones) of the order of magnitude of the losses to developing countries from lack of tax cooperation, it is necessary to take into account (i) the tax lost on the unregistered outflow of profits (whether by foreign companies or domestic residents) in any one year, and (ii) the tax loss due to the income arising abroad from the undeclared accumulated assets owned by residents. Absent official (or reliable unofficial) estimates, the loss of tax base can be estimated by drawing on estimates of unregistered (illicit) capital flows from developing countries' trade and balance-of-payments data (from World Bank data) and then calculating the accumulated stock (FitzGerald 2013).

The total global tax loss immediately before the Great Recession appears to have been on the order of 2.5 percent of developing countries' GDP, which is considerable and is of a similar size to total private capital inflows. In terms of tax revenue, the loss represents about 10 percent of revenue in developing countries but a much larger proportion (probably one-third) of corporate and income taxation revenue.

In conclusion, the tax loss for developing countries was approximately $200 to $250 billion a year in the mid-2000s—double the OECD estimate. It is likely that the figure has increased since that date due to growth in the world economy and increased financial integration. Although the current crisis may have slowed these two drivers, it has increased the level of investor risk aversion and thus the attraction of safe havens for mobile wealth.

This figure is more than double the level of official development assistance (ODA) from Development Assistance Committee (DAC) members. At an aggregate (global) level, if the tax authorities in developing countries were in receipt of these sums—with the assistance of their counterparts in developed countries and comprehensive action on tax avoidance and evasion through offshore financial centers—either of two outcomes might be achievable: (i) the total amount of international fiscal transfers (aid plus tax) available for development finance could be tripled, or (ii) development assistance could be entirely replaced by tax cooperation while doubling the net fiscal transfer.

In a WIDER study, Boadway indicated that "the clearest message that comes out of the fiscal federalism literature seems to be: *it should be fiscal equity among states rather than vertical equity among individuals that informs the design of a development financing system*" (quoted in FitzGerald 2013, 234; italics in original). This implies that redistribution of any gains from international tax cooperation should be biased toward poor countries. International fiscal equity would require that the fiscal transfer take account of the local tax "effort" and perhaps involve an additional incentive, much as national tax systems give additional incentives for voluntary household contributions. Given these difficulties in devising a suitable measure of a nation's capacity to pay, Boadway (2005) suggests that it may be necessary to fall back on a macro indicator of fiscal equity that is consistent across nations and also is a rough index of fiscal equity—in other words, the tax/GDP ratio. Extending this logic, Sustainable Development Goal (SDG) benchmarks could determine the floor for relevant public expenditure and thus the revenue requirements to be met and the scale of the required international contribution.

As pointed out in the influential WIDER study of innovative development finance:

> A . . . main source of finance for development use might be global taxation of tax bases that nations are liable to compete away because of international mobility, or that they underutilize because of monitoring problems. In principle, international agreement should be possible for a harmonized increase in taxes of these types, given that non-cooperative tax competition is responsible for their low equilibrium tax rates. (Boadway 2005, 236)

In the long run, therefore, international tax cooperation could become not only a complement to official development assistance for lower-income countries but a substitute. This transformation would not be as radical as it might at first seem because ODA is already an embryonic form of fiscal cooperation. In effect, a share of taxes raised in the donor country (ideally, of course, 0.7 percent of GDP and thus roughly 3 percent of tax revenues) is transferred to the recipient countries in the form of a budget subsidy for agreed public programs or investments.

Even if increased international CIT and PIT revenue led to some reduction in other sources of taxation, this could also be beneficial. Low-income countries—and Africa in particular—have tended to rely heavily on indirect taxation, which tends to be regressive because it is generally focused on manufactured mass consumption items. The switch from trade taxes to VAT has made the regressive effect even greater because import duties used to bear more heavily on nonessential consumer goods. The reliance on VAT has also worsened household income inequality because incidence is highest on immobile unskilled labor (OECD 2010).

Logically, the largest gains from effective international taxation of profits and assets would be made by the larger and richer developing countries—and specifically in per capita terms, the middle-income countries or regions—because these are most integrated into the world economy and generate the profits that underpin tax avoidance and evasion. As table 9.3 shows, the potential tax revenue gains to Asia and Latin America are far greater than ODA flows, which would be expected due to their larger economies, although the difference in per capita gains would be less. Leaving geostrategic considerations accounting for the ODA to the Middle East and North Africa (MENA) and Europe apart, aid allocation generally works in the other direction because ODA is focused on poorer countries and regions, particularly Africa.

International tax cooperation could not be a substitute for ODA in most of the lower-income developing countries, but it could become a complementary source of development finance. Although the funds would be channeled through different institutions (typically ministries of finance and ministries of international development from donor countries), they are both fiscal transfers from government to government, and they both have their origins in taxation. It would be logical, therefore, that the two flows should be administered in parallel, particularly because "best practice" ODA increasingly takes the form of budgetary support in cases of regular development programs as opposed to humanitarian emergencies.

Table 9.3   Estimated Potential Tax Yield to Developing Regions (US$ billions in 2006)

	Flow (F)	Stock (X)	Tax Base (Y)	Potential Yield (T)
Developing Countries	859	3060	1073	215
Sub-Saharan Africa	11	80	17	3
Asia	399	1532	507	101
Europe	186	529	223	45
Middle East and North Africa (MENA)	165	453	197	39
Latin America and the Caribbean (LAC)	97	466	129	26

Source: FitzGerald (2013).

The literature on the economic effects of aid does not address the relationship with international taxation. Domestic taxation is regarded as part of the process of fiscal response to aid to the extent that it affects government decisions on expenditure and borrowing (McGillivray and Morrissey 2004). Empirical results show that the effects are complex and varied but that aid tends to be associated with government spending increases in excess of the value of the aid. It also can have the effect of increasing borrowing and reducing tax effort. From the literature on open economy macroeconomics, it is reasonable to expect that apart from raising the rate of growth (through increased demand and import availability) the real exchange rate would tend to rise and thus exports to fall in the short run. However, the long-run effect would depend on the use of the new resources, and in particular whether they are employed to increase output and productivity in the export sector. Note that a major macroeconomic effect of increased tax receipts through identification of overseas assets (and possible legal action) would also provide a disincentive for capital flight in the first place. Retention and recovery of such assets would raise domestic investment rates and thus the rate of economic growth.

Finally, all developing countries would be in receipt of more resources, but a key exception would be those developing countries that are themselves tax havens. The scale of this loss is impossible to estimate precisely because of the opacity authorities of offshore financial centers (OFCs) deliberately create around financial assets and transactions within their jurisdictions (after all, this "confidentiality" is what attracts foreign investors). However, given that these OFCs are all closely connected with advanced economies, it would be possible to reallocate a portion of the increase in tax income to maintaining the incomes of their inhabitants and providing an alternative economic future for them. Where they are U.S. or EU dependencies, this could be done by the respective tax authorities, who would themselves be major beneficiaries of tax recovery, which would undoubtedly be at least equal to the benefits to developing countries estimated above.

Of course, expatriate lawyers and tax consultants might lose their employment, but they are fewer than the volume of financial services might imply. Most, if not all, of these services are in fact e-supplied from major onshore financial centers. Indeed, the main beneficiaries of these arrangements to prevent the exchange of information on income and wealth are not the inhabitants of these developing OFCs but are the elites of both developed and developing countries who are in a position to avoid their legal tax obligations. It would still be true that wealthy foreigners wishing to *settle* in OFCs would continue to benefit from low tax rates.

5. SLOW PROGRESS TOWARD INTERNATIONAL TAX COOPERATION

Free movement of financial assets (which need not correspond to the location of the fixed productive assets) and the geographical dispersion of firms (which allows intrafirm accounting to effectively relocate recorded profits independently of where they were generated) create fundamental challenges for tax authorities (OECD 1998; FitzGerald 2012). However, it is the location of *financial* assets, rather than their effect on real investment, that is at issue—and this is a classic collective action problem. Offshore financial centers compete for tax revenue with the countries where the productive capital is located, using very low or zero tax rates to attract financial assets without having to provide the infrastructure, labor forces, or markets needed for actual production (Slemrod and Wilson 2009).

Under these circumstances, a classic collective action presents itself. If tax authorities cooperated more effectively, the total tax base would be increased and revenue would correspond more closely to the country in which the economic activity takes place and where the real capital is located. When offshore financial centers, broadly defined, act as a destination for income streams and wealth protected from revenue authorities, they reduce the revenue available to countries that may have taxing rights in respect of that income or those assets (OECD 2010, 6).

The first model for bilateral tax agreements between countries was adopted in 1928 by the League of Nations. It was developed by a group of experts that later became the Fiscal Committee of the League of Nations. A second draft was produced in 1935, followed by subsequent models developed in Mexico (1943) favoring source-based taxation, and soon after an alternative model developed in London (1946) favoring residence-based taxation (Lennard 2008). After World War II, the United Nations, as the successor body to the League of Nations, sought to forge a compromise between the two models. In practice, a dual track emerged with the OECD representing the interests of advanced market economies and the UN representing developing countries. Their approaches differed mainly because the former were net outward investors and the latter were hosts to inward investment.

By 1958, the countries of the Organization for European Economic Cooperation, which later became the OECD, had developed the first draft of its own model convention, which firmly established residence-based taxation. This draft was amended four times through 1963, and the full model was adopted and published in 1977 through the OECD Committee on Fiscal Affairs (Owens and Bennett 2008). Meanwhile, the United Nations resumed its work on international tax cooperation in 1967, followed by the establishment in 1968 of an ad hoc group of experts on tax treaties between developed and developing countries. That group produced a "Manual for the Negotiation of Bilateral Tax Treaties Between Developed and Developing Countries" in 1979. The next year the group published a UN model convention, which was largely based on the OECD model but allowed for greater source-based taxation.

Since their development, both the UN and OECD models have been similar in many respects: both were created to prevent double taxation; both acknowledge taxing jurisdiction (permanent establishment) in similar ways; both allow for reductions to withholding taxes on outbound payments; both provide for the taxation of business profits where they are earned, which is determined under the arm's length principle; both establish a mutual agreement procedure for the resolution of tax disputes; and both models provide for exchange of information by competent authorities, either on request, automatically, or spontaneously. However, in each of these aspects, the UN model has preserved the taxing rights of countries in which production takes places, for example, through shorter time requirements to create a permanent establishment and fewer reductions of withholding taxes on charges such as fees for technical services and royalties. Moreover, the OECD model requires mandatory arbitration for unresolved tax disputes after two years, but the UN model has provided arbitration only as an option and requires consent from all parties.

Despite the fact that there are well over 3,000 bilateral tax treaties in place, these agreements have failed to address major areas of tax losses by governments, such as mismatches between country tax laws that result in double deductions or nonrecognition of income or even of taxable entities. Moreover, most information exchange still takes place upon the request of country tax administrations, and a significant number of countries and subnational jurisdictions actively promote secrecy as a business model to attract global flows of untaxed individual and corporate wealth through unregulated shell companies.

In 2001, the Zedillo Commission established by the UN identified the key issue in development financing as being the inability of developing countries to effectively tax income from capital (from foreign companies operating in their tax jurisdiction or from assets held abroad by their own residents). The commission proposed to address the tax cooperation problem from the point of view of developing countries through the creation of an International Tax Organization to: (i) compile statistics, identify trends and problems, present reports, provide technical assistance, and develop international norms for tax policy and administration; (ii) maintain surveillance of tax developments; (iii) restrain tax competition designed to attract multinationals with excessive and unwise incentives; (iv) develop procedures for arbitration when frictions develop between countries on tax questions; and (v) sponsor a mechanism for multilateral sharing of tax information (UN 2001, iii-iv).

In July of 2015, during the Third International Conference on Financing for Development, the G77 and China, with the endorsement of the UN Secretary-General (UN 2014) and other UN Experts (UN 2014a), proposed to upgrade the UN Committee of Experts on International Cooperation in Tax Matters (UN Committee) to an intergovernmental body capable of addressing all of these issues. Although a 2004 proposal to upgrade the Ad Hoc Committee recommended an intergovernmental body, members of the current UN committee serve in their personal capacities only and are not official representatives of their governments. The 2015 proposal for an intergovernmental tax body met strong opposition from the United States and the United Kingdom and resulted in lengthy and protracted negotiations of the Addis Ababa Action Agenda. In the end, the proposal was defeated, with a vague commitment to increase support for the work of the UN committee, which now meets twice per year instead of once but still lacks resources for basic operation of committee and subcommittee work.

Since 2015, the G77 and China have continued to call for an upgrade of the committee (G77 and China 2017). The government of Ecuador has championed the issue of the upgrade to address the lack of coordination and global network of secrecy and low-tax jurisdictions, which continue to erode the tax bases of all countries, but especially developing ones struggling to mobilize domestic revenues for development. The UN Economic and Social Council annually evaluates the work of the UN committee and receives inputs from member states on options for strengthening the work of the committee, but action in this regard remains to be seen. UN proposals to strengthen its powers (UN 2009, 65–66) have fallen on deaf ears.

The lack of action to strengthen international tax cooperation under the auspices of the UN is attributable in part to the emergence of the

G20. In the wake of the financial crisis of 2008–09, the G20 emerged as the self-designated "premier forum for international economic cooperation," and from the outset it included taxation as a key area of action (G20 2009). In this regard, the G20 provides mandates on issues of international taxation to the OECD directly, which receives support from the Platform of Collaboration on Tax, whose members include the OECD, IMF, World Bank, and the UN.

In addition to its fifty years of experience providing technical assistance on tax policy and administration to governments, the IMF has increased information reporting through its *Government Finance Statistics*, *Fiscal Monitor*, and Article IV reports, which now contain more information on national tax receipts, estimations of assets in OFCs, and countries' external asset positions. The World Bank also provides technical assistance and capacity-building for tax administrations, and the UN capacity-development program specializes in capacity-building issues with a focus on least developed countries. Each of the member institutions of the platform perform a nuanced role based on their respective core competencies, and all collaborate in supporting developing countries through capacity-building, such as producing "toolkits" on specific BEPS topics. The OECD, however, serves as the primary forum for the development of norms and standards on international taxation.

The UN Committee of Experts on International Cooperation in Tax Matters continues its work on updating the UN model convention, but international tax cooperation is primarily led by the G20 and directed through the OECD in two major work streams: (i) exchange of tax information related to financial accounts, and (ii) tax-base erosion and profit shifting.

EXCHANGE OF TAX INFORMATION

Over a decade before the emergence of the G20, G7 leaders mandated the OECD to address what it called "harmful tax competition" (OECD 1998). The resulting report defined "harmful tax practices," applied these standards through a Forum on Harmful Tax Practices (FHTP), and created the Global Forum on Transparency and Exchange of Information (Global Forum) to improve the exchange of information between countries. The OECD also created a "black list"' of forty-seven potentially harmful regimes within OECD countries as well as thirty-five tax haven jurisdictions, most of which were small islands or small island developing states (OECD 2001). A few years later, forty-six of the forty-seven potentially harmful regimes were removed from the list (OECD 2006) and the Global Forum was tasked to engage with both the OECD and non-OECD countries to deal with the tax haven classification through development of the "Agreement on Exchange of Information in Tax Matters" and to act as the gatekeeper for admission of non-OECD countries into the forum.

Following the 2009 London summit of the G20, at which G20 leaders pledged "to take action against non-cooperative jurisdictions, including tax havens" (G20 2009, para. 15), the Global Forum was restructured with an independent Secretariat. Currently comprised of 153 member countries, the Global Forum monitors the implementation of standards on tax transparency and exchange of information through peer-review mechanisms, country reports, and compliance ratings. Around the same time, in 2010, the United States enacted the Foreign Account Tax Compliance Act (FATCA). Under FATCA, foreign financial institutions are obliged to report to the U.S. Internal Revenue Service basic information (name, address, taxpayer identification number, and so forth) on accounts held by U.S. taxpayers or by foreign entities owned by U.S. taxpayers. Account holders who fail to report are subject to a 30 percent withholding tax penalty (26 U.S.C. §§ 1471–1474).

Soon after, the G20 moved to amend the Convention on Mutual Administrative Assistance in Tax Matters ("Multilateral Convention"), which was first developed by the OECD and Council of Europe in 1988, to allow for participation by all countries. Under article 6 of the Multilateral Convention, parties agreed to exchange tax information and sign the Common Reporting Standard Multilateral Competent Authority Agreement to participate in automatic information exchange. The Multilateral Convention is now in force in more than one hundred jurisdictions and required automatic information exchange beginning in late 2017. Notably, even though this is a multilateral instrument, the actual exchange of information occurs bilaterally only between competent authorities that agree to become exchange partners.

The G20 finance ministers requested the OECD to prepare a black list of uncooperative jurisdictions by the July 2017 G20 Leaders' Summit, at which time "defensive measures will be considered" (G20 Finance Ministers 2016). To be classified as cooperative, countries, particularly those classified as financial centers, must meet at least two out of the following three requirements: (i) a compliance rating of "largely compliant" by the Global Forum; (ii) a commitment to automatic exchange of information under the common reporting standard by 2018; and (3) participation in the Multilateral Convention or a sufficient bilateral network of information exchange. By July of 2017, the OECD reported that only Trinidad and Tobago had not yet made sufficient progress on tax transparency standards and had received a "non-compliant" rating.

TAX BASE EROSION AND PROFIT SHIFTING

Beginning in 2013, the G20 began to focus more attention on the matter of double nontaxation, and it mandated the OECD to lead reform efforts to "realign taxation with economic substance and value creation" and to tackle BEPS. In just two years, the OECD reached consensus on four minimum standards in its effort to lead coordinated reform of international tax rules: model provisions to prevent tax treaty abuse; relaunching the FHTP peer review process to address harmful tax practices and exchange tax rulings; an agreement to secure progress on dispute resolution through the mutual agreement procedure; and, probably the most significant achievement, standardized requirements for country-by-country reporting of tax information on revenues, profits, taxes due/paid, employees, and assets of each entity in a multinational corporate group. To implement country-by-country reporting, the OECD has developed the "Multilateral Competent Authority Agreement on the Exchange of Country-by-Country Reports" as well as a standardized electronic format for the exchange of information between jurisdictions.

BEPS "Associate status" in the OECD's Committee on Fiscal Affairs is now being offered to all interested countries who will commit to both the BEPS standards and BEPS implementation peer review. This "Inclusive Framework," currently comprised of 117 countries, will monitor implementation of the minimum standards and work on clarifying and developing other standards subsumed under the BEPS process, such as transfer pricing guidance, digital economy issues, and interest deductibility.

Treaty-relevant provisions, such as the primary purpose test and limitation of benefits provisions, have been included in a Multilateral Instrument to modify existing bilateral tax treaties. Similar to the matching process of information exchange under the common reporting standards, countries will indicate which alternative tax treaty measures they choose to adopt in modifying their existing tax treaties, and these measures will only take effect when both countries' preferences have matched. Despite failure to achieve consensus during the BEPS process on arbitration, particularly due to the objection of non-OECD countries, the Multilateral Instrument includes an optional provision for mandatory, binding arbitration. Notably, the United States—predominant in negotiations—has not signed on to any of the multilateral agreements, instead preferring to negotiate its own bilateral tax treaties and information exchange agreements, which are not always on a reciprocal basis. Although the United States enjoys a rating of "largely compliant" by the Global Forum, the Tax Justice Network ranks the United States second-highest on its annual 2018 Financial Secrecy Index.

In addition to global efforts of the G20 and the international tax organizations, a trend toward more focused tax coordination and harmonization efforts through regional cooperation has emerged in the past decade, both through tax cooperation within regional economic communities, such as the Association of South East Asian Nations and the European Union as well as regional tax administration forums, such as the African Tax Administration Forum and the Inter-American Center of Tax Administrations. At the same time, however, nationalist and populist reactions to global and regional integration abound in the current period.

CONCLUSIONS

In summary, the detailed Zedillo Commission recommendations for the work of an International Tax Organization have largely been taken up by the OECD and the Platform for Collaboration on Tax through the leadership of the G20, even though the proposed institutional format has been rejected. This loose governance structure, however, has not been able to effectively restrain tax competition, which makes all the difference for efforts to mobilize domestic resources and reduce inequality.

Long-term trends toward lower statutory rates for both corporate and personal income tax and greater incentives to shift tax bases have led to declining effective taxation of profits. This is largely driven by competition between countries to attract investment and a widespread belief that this will foster skill and technology transfers and economic growth despite empirical evidence demonstrating that tax exemptions and lowered rates do not contribute to long-run sustainable growth. Instead, findings from investor surveys continue to attribute investment decisions to economic and political stability and an educated and highly skilled labor force (UNIDO 2010).

For instance, the World Bank's flagship annual *Doing Business* report explicitly promotes tax competition by ranking countries based on indicators that penalize countries for levying taxes that fund education, infrastructure, health care, and basic social security (World Bank 2016). Added to this pressure, developing country governments are often lobbied by multinationals and backed by interest groups such as Chambers of Commerce—and sometimes even government representatives from a multinational company's home country—to provide preferential tax regimes that can eliminate taxable profits for decades. These tax preferences are found in double tax agreements, advanced tax rulings, special economic zones, and legislated tax exemptions, but they also may be part of investment agreements and extractives contracts. The latter is especially troubling and has been the source of significant tax losses, especially in resource-rich developing countries. Tax preferences also may come in the guise of lax enforcement, especially on transfer pricing.

Efforts to constrain tax competition between developed countries have fared no better, primarily due to the OECD's tacit acceptance of tax competition. The OECD has always made it clear that the work on harmful tax competition set out to create a conceptual and administrative distinction between "helpful" and "harmful" tax competition, with the distinction based on whether country initiatives encourage "free and fair tax competition" internationally, and thus support the "expansion of global economic growth" (OECD 2015, 11). Thus, when the BEPS process took up the issue of patent boxes (tax incentives for income from intellectual property, which is mostly parked in holding companies in low-tax, developed countries with high legal protections), there was no agreement to prohibit patent boxes, or even to set a minimum rate. Instead, the FHTP agreed to a "nexus" principle: taxpayers may only benefit from tax incentives to the extent of qualifying "research and development" expenditures made in the tax jurisdiction. It was also agreed that the only IP assets that could qualify for benefits are patents or assets similar and functionally equivalent to patents (OECD 2015). Soon after the BEPS process, countries such as the UK, Ireland, and Switzerland quickly introduced "OECD compliant" patent boxes.

Although BEPS and the movement toward automatic exchange of information has established some consensus on minimum standards, the foundational acceptance and legitimatization of tax competition remains unchecked, and post-BEPS the G20 embarked on a new work stream to provide tax certainty for investors. On the contrary, absent a single global fiscal authority, the automatic exchange of information between jurisdictions on company accounts, backed up by presumptive withholding provisions, is necessary to eliminate free riding. In addition, negotiations (similar to those for trade) on apportionment of the taxable *base* (that is, corporate profits and nonresident assets) within agreed rules is necessary to minimize externalities, even if countries continue to be free to set different income tax *rates*. Harmonization of these rates may well be the outcome, but this may turn out to be neither necessary nor inevitable. In the long run, such fiscal cooperation could substitute for the present system of international development cooperation and global public goods funding, both of which are not only underfinanced but also depend on the foreign policy discretion of individual governments.

Progressive income taxation of both corporations and individuals is an essential element of public fiscal resources, and there is no reason to believe that at present rates it significantly constrains investment, growth, or employment. Indeed, income tax revenues make a significant contribution to the reduction of income inequality, enhancing social stability and sustainable growth in the long run. The inability to effectively tax the profit income of either international investors or large domestic firms poses a serious problem for developing countries, in particular, as they seek to make investments in education, health care, and infrastructure. Indirect taxation alone—even accompanied by progressive spending—is insufficient to tilt the fiscal balance decisively toward inequality reduction.

The finding of this chapter is therefore that enhanced international tax coordination would not only reduce national income inequality (particularly when combined with appropriate fiscal policy) but could also hold the potential to replace the failing system of development aid. The efforts of the G20 in moving toward more effective international tax coordination are steps in the right direction, but there will be no sustainable progress without a fundamental commitment to replace tax competition with tax coordination.

In making such a commitment, equal participation of the G77 and China in standards and norm setting—both in form and function—is necessary. Moreover, the international organizations working on tax will be instrumental in the development and implementation of the tax coordination agenda. For this reason, all operational aspects of the international organizations, such as technical assistance, economic development projects, reports, and so forth, should be consistent with the goals of coordination instead of working against them.

Finally, the tax information exchanged by multilateral agreements should, in at least basic form, be available to all citizens to enable their full participation in fiscal governance. Numerous human rights conventions and principles require participation of citizens in government policy making, and international tax standards and norm setting should conform to these agreements (for example, the International Covenant on Civil and Political Rights, and the Maastrich Principles on Extraterritorial Obligations of States in the Area of Economic, Social and Cultural Rights).

Managing the effects of globalization, in particular tax competition, will require enhanced cooperation beyond national borders. Failure to do so has already had grave effects on income distribution globally, but especially for developing countries. Unless governments are able to provide basic services necessary to human development, conflict and global economic insecurity will increase.

REFERENCES

Aghion, Philippe, and Peter Howitt. 1998. *Endogenous Growth Theory*. Boston: MIT Press.

Auerbach, Alan J. 2006. "The Future of Capital Income Taxation." *Fiscal Studies* 27 (4): 399–420.

Boadway, Robin. 2005. "National Taxation, Fiscal Federalism and Global Taxation." In *New Sources of Development Finance*, ed. Anthony Atkinson, 210–37. Oxford: Clarendon Press for UNU-WIDER.

Bovenberg, A. Lans. 1994. "Capital taxation in the world economy." In *The Handbook of International Macroeconomics*, ed. Frederick Van der Ploeg, 116–50. Oxford: Blackwell.

Burgess, Robin, and Nicholas H. Stern. 1993. "Taxation and Development." *Journal of Economic Literature* 31 (2): 762–830.

Clausing, Kimberly A. 2011. "The Revenue Effects of Multinational Firm Income Shifting." *Tax Notes* (March).

———. 2012. "In Search of Corporate Tax Incidence." *Tax Law Review* 65 (3): 433–72.

Crivelli, Ernesto, Ruud De Mooij, and Michael Keen. 2015. "Base Erosion, Profit Shifting and Developing Countries." IMF Working Paper WP/15/118. Washington, DC: International Monetary Fund.

De Mooij, Ruud, and Michael Keen. 2015. "Taxes in Practice." *Finance & Development* 52 (1): 48–49. Washington, DC: International Monetary Fund.

ECLAC 2017. *Fiscal Panorama of Latin America and the Caribbean: Mobilizing Resources to Finance Sustainable Development.* Santiago, Chile: Economic Commission for Latin America and the Caribbean.

FitzGerald, Valpy. 2012. "Global Capital Markets, Direct Taxation and the Redistribution of Income." *International Review of Applied Economics* 26: 241–52.

——. 2013. "The International Fiscal Implications of Global Poverty Reduction and Global Public Goods Provision." Working Paper No. 2013/136. Helsinki: WIDER.

G77 and China. 2017. Statement on Behalf of the G77 and China by Carola Iniguez, Undersecretary of International Organizations of Ecuador, At the ECOSOC Special Meeting On International Tax Cooperation Matters. New York, April 7.

G20. 2009. Pittsburg Summit, Leaders Statement, September 24–25.

G20 Finance Ministers. 2016. Central Bankers Communique, July 24.

Harberger, Arnold C. 1962. "The Incidence of the Corporation Income Tax." *Journal of Political Economy* 70 (3): 215–40.

IMF. 2013. *Fiscal Monitor 2013.* Washington, DC: International Monetary Fund.

——. 2014. "Spillovers in International Corporate Taxation." IMF Policy Paper. Washington, DC: International Monetary Fund.

——. 2015. "Fiscal Policy and Long Term Growth." IMF Policy Paper. Washington, DC: International Monetary Fund.

——. 2017. *Fiscal Monitor 2017.* Washington, DC: International Monetary Fund.

Kalecki, Michal. 1937. "A Theory of Commodity, Income, and Capital Taxation." *The Economic Journal* 47 (187): 444–50.

Klemm, Alexander, and Stefan van Parys. 2009. "Empirical Evidence on the Effects of Tax Incentives." IMF WP/09/136. Washington, DC: International Monetary Fund.

Leibrecht, Markus, and Claudia Hochgatterer. 2012. "Tax Competition as a Cause of Falling Corporate Income Tax Rates: A Survey of Empirical Literature." *Journal of Economic Surveys* 26: 616–48.

Lennard, Michael. 2008. "The Purpose and Current Status of the United Nations Tax Work." *Asia-Pacific Tax Bulletin*, pp. 24–30. Amsterdam: International Bureau of Fiscal Documentation.

McGillivray, Mark, and Oliver Morrissey. 2004. "Fiscal Effects of Aid." In *Fiscal Policy for Development*, ed. Tony Addison and Alan Roe, 72–96. Basingstoke, UK: Palgrave/WIDER.

Mirrlees, James A. 1976. "Optimal Tax Theory: A Synthesis." *Journal of Public Economics* 6 (4): 327–58.

OECD. 1998. *Harmful Tax Competition: An Emerging Global Issue.* Paris. Organisation for Economic Cooperation and Development.

——. 2001. *Towards Global Tax Co-operation: Progress in Identifying and Eliminating Harmful Tax Practices.* Paris. Organisation for Economic Cooperation and Development.

——. 2006. *The OECD's Project on Harmful Tax Practices: 2006 Update on Progress in Member Countries.* Paris: Organisation for Economic Cooperation and Development.

——. 2010. *Promoting Transparency and Exchange of Information for Tax Purposes.* Paris: Organisation for Economic Cooperation and Development.

——. 2010a. *Tax Policy Reform and Economic Growth.* Tax Policy Studies No. 20. Paris: Organisation for Economic Cooperation and Development.

——. (2011) *Divided We Stand: Why Inequality Keeps Rising.* Paris: Organisation for Economic Cooperation and Development.

——. 2015. "Countering Harmful Tax Practices More Effectively, Taking into Account Transparency and Substance, Action 5—2015 Final Report." OECD/G20 Base Erosion and Profit Shifting Project.

——. 2018. *Revenue Statistics in Latin America and the Caribbean 1990–2016.* Paris: Organisation for Economic Cooperation and Development.

Ortiz, Isabel, Matthew Cummins, Jeronim Capaldo, and Kalaivani Karunanethy. 2015. "The Decade of Adjustment: A Review of Austerity Trends 2010–2020 in 187 Countries." Extension of Social Security Series No. 53. Geneva: International Labour Organization.

Ostry, Jonathan D., Andrew Berg, and Charalambos G. Tsangarides. 2014. "Redistribution, Inequality and Growth." IMF Staff Discussion Note. SDN/14/02. Washington, DC: International Monetary Fund.

Owens, Jeffrey, and Mary Bennett. 2008. "OECD Model Tax Convention: Why It Works." *OECD Observer* 269: 10–12.

Reidel, Nadine. 2014. "Quantifying International Tax Avoidance: A Review of the Academic Literature." ETPF Policy Paper 2. London: European Tax Policy Forum.

Slemrod, Joel, and John D. Wilson. 2009. "Tax Competition with Parasitic Tax Havens." *Journal of Public Economics* 93: 1261–70.

Stiglitz, Joseph. 1973. "Taxation, Corporate Financial Policy and the Cost of Capital." *Journal of Public Economics* 2: 1–34.

——. 1976. "The Corporation Tax." *Journal of Public Economics* 5: 303–11.

Uhlig, Harold, and Noriyuki Yanagawa. 1996. "Increasing the Capital Income Tax May Lead to Faster Growth." *European Economic Review* 40: 1521–40.

UN. 2001. *Report of the High-Level Panel on Financing for Development* ("Zedillo Commission"). New York: United Nations.

——. 2009. *Report of the Commission of Experts on Reforms of the International Monetary and Financial System* ("Stiglitz Commission"). New York: United Nations.

——. 2014. "The Road to Dignity by 2030: Ending Poverty, Transforming All Lives and Protecting the Planet." Synthesis Report of the Secretary-General on the Post-2015 Agenda. A/69/700, para. 115.

——. 2014a. "Report of the United Nations Special Rapporteur on Extreme Poverty and Human Rights." Magdalena Sepúlveda. A/HRC/26/28.

UNIDO. 2010. *Africa Investor Survey.* Geneva: UNIDO.

Wilson, John D. 1999. "Theories of Tax Competition." *National Tax Journal* 52 (2): 269–304.

World Bank. 2016. *Doing Business.* Washington, DC: World Bank.

Zodrow, George R. 2010. "Capital Mobility and Capital Tax Competition." *National Tax Journal* 63 (4): 865–902.

José Antonio Ocampo is a member of the board of Banco de la República (central bank of Colombia), professor in the School of International and Public Affairs at Columbia University, and chair of the United Nations Committee for Development Policy and the Independent Commission for the Reform of International Corporate Taxation (ICRICT). He has been UN under-secretary-general for Economic and Social Affairs, executive secretary of the United Nations Economic Commission for Latin America and the Caribbean, and minister of finance, minister of agriculture, and director of the National Planning Office of Colombia. He has published extensively on macroeconomic theory and policy, international financial issues, economic and social development, international trade, and Colombian and Latin American economic history.

Carlos Maria Correa is is Executive Director of the South Centre in Geneva. He has been visiting professor at several universities, consultant to various international organizations, and advisor of several governments on intellectual property, innovation policy, and public health. He was a member of the UK Commission on Intellectual Property; the Commission on Intellectual Property, Innovation and Public Health established by the World Health Assembly; and on the FAO Panel of Eminent Experts on Ethics in Food and Agriculture.

Valpy FitzGerald is professor emeritus of International Development Finance at the Oxford University Department of International Development, which he directed between 2007 and 2012, Professional Fellow at Oxford's St. Antony's College, and commissioner of the Independent Commission for the Reform of International Corporate Taxation (ICRICT). He has also taught at Cambridge, Texas, The Hague and Madrid. He has advised several international agencies on international investment regulation, debt sustainability, macroeconomic policy, and international taxation as a source of development finance. His research interests cover determinants of capital flows from developed to developing countries, international taxation issues, macroeconomic policy in emerging markets, and long-run economic growth and welfare in Latin America.

Davide Furceri is a senior economist in the International Monetary Fund's Research Department. He previously worked at the European Central Bank and the Organisation for Economic Co-operation and Development. He has published extensively in academic journals in the fields of international macroeconomics and public finance. He holds a PhD in economics from the University of Illinois and a doctoral degree in regional economics from the University of Palermo.

Kevin P. Gallagher is a professor at and director of the Global Development Policy Center at Boston University's Pardee School for Global Studies. He cochairs the T-20 Task Force on An International Financial Architecture for Stability and Development at the G20. He has served as an advisor to the Department of State and the Environmental Protection Agency in the United States, to the United Nations Conference on Trade and Development, and to the United Nations Economic Commission for Latin America and the Caribbean. He has also been a visiting professor at several universities in the United States, Latin America and China.

Eric Helleiner is a professor in the Department of Political Science at the University of Waterloo, and coeditor of the book series Cornell Studies in Money. He was a member of the Warwick Commission on International Financial Reform and the High Level Panel on the Governance of the Financial Stability Board. His research interests include global financial crises and regulation, shifting power in the international monetary system, the origins of international development, and the history of international political economy. He has published extensively on the history of the international monetary system, the recent politics of China in relation to that system, and the politics of financial regulation.

Lise Johnson is the head of Investment Law and Policy at the Columbia Center on Sustainable Investment (CCSI). Her work at CCSI centers on analyzing the contractual, legislative, and international legal frameworks governing international investment and examining how those frameworks shape outcomes and impacts. She focuses, in particular, on analyzing international investment treaties and the investor-state arbitrations that arise under them, examining the implications those treaties and cases have for host countries' policies and sustainable development strategies.

Guillermo Lagarda is senior economist for the Inter-American Development Bank and a research scholar at Boston University's Global Economic Governance Initiative. He previously worked for Latin American and Caribbean Poverty Reduction Management at the World Bank and in the Ministry of Finance of Mexico. His research is focused on macro financial linkages, financial stability, and global fiscal rules. His recent work includes the impact of financial sanctions, correlations between capital openness and inequality, the global impacts of the recent U.S. tax reform, the effects of noncompliance with rules on anti-money-laundering, and combating the financing of terrorism.

Jennifer Linares is an economist for the Country Department of Central America, Mexico, Panama, and the Dominican Republic of the Inter-American Development Bank. Before working for the IDB, she was an economist and research analyst in the Florida TaxWatch Research Institute, and a Fellow at the Panama Canal Authority.

Her research interests include the economics of education, labor markets, immigration, and the economics of income distribution and poverty.

Prakash Loungani is an advisor in the International Monetary Fund's Independent Evaluation Office. Previously he worked for the IMF's Research Department, the Federal Reserve Board, and the University of Florida. Since 2001, he has been an adjunct professor at Vanderbilt University's Owen School of Management. His research publications focus on the inability of economists to forecast recessions, the cyclical sources of unemployment, declining U.S. labor mobility, and the impacts of austerity and openness on inequality. He blogs as The Unassuming Economist.

Manuel F. Montes is a permanent observer to the United Nations and senior advisor on finance and development at the South Centre. He was previously chief of the development strategies branch in the United Nations Department of Economic and Social Affairs, United Nations Development Program's regional program coordinator for Asia Pacific Trade and Investment Initiative based in Sri Lanka, program officer for International Economic Policy at the Ford Foundation in New York, senior fellow and coordinator for economics studies at the East-West Centre in Honolulu, and associate professor of economics at the University of the Philippines.

Jonathan D. Ostry is deputy director of the Research Department at the International Monetary Fund. His recent responsibilities include leading staff teams on IMF-FSB Early Warning Exercises on global systemic macrofinancial risks; vulnerabilities exercises for advanced and emerging market countries; multilateral exchange rate surveillance; international financial architecture and reform of the IMF's lending toolkit; capital account management and financial globalization; fiscal sustainability issues; and the nexus between income inequality and economic growth. He also led the division that produces the IMF's flagship multilateral surveillance publication *World Economic Outlook*. He is the author of several books and articles on international macroeconomic issues, financial globalization, and macroeconomic policies and inequality.

Osvaldo Rosales is a professor at the MBA in the University of Chile on "Topics of International Economy," and at the Chilean Diplomatic Academy on "International Economy and Trade Negotiations." He was director of the Division of International Trade and Integration of the United Nations Economic Commission for Latin America and the Caribbean, vice-minister of trade of Chile, and chief negotiator in 2000–04 of the FTAs for Chile with the United States, the European Union (Trade Pillar), and South Korea. He has published and advised a number of governments and business organizations on trade policy, trade negotiations, and regional integration in Latin America and Asia.

Lisa Sachs is the director of the Columbia Center on Sustainable Investment (CCSI). Since joining CCSI in 2008, she established and oversees CCSI's three areas of focus: investments in extractive industries, investments in land and agriculture, and investment law and policy. She teaches at Columbia Law School and Columbia's School of International and Public Affairs. She is also a cochair of the UN Sustainable Development Solutions Network's group on the Good Governance of Extractive and Land Resources and is a member of the World Economic Forum's Global Future

Council on the Future of International Governance, Public-Private Cooperation, and Sustainable Development.

Erika Dayle Siu is a tax and development policy specialist and currently manages a team based at the University of Illinois at Chicago that builds research capacity on health taxation in 22 think tanks across 17 countries. She has previously worked for the United Nations Development Program, the International Centre for Taxation and Development, and most recently directed the Independent Commission for the Reform of International Corporate Taxation (ICRICT). She is a member of the New York Bar and New Jersey Bar.

INDEX

Page numbers in *italics* indicate figures or tables.

120–23, 132–33; ownership and, 122, 132–33, 138n8; policy and, 119–22; regulation defense and, 121; wealth and, 121–22

government expenditures, 55, *56*

Government Finance Statistics, Fiscal Monitor (IMF), 264

governments, 116; access to, 130–33; impartiality of, 132; legitimate expectations from, 130–31; subsidies from, 129, 134

government spending, 76–77

GPG. *See* global public goods

Great Depression, 43

Great Recession, 150, 173n6

GREENBOOK, 151

"green-zone" countries, 72, 78n5

gross capital flows, 148, 173n3

gross domestic product (GDP), 25n8, 151–52, 154, 212; capital flows related to, 148, 173n2; CIT and, 249–50; global tax loss and, 257; government expenditures and, 55, *56*; of low-income countries, 161–62

growth, 3, 77n2; duration of, 64, *65*; FDI and, 66; inequality related to, 57–58, 60–61, *62, 63*, 63–64, *65*, 77nn1–2; openness and, *65*, 65–66

growth and redistribution, 59; correction for, 60–61, *62, 63*, 63–64, 77nn1–2

Guariglia, Alessandra, 102

GVC. *See* global value chains

Hakelberg, Lukas, 47

Hansen tests, 77n1

Hellmann, Thomas F., 145

high-income countries, 155, 158, 163, 172, *176–77, 178*

Hodgson, Mélida, 227

Hodson, Mathew, 138n10

host states, 105, 108n14, 113; IIAs and, 114–15, 117–18; MNEs and, 118–19, 122–24, 127–28, 134

Howitt, Peter, 255

human capital investment, 255

IAB. *See* Inter-American Bank

IBRD. *See* International Bank for Reconstruction and Development

ICRICT. *See* Independent Commission for the Reform of International Corporate Taxation

ICS. *See* International Court System

ICSID. *See* International Center for Settlement of Investment Disputes

IIAs. *See* international investment agreements

Ikenberry, John, 43

ILAs and property rights, 137, 140n43; FET and, 127–30, 134–36, 139n26; legitimate expectations in, 130–36; protected expectations in, 130; status quo in, 133–36

ILO. *See* International Labor Organization

IMF. *See* International Monetary Fund

impulse response functions (IRFs), 77n3

inaudita altera parte, 206n51

income, 55, *57*; policy related to, 121–22. *See also specific topics*

income per capita, 2–3, 24n2

income stagnation, 55, *57*

Independent Commission for the Reform of International Corporate Taxation (ICRICT), 21–22, 25n11

India, 48, 100, 104, 106–7

"indirect expropriation," 10, 22–23

industrial policies, 235

inequality, 2–3, 146, *147*; awards related to, 103–4, 137, 149n43; backlash from, 57; from capital account liberalization, 69–71, *70*; in emerging markets, *57*; growth related to, 57–58, 60–61, *62, 63*, 63–64, *65*, 77nn1–2; new form of, 11–12; policy related to, 57–59; redistribution and, 57–58, 60–61, *62, 63*, 63–64, *65, 66*, 77nn1–2; within-country, 55, *57–58*, 82. *See also specific topics*

infrastructure, 130

Initiative for Policy Dialogue (IPD), 1–2

Inklaar, Robert, *56*

Schreuer, Christoph, 108n11
Schumpeter, Joseph A., 59
SDGs. *See* Sustainable Development Goals
secondary patents, 198–99
"second globalization," 1
secrecy: of BITs, 84, 103–4; in
    international tax competition, 251; of
    U.S., 267
shocks, 153–54; capital openness results
    and discussion, and, 150–52, 168–72,
    169, 173nn9–10
short-run trade-off, 73–74, *74*
"side letters," 190–91, 240n30
Singapore, 231
small and medium enterprises (SMEs),
    235
social policy constraints: on black
    economic empowerment, 96–97;
    on environment policy, 99–100; on
    land reform, 97–98; on minimum
    wage, 97, 108n12; on water services,
    98–99
social security, 31–33
SOEs. *See* state-owned enterprises
sofosbuvir, 199, 206n52
Solt, Frederick, *57*, 61
South Africa, 48, 95–97, 100
South America, *91*, 91–92. *See also*
    specific countries
Standardized World Income Inequality
    Database (SWIID), 61, 146
state-owned enterprises (SOEs), *216*,
    216–18
Stiglitz, Joseph E., 145
strong institutions. *See* capital openness
    results and discussion
Subramanian, Arvind, 146
Sub-Saharan Africa, 91–92, *92*, *147*, *259*
subsidies, 129, 134
Supreme Court, U.S., 131
"survival clause," 85–86
Sustainable Development Goals (SDGs),
    46, 52n1, 180, 258
SWIID. *See* Standardized World Income
    Inequality Database
system-GMM, *62*, 63, *63*, 77n1

tariffs, *216*, 234–35; GATT on, 38,
    204n28, 233
taxation, 260; capital income, 253–56;
    CIT, 16, 243–45, *244*; evasion of,
    251; globalization and, 234–36;
    ICRICT, 21–22, 25n11; legitimate
    expectations and, 131; MNEs and, 12,
    25n6, 116; OECD on, 17, 245–46;
    PIT, 16; TPP and, 229–30; U.S.
    and, 47. *See also* international tax
    competition; profit taxation
tax havens, 41, 213, 249–50, 260, 264–65
technology, 69, 102, 126, 179–80, 221
test data protection: commercialization
    and, 193–94, 205nn34–35, 205n38;
    compulsory licenses/government
    use of, 194; early working of, 194;
    exclusion of, 192, 194, 202, 205n33;
    period of, 192; process for, 192,
    205n35; products in, 193; scope of,
    193, 205n38; termination of, 194–95;
    undisclosed date and, 193
Therapeutic Goods Act 1989, 201
Third International Conference on
    Financing for Development, 263
Timmer, Marcel P., *56*
TiSA. *See* Trade in Services Agreement
TPA. *See* Trade Promotion Authority
TPP. *See* Trans-Pacific Partnership
Trade Act, U.S., 195
Trade in Services Agreement (TiSA), 216
trade openness, 153
Trade Promotion Authority (TPA),
    214–16, 220
Trade-Related Aspects of Intellectual
    Property Rights (TRIPS), 23–24,
    180, 202, 203n3; Bolar exception
    and, 186–87; ceilings and, 182;
    Doha Declaration and, 15, 186–87,
    204n15, 204n17; FTAs and, 218–20,
    239n5, 240n8; IPRs and, 218–20,
    239nn5–6, 240n7; TRIPS-extra,
    14–15, 182–83; TRIPS-minimum, 14,
    181; TRIPS-minus, 182, 203nn5–6;
    TRIPS-plus, 14–15, 181–83; WTO
    and, 14–15, 182, 186–87, 203n7